MW01293052

A Giant among Giants

A Giant among Giants

The Baseball Life of Willie McCovey

CHRIS HAFT

University of Nebraska Press
LINCOLN

Chapter 22, "The Final Chapter," previously appeared in
the *San Francisco Giants 2019 Yearbook*, pp. 38–52.

The University of Nebraska Press is part of a land-grant institution
with campuses and programs on the past, present, and future
homelands of the Pawnee, Ponca, Otoe-Missouria, Omaha, Dakota,
Lakota, Kaw, Cheyenne, and Arapaho Peoples, as well as those
of the relocated Ho-Chunk, Sac and Fox, and Iowa Peoples.

Except where noted, all photographs appear
courtesy of the San Francisco Giants.

Library of Congress Cataloging-in-Publication Data
Names: Haft, Chris, author
Title: A giant among Giants: the baseball life
of Willie Mccovey / Chris Haft.
Other titles: Baseball life of Willie Mccovey
Description: Lincoln: University of Nebraska Press, [2024] |
Includes bibliographical references and index.
Identifiers: LCCN 2024011391
ISBN 9781496241979 (pdf)
ISBN 9781496241962 (epub)
ISBN 9781496236241 (hardback)
Subjects: LCSH: McCovey, Willie, 1938–2018 | African American
baseball players—Biography | San Francisco Giants (Baseball
team)—Biography | San Francisco (Calif.)—Biography |
BISAC: BIOGRAPHY & AUTOBIOGRAPHY / Sports | SPORTS
& RECREATION / Baseball / History | LCGFT: Biographies
Classification: LCC GV865.M2934 H34 2025 |
DDC 796.357092/396073—dc23/eng
LC record available at https://lccn.loc.gov/2024011391

Set in Arno Pro by Scribe Inc.

To Bill Hill, Bill Neukom, and of course, Allison McCovey,
for loading the bases with their faith in this work

A part of him lives in all of us.

—Vida Blue (1949–2023) on Willie McCovey

CONTENTS

ACKNOWLEDGMENTS

Here comes the page or two I feared writing the most—not because I'm ungrateful but because I know good and well that I'll forget to cite several people who were essential to the completion of this book. Regardless, here goes (for simplicity's sake, the deceased are mixed with the living):

C. David Burgin, Dinn Mann, Blake Rhodes, and John Schlegel, thank you for placing me in the position that enabled me to cover the Giants for mlb.com, meet Willie McCovey, and write the stories that serve as the foundation for much of this book.

Josh Rawitch and his staff at the Baseball Hall of Fame proved invaluable by providing a mother lode of McCovey-related press clippings. Rawitch's predecessor as hall president, Jeff Idelson, was an MVP by setting up interviews with the likes of Ferguson Jenkins, Johnny Bench, and Dave Winfield.

This project never would have gained momentum without the encouragement of Estela, McCovey's widow, who provided constant encouragement early in the process, and Lise Peters, who literally unlocked the doors to the first batch of McCovey clippings that gave me essential information—and confidence.

Fresh off his innovative collaboration with Willie Mays—*24: Life Lessons from the Say Hey Kid*—John Shea of the *San Francisco Chronicle* remained my cleanup hitter from start to finish. John provided advice regarding my table of contents, helped put me in touch with several interviewees, and suggested how I might transition from one phase to the next.

Scott Emmert of the San Jose Sharks was generous and trusting enough to share his collection of McCovey scrapbooks that were nothing short of mind-blowing.

The kind staff at the Mobile, Alabama, Public Library helped point me in the right direction with the press clippings they sent.

Thanks to Matt Chisholm, the Giants' vice president of communication, and community relations directors Staci Slaughter (past) and Shana Daum (present) and their staffs. Mark Ling of the Oakland A's media relations staff also provided valuable assistance.

This entire book bears the stamp of Mario Alioto, who in 2023 observed his 50th season with the Giants—from batboy to executive. Early in my tenure as a Giants beat writer, Mario bridged the gap between me and McCovey for interviews. Without Mario's assistance I never would have developed the comfortable relationship I had with McCovey, giving me material that later proved essential.

Mike Murphy, with whom I obviously share a lot (you still can purchase *From the Stick to the Cove*, Murph's autobiography written with me), always boosted my spirits when we crossed paths.

Annabella Pidlaoan, my youthful aunt who nurtured my love for sports, never let me get lazy as I strove to complete this book.

Many thanks to my interviewees. Not all of them reached print, but each of them helped tell Willie McCovey's story: Pat Gallagher, Jim Davenport, Jack Hiatt, Mike Krukow, Robin Roberts, Eddie Bressoud, Ellis Burks, J. T. Snow, Mike "Tiny" Felder, Roger Angell, Hobie Landrith, Mike Murphy, Larry Dierker, Rocky Dudum, Jeff Dudum, Bob Lurie, Jim Maloney, Joe Amalfitano, Darrell Evans, Vida Blue, Barry Tompkins, Bob Bolin, Billy Williams, Dave Righetti, Travis Ishikawa, Buster Posey, Frank Robinson, Larry Baer, Gary Lavelle, Kevin Frandsen, Chris Speier, Tim McCarver, Jeff Torborg, Tommy Davis, Randy Winn, Jim Lefebvre, Dan Rusanowsky, Juan Marichal, Don Sutton, Randy Cross, Orlando Cepeda, Bill Madlock, Mike Yastrzemski, Gary Matthews, Hal Lanier, Jon Miller, Cameron Palmer, Jim Barr, Matt Levine, Connie Lurie, Bill White, Mike McCormick, Todd Hundley, Dave Bristol, Ferguson Jenkins, Johnny Bench, Dave Winfield, Clauzell McCovey, Angelia Steen Guillot, Carolyn Campbell, Terry Whitfield, Matt Duffy, Ken Henderson, Rudy Law, Bengie Molina, Bill Arnold, Steve Blass, Mark Purdy, Al Klein, Kevin Mitchell, Steve Mesenburg, Karen Booker, Dusty Baker, Bobby Richardson, Ralph Terry, Randy Jones, Chris Russo, Bob Melvin, Pete

Rose, Matt Cain, Madison Bumgarner, Mike Matheny, David Bell, Steve Stone, Eddie Montague, Mike Aldrete, Tito Fuentes, Larry Herndon, Brian Murphy, Bob Burda, John D'Acquisto, Will Clark, Shawon Dunston, Cliff Floyd, Luis Gonzalez, Allison McCovey, Rich Murray, Estela McCovey, Al Downing, Dick Ellsworth, and Jim Kaat.

Special thanks to Patrick Quinlan, Dan Taylor, John Erardi, Mike Swanson, Ryan Lefebvre, Susan Slusser, Dan Brown, Alyson Footer, Carrie Muskat, Ken Gurnick, Rob Butcher, F. P. Santangelo, Erwin Higueros, Gene Dias, Jay Horwitz, Anthony Di Como, Bryan Hoch, Greg Casterioto, Scott Reifert, JP Nolan, Joan Ryan, Anne Rogers, and Lyle Spencer.

God bless the souls of Mom, Dad, Lola, Uncle Larry, and Aunt Helene.

Blessings, too, upon my daughters, Samantha Allen and Stephanie Haft; my son-in-law, Brenton Allen; and my dear grandson, August.

Willie Lee "Stretch" McCovey must receive the final salute. With this book and the perspective of time, perhaps more people will realize what a marvel he was.

A Giant among Giants

Introduction

He was iconic.

—Hall of Fame catcher Johnny Bench

Speakers at the celebration of Willie McCovey's life, which was held at San Francisco's Oracle Park on November 8, 2018, accented their remembrances with intense emotion, evoking the power—the powerful feelings, the powerful presence—that the legendary Giants first baseman displayed in a Major League career that spanned four calendar decades.

Mike Krukow choked back tears as he recalled how he wanted to emulate McCovey's character. Barry Bonds remembered asking the imposing McCovey as a youth if he could call him "Uncle Willie" (permission granted). Longtime Giants coach Joe Amalfitano, a teammate of McCovey's in the Minor and Major Leagues, referred to the slugger's "love affair" with San Francisco, where he remained a favorite son long after he played his final game in 1980.

The most moving tribute of all may have been the nonverbal one delivered by Mike "Tiny" Felder, who brought his 1992 Willie Mac Award plaque to the sun-splashed event. Felder, a former Giants outfielder who won the award that's emblematic of the ballclub's most inspirational player, clutched the home plate–shaped totem to his chest through much of the ninety-minute tribute to McCovey, who died eight days earlier on October 31 at age eighty of ongoing health issues. The plaque spoke eloquently for Felder.

"It was a no-brainer," Felder said of his decision to bring the trophy. He related that upon arising that morning at his Richmond, California, residence, he declared to himself, "I've got to bring my Willie Mac award and show what Willie Mac meant to me."

Felder didn't just express the depth of emotion that McCovey stirred within him. He also demonstrated how legions of others felt about the man. "The more people saw him and the more people reacted to him, the more people loved him," former Giants owner Bob Lurie said. "When you got to know Willie, you had to love him."

McCovey's home in Woodside, California, afforded him views of his kingdom of fans. Unbeknownst to them, he could see them drive past on Highways 101 or 280. San Francisco International Airport was visible too. Imagine how thousands of commuters would react if they sensed that Willie McCovey could be staring down at them. The distraction would cause some nasty pileups.

"I'm still amazed [by] how much you can touch people and how much you mean to them," McCovey said less than a year before his death. "I don't know how to explain it. I've met people who tell me, 'You were the only reason my grandmother or somebody lived the last few years, because of you.' Things like that, you listen to it, and you wonder, 'God, that's amazing.'"

Baseball purists everywhere admired McCovey for his hitting prowess and defensive flair. Cincinnati's Johnny Bench, the finest catcher of his generation and perhaps all others, adored McCovey so much that he couldn't bear to witness the big man's physical erosion. "It hurt me so much to see his demise," Bench said, "and his wheelchair was the saddest thing I ever had to see.

"He was too much of a hero to me. He was iconic."

Bench was among those who understood McCovey's true significance, which lay in the personal warmth that he exuded and others reciprocated. McCovey's life wasn't measured in his home run and RBI totals. For him, it was all about respect and love.

"You hit it on the head," former Giants shortstop Chris Speier said. "Among people who played with him or against him, those are the words that come out." They echo, too, among his closest friends—most notably, the Dudum family. "I've known Willie McCovey all my life," Jeff Dudum said of his godfather. "He's like family to me."

I began one conversation during the early portion of the interviewing process for this book and quickly felt as if a dog were sniffing at my shoe-tops. Except this was no ordinary canine. This was a Doberman named Vida

Blue, fully prepared to deliver a crippling bite to my integrity if he didn't like my answers to his questions. I pictured Blue firing dozens of phone and text messages like so many fastballs, all warning fellow Major League alumni not to speak to me. This project would have ended before it began. Said a wary Blue, "First, let me ask you—why are you writing something about Willie McCovey?" I responded to the marvelous left-hander—who asked McCovey to serve as the best man at his 1989 wedding—by essentially repeating what I had said to Speier. "I just think it needs to be written, Vida," I replied. "He shouldn't fade from the consciousness of people on this earth without somebody trying to point out how much respect he commands and how much love he inspires."

That was good enough for Blue, who started reminiscing happily about receiving the dressing stall next to McCovey's after being sent from Oakland to San Francisco for seven players in the March 15, 1978, trade that revitalized the Giants franchise. Blue also remembered that Joe Liscio, San Francisco's head athletic trainer, had a distinctive way of honoring McCovey. Perhaps McCovey's name would come up in conversation. Or McCovey himself would pass through the clubhouse or stop by the trainer's room. Whatever the prompting was, Liscio would be moved to say, "He's a giant among Giants."

The Giants' rosters were graced with three demigods at various junctures since the franchise moved from New York to San Francisco before the 1958 season. Each member of this triumvirate attracted a distinct following.

Willie Mays was the most admired Giant for his multitalented greatness, though he remained underappreciated for years after the franchise moved west from New York following the 1957 season. Many Northern Californians refused to embrace him because he wasn't "theirs." They regarded him as an interloper from Manhattan. That abruptly and fortunately changed on May 4, 1966, when Mays belted his 512th career home run to set a National League (NL) mark. League records are largely overlooked in this era, but in Mays's day—his "Say Hey day," if you will—they carried deep significance. The prolonged ovation Mays received from the onlookers at San Francisco's Candlestick Park that night signaled the fans' acceptance of him.

Barry Bonds was reviled on the road but hailed in San Francisco, where fans awaited his every swing with delicious anticipation for 15 seasons. Like his godfather, Mays, and his father, Bobby, Barry possessed baseball's five classic "tools"—the ability to hit for average as well as power, speed, throwing skill, and fielding deftness. His slugging particularly captivated Giants fans, who hardly seemed to care about the rumors of performance-enhancing drug use that swirled around him. Bonds gave Giants fans one more big thrill by becoming baseball's all-time home run leader by hitting no. 756 off Washington's Mike Bacsik on August 7, 2007. That merry-go-round stopped a little more than a month later, when the Giants announced that Bonds wouldn't be signed for the 2008 season.

McCovey was the one who people wanted to hug the most. "I think he radiated a gentleness that was easy to pick up," said Bob Lurie's wife, Connie. "He was sort of a gentle Giant, truly. He was just very kind, very sweet." Even opposing players sensed McCovey's warmth. "His big grin was always a welcome sight," Bench said. Giants nemesis Tommy Davis described McCovey thusly: "Easy-going, easy-talking, long-ball hitting." Listening to Davis, it was no wonder that McCovey was nicknamed "Easy," an alternate sobriquet to the more commonly used "Stretch." Davis added, "People couldn't dislike him." Indeed, teammates revered him. "He commanded respect with his presence. You could always talk to Willie Mac. His locker was always open," reliever Gary Lavelle said.

He also could be refreshingly down-to-earth. One afternoon in the mid-1980s, Connie Lurie was playing a round by herself at Lake Merced Golf Club in Daly City when she encountered McCovey, who was also playing solo. They joined forces for the last few holes, which were highlighted by some well-intentioned advice from McCovey. "He told me one of the funniest things," Connie Lurie said. "After I teed off, he told me I needed to get my butt more in my swing. That really tickled me. And it still does. He was absolutely right, I'm sure."

Blue was born in 1949 and faced McCovey in the 1971 All-Star Game before becoming his friend and teammate. Catcher Buster Posey was born in 1987 and knew of McCovey's baseball career only by reputation or as part of a history lesson. Yet their remarks about McCovey were virtually identical.

"He was the kindest, gentlest guy I've ever met," Blue said. "I don't know if he had any anger in him." Echoed Posey, who joined McCovey in the Giants' fraternity of National League Most Valuable Player Award winners in 2012, "He always exuded kindness whenever I was around him."

In a business where confidence ebbs and flows, McCovey remained a valuable presence simply because he made people feel good about themselves. Players relished encountering him in equipment manager Mike Murphy's office in the Giants' clubhouse, whether it led to a dissertation on hitting or just a simple hello.

"Willie McCovey was one of the greatest guys I ever met," first baseman J. T. Snow said. "I talked to him a lot when I played. He had a way about him. He always called me 'Kid.' I remember talking to him when I was struggling at the plate. He'd say, 'Just hang in there, Kid; keep swinging.' He always had nice things to say about my defense and admired the way I played. To me, Willie McCovey was my favorite ex-Giant of all time."

Will Clark, another appreciative first baseman, does his best to keep McCovey's spirit alive. He displays not one but two autographed photos of McCovey in his home office.

"Stretch and I, we had a bond," Clark said. "It was really special for me to get to know him as a person. He was always very forthcoming with advice. He would talk about the wind patterns and wind currents and what to look for."

Said right-hander Matt Cain, "He earned your respect very easily with his mannerisms and how he talked to people. That meant a lot to a lot of the guys. He didn't come in with this arrogance about himself. He'd want to get to know guys. He'd want to share. I think the biggest thing that Willie did was, he always had a positive attitude toward the guys. Whether things were going great or bad, he had this kind of even-keeled calmness about him that kind of filtered through his handshakes into you. Man, that's a powerful man right there on so many different levels. He was a big man in stature and the way he carried himself."

What's fascinating about Cain's remarks is that McCovey always was on crutches, in a wheelchair, or strapped to a gurney when they crossed paths. And yet Cain spoke of how McCovey "carried himself." Such was McCovey's aura.

Willie Lee McCovey was a highly uncommon gentleman in many ways. He was never unencumbered by injury for a single day in his 22-year Major

League career. Yet he became only the 16th first-ballot inductee in his sport's Hall of Fame, and he retired as the National League's most prolific left-handed-batting home run hitter ever.

For all the accolades that Mays and Bonds have received—and richly deserve—it's McCovey's name that's synonymous with the Giants' highest honor. That would be the Willie Mac Award, given to the team's most inspirational player. And it's his name that identifies the most novel landmark at the team's ballpark. McCovey Cove, of course.

Opposing pitchers approached McCovey with something akin to fear. Mays, who mostly batted ahead of him for 13 seasons, prompted a divergent strategy. Hoping to neutralize Mays, perhaps the finest ballplayer ever, rival pitchers constantly threw at him in attempts to unnerve him or weaken his resolve. Mays's reflexes and pitch recognition were so sharp that he was never hit by more than 4 pitches in any year. But the tension conveyed by the potential for brushback pitches often accompanied him to the batter's box.

Not so with McCovey. He was struck by 69 pitches during his career, exceeding Mays's 44. But pitchers simply tried to move the left-handed-batting McCovey away from home plate and sometimes hit him instead of the inside corner. "He had such long arms, his bat head would extend into the other batter's box," former Dodgers catcher Jeff Torborg said. NL pitchers realized that the 6-foot-4, 200-pound McCovey, who ranked among the biggest of big leaguers at the time, wouldn't retreat from a challenge. So they knew that he knew—or at least they *hoped* that he knew—that they never confronted him with malice aforethought. "You didn't want to intimidate him," said Hall of Fame left fielder Billy Williams, who, like McCovey, was raised in Mobile, Alabama. "You didn't want to make him mad on a baseball field. He looked like he would pinch your head off. He was such a big guy."

Seemingly everything about McCovey was hugely proportioned. His home runs rarely scraped the top of the outfield barrier. They typically carried deep into the bleachers or the upper deck. He tended to drive big cars. Given his physical stature, how could it be otherwise?

"I squatted behind him, and I felt like a little kid," Torborg said.

Being left-handed, Dave Righetti identified with McCovey, who became his favorite player. Growing up in San Jose, about forty-five miles south of

San Francisco, Righetti joined the legion of Bay Area youths who worshipped the Giants. "Besides Frank Howard, he filled up the whole TV screen," said Righetti, who initially gained fame as the Yankees' closer in the mid-1980s before helping the Giants capture World Series titles in 2010, 2012, and 2014 as their pitching coach. "Back then, players weren't that big. But McCovey . . . oh, my God."

Preparing the Giants' pitchers for each game understandably preoccupied Righetti. But he always had time to check in with McCovey, the man who initiated his big league dreams and attended virtually every Giants home game once they moved into the ballpark at Third and King Streets in the year 2000. "I don't think a day went by when I didn't say hello to him," Righetti said.

As a run producer, McCovey's stature was virtually unmatched during his peak. He had his best years while NL starting pitching overall ascended to a phenomenal level, as future Hall of Famers such as Don Drysdale, Bob Gibson, Ferguson Jenkins, Sandy Koufax, Don Sutton, Phil Niekro, Tom Seaver, and Giants teammates Juan Marichal and Gaylord Perry achieved prominence. From 1965 to 1970, McCovey simply was the best hitter in baseball. During that 6-season span, he and Hank Aaron shared the Major League lead in home runs (226). Meanwhile, McCovey alone topped the Majors in on-base percentage (.405), slugging percentage (.578), and his favorite statistic, RBIS (636).

"Maybe it's because when you faced a Hall of Fame pitcher, you had to get up for it," said all-time hits leader Pete Rose of McCovey's proficiency. "You were gonna get your hits off the lambs. You had to struggle and bear down against the lions. Because they'd eat you alive. I happened to play in an era when there were a lot of lions out there pitching."

McCovey's big heart matched his huge numbers. He participated in numerous charitable events, even after he was confined to a wheelchair and a gurney in his later years by knee trouble, back pain, and infections. His widely known nickname, "Stretch," gave meaning and momentum to the Giants' most intensive charitable fundraising event of each season, the Junior Giants Stretch Drive.

The concept of family truly stirred McCovey's soul. Growing up as the seventh of ten children obviously influenced his outlook. "Baseball and family together have shaped my character, my values, and my career," he said in his Hall of Fame induction speech. Though he rarely visited Mobile, his relatives understood that his loathing of the South's bigotry prompted him to stay in California when given the choice. Asked how proud he was of his older brother, Clauzell McCovey said, "On a scale of one to 10, with 10 being best . . . 10."

McCovey's popularity among Bay Area sports fans—and the sincerity of his gratitude toward them—cannot be measured. He served as the San Jose Sharks' celebrity captain during their 1991–92 inaugural season, when the National Hockey League expansion team needed a figure who people believed in to bolster the franchise's efforts to establish itself in the Bay Area. He set the mood on one Valentine's Day in the mid-1980s when he strode through downtown San Francisco's Financial District and gave a rose to any surprised yet thrilled woman who wanted one. The combination of respect and love that helped define him, said outfielder Larry Herndon, "might not be superrare. But he did it better than anybody."

Bent on preserving his privacy, McCovey never wanted a book-length work published about him while he was living. But his story is too great to be allowed to fade into oblivion.

"You never hear much about Willie anymore," infielder Jim Davenport, who spent all 12 years of his big league career with McCovey as a Giants teammate, said in 2009. "But people who have been around him know how great a player he was and how great a person he is."

The tale truly began on July 30, 1959.

1

Instant Success

> You could tell that Willie was going to be a problem for a lot
> of guys, not just me.
> —Robin Roberts

The 1959 San Francisco Giants exuded confidence as they approached late summer. They considered themselves legitimate contenders for the National League pennant. They had an enviable starting rotation consisting of right-handers Sam Jones and Jack Sanford as well as lefties Johnny Antonelli and Mike McCormick. Stu Miller, one of baseball's most versatile pitchers, could handle every role imaginable. Orlando Cepeda was on his way to improving upon the statistics he assembled a season earlier, when he won the NL's Rookie of the Year Award. Jim Davenport was developing into a top-tier third baseman. And of course, the Giants had Willie Mays, already considered a sure Hall of Famer at age twenty-eight.

San Franciscans welcomed the Giants enthusiastically when the franchise moved west from New York before the start of the 1958 season. The inaugural San Francisco club spent forty days in first place following a lackluster 69–85, 7th-place finish in its final New York season. Hence, the Giants' newly minted fans assumed that this progress would continue and that winning the pennant would be possible in '59. So when the Giants moved into first place on July 4, the zealots who regularly packed 22,000-seat Seals Stadium, the team's home ballpark at the intersection of Sixteenth and Bryant Streets, expected nothing less. At least until October, when the World Series would be played.

Fans are the same everywhere. They can't be blamed for neglecting to curb their expectations. Giants fans had no way of knowing what the near future would teach them: the 8-team National League, which expanded to 10 teams in 1962, was a rugged bunch. A different team finished first each year from 1960 to 1964. The elevated level of competition was evident in '59 too. On June 8, the Giants owned an ordinary 30-24 record. Yet they stood in second place, 3 games behind the Milwaukee Braves. Three other teams, the Dodgers, Pirates, and Cubs, trailed Milwaukee by 5 games or fewer. Everybody was beating up each other.

The Giants owned or shared the league lead from July 4 through July 28. However, manager Bill Rigney worried about the team's offense, which was vulnerable when compared with the lineups fielded by the Milwaukee Braves and Los Angeles Dodgers, San Francisco's chief rivals. Milwaukee complemented Hall of Fame sluggers Hank Aaron and Eddie Mathews with Del Crandall and Joe Adcock. Five Dodgers would finish the season with at least 18 homers: Don Demeter, Gil Hodges, Wally Moon, Charlie Neal, and Duke Snider. By comparison, Mays and Cepeda gave the Giants plenty of pop. But their only other true threat was right fielder Willie Kirkland, a left-handed batter who frequently was benched against left-handed starters.

Rigney knew that the Giants couldn't sustain their pennant drive without adding an impact bat to the lineup. In a 3–2 loss to the Dodgers and Don Drysdale on July 20, Davenport, Kirkland, Mays, and Cepeda—batting first through fourth, respectively—went a combined 0-for-14. The next day, Roger Craig, the future Giants manager, yielded 3 hits in a 1–0 victory that sealed the Dodgers' sweep of a 2-game series. The Giants recovered by winning 3 games in a row, which kept them in first place. Then came four straight defeats, including a frustrating setback on July 29, when Antonelli allowed only 3 hits in a complete-game effort but lost to the last-place Phillies, 3–1. The Dodgers clambered atop the NL standings, a ½ game in front of the Giants and 1 game ahead of Milwaukee.

After the loss to the Phillies, Rigney spent more time than usual at his tiny desk in his tiny office in the tiny Giants clubhouse at tiny Seals Stadium, which was beautiful but doomed. A 22,000-seat ballpark had no future as a Major League venue, even in the quaint 1950s. Candlestick Park, which would accommodate crowds exceeding 42,000, already was under construction.

But Seals Stadium would enjoy one more proud day, serving as midwife to the spectacular birth of an outstanding big league career.

Mike Murphy, the assistant clubhouse manager who tended to both the home and visitors' quarters, worked just as late as Rigney. "Murph" helped clubhouse manager Eddie Logan scrape the dirt off each and every pair of spikes besides emptying the "wet bags" of their contents—game-worn uniforms that had to be laundered before the following afternoon's series finale against Philadelphia. Shortly before leaving the ballpark, Murphy was stopped by a beaming Rigney. "Hey, we're bringing up a big Irishman tomorrow," Rigney said. "Wait until you see *this* guy."

Being half Irish, a thrilled Murphy left for Seals Stadium earlier than usual the next day. But the "big Irishman's" flight from Phoenix, home of the Giants' Triple-A affiliate, wasn't due to land at San Francisco International Airport until 11:00 a.m. Soon after that time, a stranger, as tall as he was trim, entered the clubhouse. He certainly looked distinctive. But he was Black, not the red-haired, freckle-faced lad Murph envisioned. He nevertheless impressed Murphy with his sheer size. "I thought Paul Bunyan had come to life," Murphy recalled. "The clubhouse was small to begin with, and this guy took up whatever space was left." The rookie stared at the clubhouse floor, apparently shy and ill at ease. But he looked squarely at Murphy when the clubbie approached. "Hi. I'm Willie McCovey," the rookie said, flashing the smile that ultimately endeared him to legions of people—teammates as well as fans. "When he smiled, he lit up the room," Murphy said. "I've loved Stretch ever since."

Hobie Landrith, a Giants catcher from 1959 to 1961, saw significance as well as brilliance in McCovey's smile, which revealed a chipped front tooth (a dentist capped it before too long). "If he walked into a room and smiled, everybody smiled," Landrith said. "When you can create that kind of environment, you're a special person." McCovey would maintain this trait throughout his career. "He has that poker face, but he also has that great smile," said Pat Gallagher, a longtime Giants executive.

Smiles creased the faces of virtually everybody in the Giants' clubhouse that morning. McCovey had spent some time in spring training that year, so the veterans knew how to get under his skin. Antonelli was the first to greet him. "Lovey-Dovey McCovey!" he singsonged, followed by choruses of teammates giving the rookie a good-natured, big league ribbing.

Behind the teasing was hope that McCovey could spark the indifferent offense. He certainly seemed ready for the Majors when Triple-A Phoenix manager John Davis told him after a doubleheader the night before to catch a flight to San Francisco. In 95 games with Phoenix, McCovey compiled a .372 batting average, 29 homers, and 92 RBIs. "I had nothing to prove in that league," McCovey said.

One of McCovey's primary concerns as he prepared to leave Phoenix had nothing to do with baseball. "After I got over the shock, I think my first [telephone] call was how was I going to collect all my records," he said. McCovey explained that having also played in Phoenix the year before, he had befriended numerous people, including some from whom he borrowed various 33s, 45s, and 78s. "It didn't occur to me that they could mail them," McCovey said.

His focus soon returned to baseball. "I was up all night with excitement," he said. He wouldn't have slept much regardless of his temperament, since Phoenix's doubleheader didn't conclude until late evening, and he had to take an early flight to be in uniform for the Phillies-Giants 1:30 p.m. start.

About that uniform: McCovey felt proud to receive jersey number 44—the same number worn by Aaron, a fellow Mobile, Alabama, native who had established himself as one of the game's elite performers. Finding other gear proved to be more challenging. "I had to borrow somebody else's pants. They were a little tight, but I didn't care," said McCovey, who, at 6 foot 4 and 200 pounds, possessed a longer and slimmer build than just about every other Giant. "Somebody else," for the record, turned out to be 6-foot-3 infielder Andre Rodgers.

Due to the wardrobe issues, his slightly delayed flight, and the airline's failure to ship his bats from Phoenix on time, McCovey missed batting practice. With his preferred lumber AWOL and none of his bats left over from spring training, McCovey searched the bat rack for a model that felt comfortable. He settled on infielder Ed Bressoud's Hillerich & Bradsby U1. "Thirty-five inches, 33 ounces," Bressoud recalled.

Finding a bat was necessary for McCovey. Rigney installed him in the lineup at first base. This uprooted Cepeda, who moved across the diamond to third base—the position he tried (and failed) to handle when the Giants initially signed him in 1955. Rigney also announced that McCovey would bat third. "You know who normally hits third," McCovey said. That would be Mays, destined to join the short list of players considered to be the greatest ever. Rigney elevated Mays to the second slot in the batting order.

McCovey betrayed no anxiety about displacing the team's two premier hitters, though, as Rigney said, "I dropped him into a tough spot." Facing Phillies right-hander Robin Roberts, McCovey settled into the left-handed batter's box with 2 outs and the bases empty in the 1st inning and launched the routine that became familiar for 22 seasons. He pounded home plate once with the barrel of his bat—nothing too ferocious or showy, but solidly enough to convey assertiveness. Then he established his timing by taking a brief series of half swings. Against a pitcher such as Roberts, who worked quickly, McCovey might prepare himself with just two swings. Against more deliberate pitchers, the number could increase to four. Either way, McCovey conveyed the sense that he was generating momentum with each cut. He announced his presence immediately by singling in that initial plate appearance, then proceeded to go 4-for-4 by adding a lead-off triple in the 4th inning, an RBI single in the 5th, and a run-scoring triple in the 7th. He also scored 3 runs. The Giants returned to first place, a ½ game ahead of Milwaukee, with a 7-2 win.

Lon Simmons, the beloved Bay Area broadcaster who befriended McCovey and was behind the microphone for his debut, relished the afternoon decades later. "Stretch hit them off the batter's eye," Simmons said. "They were such bullets that the fielders couldn't catch up with them."

The triples constituted the most startling aspect of McCovey's effort, given his career-long knee problems. But he had endured only one knee surgery at this juncture. "I think the marvel was to see how fast he was," said McCormick, who complemented McCovey by pitching a 7-hit complete game. The fact that Roberts was a future Hall of Famer is inevitably mentioned in conjunction with McCovey's fabulous debut. But Roberts's excellence, which is often ignored, makes McCovey's debut all the more impressive. Between July 1952 and June 1953, Roberts completed 28 consecutive starts. He led the NL in wins for 4 seasons in a row (1952–55) and topped the Majors in that category for the last 3 years of that span. He was a 7-time All-Star who lasted

19 years and won 286 games in the big leagues. This was not a borderline Hall of Famer who McCovey victimized. "Robin's one of the best pitchers ever. *Ever,*" said outfielder Gary Matthews, one of McCovey's Giants teammates who became steeped in Phillies culture when he was a broadcaster for the club during his retirement.

"He got four bloop hits off me. Tell Willie I said that," Roberts joked in a 2009 interview. Turning serious, Roberts added, "You could tell that Willie was going to be a problem for a lot of guys, not just me." Said McCovey, "All I know is I was just up there hacking. I remember that Robin had good control, so I knew he was going to be around the plate."

Antonelli couldn't restrain himself from poking a little more fun at McCovey after the game. "Nice going, Stretch! The drinks are on you," Antonelli scrawled on the clubhouse chalkboard.

In retrospect, it can be suggested that the baseball gods worked overtime on this date, sowing the seeds of drama and greatness. Bob Gibson, a rookie right-hander with the St. Louis Cardinals, recorded his first Major League victory with an 8-hitter in a 1–0 decision at Cincinnati. After his own fabulous Hall of Fame career ended, Gibson called McCovey the most formidable hitter he ever confronted. Stan Williams, who would figure prominently in one of the Giants' biggest triumphs in their history, pitched and lost for the Dodgers in a 12-inning, 5–4 duel against Pittsburgh. Billy O'Dell, a top pitcher for the pennant-winning Giants of 1962, started for Baltimore and was knocked around by Detroit in an 11–2 loss. Warren Spahn, who surrendered Mays's first Major League homer in 1951, collected career win no. 260 of 363 in a 6–2 victory over the Cubs. Aaron backed Spahn with his 27th homer of the season. The Cubs' lineup included Bobby Thomson—yes, *that* Bobby Thomson—and future Giants manager Alvin Dark.

After the game, McCovey joined teammates Leon Wagner and Kirkland for dinner. His already budding fame followed him to the restaurant. A nearby newsstand displayed copies of the *Call-Bulletin,* an afternoon newspaper. The *Call-Bulletin's* latest edition featured details of McCovey's big day. The boldface headlines grabbed his attention. "That was the first time I had ever seen my name like that, so that was exciting," he said. "I think I bought all the papers that were on that stand." Roberts gained a measure of revenge on

September 11, when he limited the Giants to 3 hits in a 1–0 triumph. McCovey went 0-for-3 with a walk.

It's intriguing to note that the Phillies' second baseman in both of those games was George Anderson, who was better known in baseball circles by his nickname, "Sparky." McCovey must have lodged himself in Anderson's considerable memory. Anderson, who would later gain fame as the manager of the Cincinnati Reds, consistently ordered his pitchers to approach McCovey as if he were capable of going 4-for-4, not 0-for-3, in every game.

McCovey's arrival galvanized the Giants. His debut, which ranks among the finest in any professional sport, launched a surge of 10 victories in 12 games that put San Francisco back atop the NL standings by 3 games. "I kind of created a spark that resonated through the rest of the team," he said. No kidding. He started at first base in the first 11 games following his promotion to the Majors. In his first 7 games, he batted .467 (14-for-30) with 9 runs scored, 9 RBIs, and 3 homers. The night after McCovey's debut, the Giants had to turn away four thousand fans, most of whom doubtlessly came to see him. McCovey didn't disappoint those who succeeded at squeezing into Seals Stadium, rapping a 2-out, 8th-inning single to drive in Mays with the tiebreaking run in a 4–3 victory over Pittsburgh. On August 1, McCovey went 3-for-5 with 2 doubles and 3 runs scored. He went only 1-for-5 on August 2, but his lone hit was his first Major League home run, a 2-run clout off Pittsburgh's Ron Kline that led the Giants' surge from a 3–0 deficit in a 5–3 win. On August 5 he homered twice off Milwaukee's Bob Buhl for his first of 44 career multiple-homer games in a 4–1 Giants win.

But accommodating McCovey meant benching a player who previously occupied a regular role. And the Giants needed Cepeda's bat in the lineup, considering he entered August batting .319 with 21 homers and 71 RBIs. So Rigney switched Cepeda to third base, a position that left-handers such as McCovey never play. Deploying Cepeda at third meant benching Davenport, a superb defender. Or Rigney would station Cepeda in left field, replacing Jackie Brandt. This also weakened the Giants' defense, given that Brandt would win a Gold Glove for fielding excellence that year.

Thus began an ongoing debate that lasted until the Giants traded Cepeda to St. Louis on May 4, 1966: What's the best way to keep both McCovey and Cepeda in the lineup? Said Rigney in Mike Mandel's outstanding 1979 oral history, SF *Giants*, "I talked like a bloody Dutch uncle to get Cepeda to play left field, because he could have. And then I could have had both of them in the lineup. He wouldn't do it. He just wouldn't do it. . . . I showed him what the lineup would look like, he and Mays and McCovey hitting back to back to back where there would be no easy inning for anybody."

Cepeda instantly demonstrated that trouble was imminent. He said all the right things upon seeing himself assigned to third base on the morning of McCovey's debut: "I don't like it but I have to play it. I'll give it 100 percent." He wasn't at all sanguine after the game, however. "I don't belong on that base anymore," Cepeda said.

The McCovey-induced boost lasted through September 17, when the Giants whipped Milwaukee, 13–6. After Braves ace Warren Spahn faced only 4 batters, San Francisco seized upon his absence. Putting his U1 model to good use, Bressoud banged out 3 hits and scored 4 runs from the leadoff spot. Mays went 4-for-4 with 5 RBIs. Davenport homered to fuel a 4-RBI effort, and Cepeda had a run-scoring single among his 2 hits. With the Giants leading 8–5, McCovey contributed a 2-run double in the 7th inning that essentially determined the outcome. This game demonstrated the awesome potential of the Giants' offense; their 13-run total was 1 shy of their season high. Moreover, the outcome lengthened San Francisco's lead in the NL standings to 2 games over Milwaukee and Los Angeles with 8 to play. Giddy fans wondered whether Candlestick Park's construction was far enough along to accommodate World Series crowds.

Two days later, however, the Dodgers captured both ends of a day-night doubleheader at Seals Stadium, 4–1 and 5–3. The Dodgers completed the series sweep with an 8–2 win on September 20. The Giants trailed first-place Los Angeles by 1 mere game, but back-to-back, last-at-bat losses to the Cubs at Wrigley Field broke the Giants' spirit. San Francisco ultimately finished third, 4 games behind the Dodgers and 2 behind the second-place Braves, with an 83-71 record and 7 losses in its last 8 games.

The NL Rookie of the Year vote wasn't nearly as competitive as the pennant race. McCovey received all twenty-four votes from members of the

Baseball Writers' Association of America. He joined Cepeda (1958) and Cincinnati's Frank Robinson (1956) as the award's only recipients to win the vote unanimously.

The election's most remarkable aspect was that McCovey appeared in only 52 games for the Giants, approximately one-third of the schedule. Yet the strength of his performance was undeniable. He batted .354 with 13 home runs and 38 RBIs, garnishing those figures with a .429 on-base percentage and a .656 slugging percentage. That gave him an otherworldly OPS (on-base plus slugging percentage, a statistic that had not yet been discovered) of 1.085.

Consistent? He sustained a 22-game hitting streak from August 17 through September 10, batting .378 in that span. Resilient? On August 31 at Los Angeles, he struck out and fouled out in his first two plate appearances against Sandy Koufax. He homered in his third at bat. "The Giants in those days had so many guys that made a big impact, you had to be great to stand out," Simmons said. "And he did."

Rigney praised McCovey's mastery of hitting basics: "He takes a short stride and keeps his head still. That's why he times the ball so well. He stays on top of the ball and he doesn't uppercut it. He has a near-perfect swing, a picture swing, and he doesn't go after too many bad balls. He can hit right-handers and left-handers just the same." In fact, McCovey batted .360 off right-handers and .340 off lefties. Emboldened by their success with signing and developing talent—in 1960 they would unveil right-hander Juan Marichal—the Giants envisioned a bright future for themselves.

2

Man from Mobile

We had this big vision in our heads that someday we might
play in the Major Leagues.
—Hall of Fame outfielder Billy Williams

Willie Lee McCovey was born on January 10, 1938, at 906 South Hamilton
Street in Mobile, Alabama. He was the seventh of ten children brought into
this world by Frank and Ester McCovey. A younger Frank topped the roster
of McCovey kids, followed by Frances, Wyatt, Ethel, Arthur, Richmond,
Willie, Walter, Clauzell, and Cleon.

By the time Willie came along, members of the McCovey brood sensed
when their family was about to grow. Ester's maternity wear was the giveaway
clue. "They knew she was getting ready to have another kid because she would
set out those funny-looking clothes," said Angelia Guillot, Ethel's daughter
and one of Willie's nieces who serves as the family's unofficial historian.

The McCoveys met under less-than-romantic circumstances. Ester was
among the employees whom Frank supervised on a farm in Shipman, Missis-
sippi. For this reason Ester continued to call Frank "Mister Frank" throughout their relationship. The children called Ester "Big Mama," despite her
diminutive stature, or "Sugar." Potatoes, corn, and onions were among the
primary crops produced at the farm.

The McCoveys moved to the Hamilton Street house after Mister Frank
got a job with the Gulf, Mobile and Ohio Railroad. They maintained their
close ties with relatives from Shipman who also went to work for the
GM&O. They'd spend the night at the McCoveys' when passing through
Mobile.

The McCovey siblings grew to know each other extremely well under these circumstances. The children would sleep atop wooden pallets covered by blankets. There just wasn't much room at 906 South Hamilton, which was known as a "shotgun" house. "When you stood at the front door, you could see all the way to the back door," Angelia related.

Said Willie, "You could very easily go walking in the wrong house, they all looked so much alike. It was an all-black neighborhood that some people might call a ghetto, but I've seen some areas now since I've grown up that are considered ghettos and I think we were a lot better off than some of those neighborhoods."

The house wasn't immediately equipped with electricity, forcing the children to do their homework by the light of a kerosene lamp. The McCovey kids thus became efficient scholars. And when the logs had burned their last, it was bedtime, no questions asked. Occasionally, Mister Frank, who loved sweet potatoes, roasted a yam or two in the fire's ashes for a treat.

Fishing food from the flame was part of Frank McCovey's mystique. While so many children and guests came and went, he was the figure around whom everything revolved. "He was quiet, but he was the authoritarian of the household," Clauzell said.

It wasn't surprising, then, that Willie inherited his father's strong, silent persona. "Willie was just like Daddy. Two peas in a pod," Clauzell said. "They mostly didn't have much to say. But when one of them was saying something, you knew it."

Willie preferred to announce his presence as a youth with his athletic ability. He played football, basketball, and softball—the intensely competitive fast-pitch variety, not the social, let-'em-hit-it slow-pitch version. "They didn't do anything slow," Clauzell said of Willie and his athletically inclined cohorts.

As was the case in most of America at the time, baseball remained the "in" sport to play, particularly among young Blacks intent on emulating Jackie Robinson's bold integration of the Major Leagues in 1947. "I guess all kids have idols, and naturally Jackie Robinson was to all black kids," McCovey said. "Jackie Robinson gave us hope that maybe we could get to the big leagues." McCovey showed enough early promise to earn a spot on local sandlots playing with adults on Sundays.

When McCovey and his friends couldn't muster enough equipment or find a diamond or vacant lot for a ball game, they improvised by playing "top ball." They substituted bottle caps—hence the word *top*—for balls. Imagine the movement and velocity a pitcher could impart upon a bottle cap. Consider the technically sound swing a hitter had to employ to make meaningful contact. And the fact that the sweet spot on the so-called bats that top-ball players used was extremely sparse. "Most of the bats were mop handles, broom handles, whatever you could get your hands on," Clauzell said. "We'd play with them until nightfall."

In fact, watching Willie dominate his peers in top ball gave Clauzell the earliest notions that his big brother could someday be a big leaguer. "He was pretty good at hitting those caps," said Clauzell, who was ten years younger than Willie.

Ideally, the McCovey brothers and other aspiring ballplayers never would have had to play a single game of top ball. But segregationist Jim Crow laws denied Blacks access to many fields. "Most of the places in Mobile, blacks couldn't go," Clauzell said. "That's why we were on the street, hitting bottle caps."

McCovey's dreams of reaching the Majors seemed closer to fruition when he received an opportunity to meet the great Robinson. Giants scout Alex Pompez, who urged the club to sign McCovey, was traveling with Robinson's barnstorming team when it visited Mobile during one off-season. "Alex made sure to call me and took me down in the clubhouse and introduced me to Jackie," McCovey said. "It's funny because during that time, we didn't think of asking for autographs. Just meeting him and shaking his hand was enough for me."

Willie dropped out of Mobile's Central High School after his junior year, ostensibly to earn extra money for the family. He quite literally was pulling in additional dough by making biscuits at a local bakery. He tried to join the Navy but, at sixteen, was too young. There also was talk of his joining his elder brother Wyatt in Los Angeles, where work was said to be plentiful. But ultimately, the fact was that freeing himself from the encumberment of school enabled Willie to embrace his true ambition. "His whole focus was baseball," said his first wife, Karen Booker. "And that basically lasted throughout his entire life."

While visiting Wyatt during the 1954–55 holiday season, Willie was sum-moned home. Renowned "bird dog" scout Jesse Thomas had endorsed McCovey and other Mobile-area prospects to Pompez, the scout who built his Hall of Fame credentials largely on the talent he provided to the Giants. Pompez thus invited McCovey and a couple of dozen other youths to a tryout at the club's Minor League training facility in Melbourne, Florida. However, a significant obstacle stood between Willie and the start of his professional career: Mister Frank. The family patriarch was a deacon in the Baptist church and ran his household accordingly. "We were in church every week. Sometimes twice a week," Clauzell said. With this mindset came an unassailable rule: no games that could be remotely construed as gambling or could lead to betting were permitted at the McCovey home. The forbidden list included card games, checkers, chess, and virtually everything recreational. Playing sports outside the house as Willie did was barely tolerated. Surely he wouldn't be allowed to pursue baseball as a career. As one can imagine, the argument was loud and long. But Willie—with surprise support from Big Mama—got his wish.

Jack Schwarz, the Giants' director of Minor League operations, saw noth-ing impressive about the first twelve players to try out. In fact, the club's talent evaluators were so discouraged that they considered canceling the workout for the second group of players. But Schwarz was a little less pessi-mistic. "We're talking about $156," said Schwarz, referring to the bus fare for the next thirteen players. Again, the tryout was held. Again, twelve players were deemed lacking in big league talent. The thirteenth was McCovey. He agreed to a contract worth $175 per month, a deal that had to be signed by his mother. Ester McCovey did so but asked the Giants to include a $500 bonus. "Carl Hubbell, our chief of scouts, was in the office when I opened her letter," Schwarz said. "We looked at each other and agreed at once."

Never afraid to obtain players from any ethnic background after Robin-son broke the color barrier, the Giants also signed Puerto Ricans Orlando Cepeda (as a third baseman) and infielder Jose Pagan in 1955. As for McCovey, Schwarz assigned him to Sandersville in the Class D Georgia State League and admitted to having some "misgivings" over sending him to a spot in the Deep South, given racial attitudes. But, said Schwarz, "he became a great favorite down there." McCovey finished the season with a .305 batting average, 19 home runs, and a league-high 113 RBIs.

McCovey returned home in style. He reached South Hamilton Street behind the wheel of a green Oldsmobile, stopped the car, shut down the ignition, and gave Mister Frank the keys. "That's the only time I ever saw my father smile," Clauzell said. Yet never, not even once, did Frank McCovey see his son play a professional ball game in person.

In 1956, McCovey advanced to Danville, the Giants' Class B Carolina League affiliate, and outclassed his foes while batting .310 with 29 homers, 89 RBIs, and a league-best 38 doubles. After one of these first two seasons, McCovey befriended Billy Williams, the future Hall of Fame outfielder who spent most of his career with the Chicago Cubs. They met through Williams's brother, Franklin, an infielder-outfielder in the Pirates' system who played against McCovey in 1955 in the Georgia State League. "They got in a conversation and each of them didn't know the other guy was from Mobile," Williams said. "This was about '57, I think it was. After the season we spent so much time together. I was in Whistler, and he was in a town called Maysville—not named after Willie Mays. We lived about six miles from each other. We had this big vision in our heads that someday we might play in the major leagues."

They did, though Williams wasn't initially certain about his friend. McCovey endured the same fate that many players with unusual names encountered: their names got Americanized. The great Roberto Clemente, for example, was widely known as "Bob" Clemente in the 1950s and '60s. In McCovey's case, his surname was pronounced one way down South and another way elsewhere. "I knew him as Willie Mac-COH-vee," Williams said. "When I got to the big leagues, I asked, 'Who's Willie Mac-CUH-vee?'" Asked if certain family members still employ the name's "Mac-COH-vee" version, Clauzell McCovey said, "Most of us still do."

Decades earlier, Mobile natives and Negro League legends Satchel Paige and Ted "Double Duty" Radcliffe helped put the city on the baseball map. Hank Aaron, another Mobilian, guaranteed that it would stay there. To McCovey and Williams, he was an icon. When Aaron elevated himself into the elite level of stars by finishing third, first, and third, respectively, in the National

League Most Valuable Player Award voting from 1956 to 1958, he ensured that Mobile's baseball heritage would remain fruitful and multiply with the likes of center fielder Tommie Agee, one of the Mets' top performers in their 1969 World Series–winning season; Cleon Jones, the leading hitter for those '69 Mets; Amos Otis, five-time All-Star outfielder with Kansas City; and Ozzie Smith, who rewrote how to play shortstop during nineteen years in the Majors.

"We had to uphold a standard," Williams said. "We had a lot of pride. One Mobile guy would inspire the other one, like Aaron inspired McCovey and myself; we both were Rookies of the Year. And we inspired Tommie Agee, who started out with the White Sox and was a Rookie of the Year. So we had three guys from Mobile being Rookie of the Year. So many home runs, so many batting titles; so many MVPs."

Each year brought McCovey closer to the Majors—which was the same as saying that he came closer with each passing day to leaving the racist South. Intent on leaving behind this part of his past, he returned home on only a few occasions: following his wildly successful rookie season, for the funerals of his parents, and for a sports banquet. There might have been three or four other trips home, but no more than that.

McCovey was reminded of the region's ugly racial attitudes while playing for the Giants' Double-A Dallas affiliate in 1957. "We couldn't go to Austin," he said. "Black players couldn't play in Austin. We didn't even make the trip there. Weren't allowed. We usually played in Houston before we went to Austin, so we'd stay in Houston when the rest of the team went to Austin. Then we met them in the next city."

Two of Willie's nieces, Angelia and Carolyn, recalled the suffering that various cheerleading corps endured during the Black-only Mardi Gras parades when they stepped on planks of wood with nails, their sharp ends exposed, driven through them. "It was nasty down here," Clauzell said. "That was when [Alabama governor] George Wallace was telling everybody to go back to Africa. The Jim Crow thing was really what drove Willie away from here. Willie wouldn't even come back when they had his 'Day' here. My mother had to go out there and get his accolades."

An incident that occurred at the McCovey home demonstrated Blacks' vulnerability to harassment, as Clauzell related. Late one night, the family was awakened by loud knocking at the front door. "Open up! It's the law!" Frank McCovey quickly grabbed his gun and had it within reach if anything drastic were to happen. Nothing did; the officers were pursuing an escapee from prison who obviously wasn't being harbored by the McCoveys.

Interestingly, McCovey also encountered the type of behavior that prompted him to desert Mobile when he reported to San Francisco police that a rock was thrown through the window of his front door shortly after midnight on July 4, 1963. The brief story in *The Sporting News* read, in part, "Police were at a loss to explain the incident because there had been no racial trouble in the area. 'McCovey is a hero out here,' said Mrs. C.F. Chamberlain, a neighbor. 'The youngsters can't wait for him to get home so they can get a look at him.'"

3

Starting to Struggle

I hit best inside. And where were they pitching me? Inside.
They were jamming me. They knew I was a fraction of a
second behind in my swing.
—Willie McCovey

The Giants entered the 1960 season seemingly bent on prompting baseball's Hall of Fame to waive its eligibility standards for Willie McCovey. Following his 1959 performance, why wait for the mandatory five years to pass after his retirement to assign him a spot in Cooperstown? Rigney felt certain that his budding star would avoid the "sophomore jinx" that plunges many promising rookies into mediocrity. "He's one guy who I'd say would be immune," Rigney said. "His hitting is fundamentally too sound. He could be baseball's next .400 hitter."

The prospect of having McCovey in the lineup for an entire season left Rigney almost giddy with excitement. Moreover, left-handed-batting pull hitters such as McCovey were expected to thrive at Candlestick Park, the Giants' new home, due to the breezes that would carry fly balls toward right field. "How many home runs will he hit? I'll put it at a conservative 30," Rigney said.

For a team that hadn't risen to the top of the National League since 1954, the 1960 Giants sounded like a ballclub that was lounging comfortably on the observation deck. "A lot of people thought that if the Russians didn't attack, we'd win the pennant by fifteen [games]," Rigney said.

Things didn't quite turn out that way. Not for McCovey. Not for the Giants. And definitely not for Rigney. On May 29, the Giants were 25-14 and held a share of first place with eventual NL champion Pittsburgh. Then the "June Swoon," a malaise that typically overcame the Giants as they approached the summer solstice, struck them again. The swoon initially plagued the Giants in 1958, when they entered the month in first place and emerged from it in third place after a 10-17 finish. The Giants posted a respectable 17-14 June mark in 1959 but regressed to 11-16 in '60.

There had been little talk of a swoon when Monday, June 13, dawned. The Giants (32-21) trailed Pittsburgh (32-20) by a mere ½ game. In that day's series finale against Milwaukee, they scored 4 1st-inning runs off formidable right-hander Lew Burdette. But Jack Sanford, one of San Francisco's most dependable starters, was removed during the 2nd inning as the Braves amassed 4 runs to tie the score. They pulled away with 5 9th-inning runs to rout the Giants, 12–5.

That started a 4-game losing streak that was particularly ominous for the Giants, since it was Pittsburgh, the eventual NL champions, who dealt them the next three defeats. The aggregate score for the series was 30–16, making the Pirates' sweep look all the more definitive.

The lopsided results reflected the unusually feeble efforts that the Giants delivered. Errors by shortstop Eddie Bressoud and second baseman Don Blasingame generated 4 unearned runs in the series opener, which Pittsburgh captured, 6–3. During Pittsburgh's 14–6 thumping in the next game, San Francisco used six pitchers, a common occurrence in contemporary big league baseball but an astonishingly high number in that era. The third game—and the series—would have seemed like even more of a mismatch had the Giants not scored 5 meaningless 9th-inning runs in a 10–7 decision.

The Giants broke their slump with a 7–3 win over Philadelphia on June 17. That didn't prevent owner Horace Stoneham from firing Rigney, despite the Giants' 33-25 record. San Francisco trailed Pittsburgh by 4 games, which was hardly insurmountable. But Stoneham had lost confidence in Rigney, probably dating back to the previous season's pennant race. "We were being outhustled," Stoneham told reporters. "I've been thinking about a change for some time."

Tom Sheehan, one of Stoneham's top scouts, succeeded Rigney. Sheehan became primarily known for his bloated physique, which forced the clubhouse staff to struggle to find him a jersey that fit properly. "He wore size 46 pants and a 58 shirt," said clubhouse and equipment manager Mike Murphy, still sounding incredulous more than a half century later.

Everybody knew that Sheehan would serve as just an interim manager until the Giants could find a more qualified replacement during the 1961–62 off-season. Lacking the daily focus that ballplayers need to excel, the Giants staggered to a 46-50 record under Sheehan. Said Murphy, "'I'm not saying the team gave up on him, but the unofficial team slogan became, 'Shut up and deal.'"

McCovey struggled no matter who was managing. He began the season ranked among the National League leaders with 9 home runs and 32 RBIS by the end of May. He hit his first career grand slam on June 12 against Milwaukee's Carlton Willey to spark a 16–7 Giants rout, then went 2-for-4 the next day to lift his batting average to .255. That figure never climbed higher for the rest of the season. In the 19 games following that brief binge, McCovey hit .208 with no home runs and 2 RBIS, prompting his demotion to Triple-A Tacoma on July 17. "He took it like a man," recalled Cepeda, who returned to first base after playing left field regularly.

McCovey's demotion enabled the Giants to summon Juan Marichal, another Alex Pompez–inspired "find," from Tacoma. The twenty-two-year-old right-hander made his Major League debut on July 19 against Philadelphia at Candlestick Park and was 4 outs away from a no-hitter when pinch hitter Clay Dalrymple singled softly but cleanly into center field. That would be the Phillies' lone hit off Marichal, who walked 1 and struck out 12 in the Giants' 2–0 triumph. Thus another star was born. Marichal reached the 20-win level six times, was named to ten All-Star teams, led the Majors with 191 victories in the 1960s, and joined McCovey, Mays, and Cepeda in the Hall of Fame. "When Juan pitched," McCovey said, "that was 'win' day."

McCovey returned to the Giants for the season's final two months but impressed nobody. He hit .216 (11-for-51) with 2 home runs and 11 RBIS in 30 games. Sheehan saw fit to start McCovey in only 8 of those games. The NL's reigning Rookie of the Year hit .238 with 13 homers in 101 games (65 starts). To many, it appeared to be a disastrous regression.

Or was it really that bad? McCovey accumulated 13 homers and 51 RBIS in just 260 at bats. Those were better ratios than Willie Mays (29 homers,

103 RBIS, 595 at bats) or Orlando Cepeda (24 homers, 96 RBIS, 569 at bats) compiled. To a considerable degree, McCovey and his teammates shared an extremely large problem: playing at Candlestick Park, their new home. It was uncomfortable at best and unfair at the worst. Candlestick's chilly, windy conditions weren't conducive to generating offense. Basic statistics illustrated this. At home, the Giants batted .244, recorded a .367 slugging percentage, hit 46 homers, and scored 296 runs. Their corresponding numbers on the road were .265, .416, 84, and 375.

Hitters pointed accusatory fingers at the yawning outfield dimensions, which included 420 feet to center field and 397 feet to the left-field power alley. According to a widely circulated quotation attributed to McCovey, he allegedly said of Candlestick, "The peanut shells get in your eyes." About fifty years later, McCovey denied making that remark.

McCovey, who would finish his career as the most prolific hitter in Candlestick history, performed there through most of 1960 as if he'd rather be anyplace else. He batted .204 at home with 4 homers and 20 RBIS in 47 games. But McCovey hit capably in 54 road games, batting .270—his ultimate lifetime average overall—with a .916 OPS that put him on a par with All-Stars. Moreover, he hit when it counted, though his opportunities were limited. With 2 outs and at least 1 runner in scoring position, McCovey batted .300 (9-for-30) with a 1.010 OPS. He thrived in late-inning pressure situations, hitting .291 (16-for-55) with a 1.085 OPS. (A late-and-close opportunity is defined as a plate appearance in the 7th inning or later when the batter's team trails by 3 runs or fewer, is tied, or is ahead by only 1 run. Bases-loaded plate appearances also fit this category when the batting team trails by 4 runs during any at bat in the 7th inning or later when the batter's team trails by 3 runs or fewer, is tied, or is ahead by only 1 run. If the bases are loaded and the batting team trails by 4 runs, this also counts as a late-inning pressure situation.)

Nevertheless, .238 is still .238. Being approximately twenty pounds overweight affected McCovey's production, he told the *San Francisco Examiner*. "I hit best inside," he said. "And where were they pitching me? Inside. They were jamming me. They knew I was a fraction of a second behind in my swing." Sheehan's summary of McCovey's performance was succinct and somewhat cruel: "He can't run, he can't field, he can't hit."

Even the great Mays couldn't overcome Candlestick. He continued to excel, batting .319 while rapping a big league–high 190 hits. But his total of 29 homers was his lowest for a full season, primarily because he clouted only 12 of them at Candlestick. The Giants' bullpen was initially situated in the park's left-field foul territory, where relievers routinely watched Mays belt drives with home run trajectory that died at the warning track, struck down by the capricious breezes. Mays's OPS at home, a commendable .875, soared to .990 on the road.

Mays needed relatively little time to adjust to Candlestick, however. He was *that* talented. He remained mostly a pull hitter, but he learned to capitalize on the right field–bound jet stream. Consider that he recorded two of the most important hits of his career by driving the ball to the opposite field—his 9th-inning double in Game 7 of the 1962 World Series and his 512th home run, which he hit off Dodgers lefty Claude Osteen on May 4, 1966, to become the NL's all-time home run leader.

As the Giants began spring training in 1961 under new manager Alvin Dark, McCovey remained under intense scrutiny. Dark wanted to maintain a mostly set lineup throughout the NL's annual dogfight that masqueraded as a baseball season. A steady year from McCovey at first base would enable Dark to stabilize the lineup by keeping Cepeda in left field. Dark then could limit his daily personnel debate to fielding the club's best defensive lineup, which would put Jim Davenport at third base. Or Dark could emphasize offense. That meant starting Harvey Kuenn, the 1959 American League (AL) batting champion with Detroit, instead of Davenport.

Expectations remained high for the Giants. So when they failed to fulfill the hopes of the fans by finishing third, 8 games behind Cincinnati, the public needed a scapegoat to absorb the blame. McCovey became a convenient target. His total of 50 RBIs ranked sixth on the team and was virtually identical to the 51 he amassed in 1960. But he also hiked his home run output from 13 to 18, scored 59 runs compared to 37 the year before, lifted his batting average 33 points to .271, and inched his OPS higher from .818 to .841. He also batted a blistering .426 (23-for-54) with 5 home runs in August.

That didn't completely temper the fans' skepticism. *San Francisco Chronicle* sports editor Art Rosenbaum described a scene from a May 21, 1961, game against the Dodgers at Candlestick in which McCovey struck out as a pinch hitter to end the 8th inning. Never mind that the pitcher was the fabulous Sandy Koufax, who was in the process of finishing a 4-hit, complete-game effort in a 3–2 Los Angeles triumph. Rosenbaum cited a seven-year-old boy who "booed his lungs out" at McCovey. Asked why he was booing McCovey, the kid replied, "Because everybody else is." After the game, Rosenbaum gave the embattled scapegoat a chance to speak. Said a shaken yet determined McCovey, "I know I can hit some more. I know it. I know it."

McCovey evolved into a polarizing figure. His success was met with skepticism; his effort caused ennui. McCovey was prone to defensive lapses. What young player isn't? Except when he goofed, Giants fans were apt to remember and slow to forgive. Booing therefore followed McCovey wherever he went on the field—not perpetually, but often enough to be noticed. Of course, many fans had climbed onto Cepeda's bandwagon during his 1958 Rookie of the Year campaign and wouldn't budge. They remained enamored of Cepeda as a first baseman. If Cepeda committed an error while playing one of his alternate positions, left field or third base, that was McCovey's fault—because, they reasoned, if Cepeda had been stationed at first base, the misplay wouldn't have happened.

McCovey also seemed to attract more than his share of bad luck. During the 1960 season, he belted a particularly vicious home run at Philadelphia that a rainout washed away. In '61, he scorched a line drive to center field that mutilated the fielding glove of his idol, Hank Aaron. The official scorer, giving McCovey no credit for hitting a ball so hard that Aaron could not field it, ruled the play a 2-base error instead of a double.

One newspaper columnist, the *San Francisco Chronicle*'s Charles McCabe, was especially harsh on McCovey, which fanned the flames of the public's discontent. At one point, McCabe, known as the "Fearless Spectator," urged the Giants to trade McCovey to their Tacoma Triple-A affiliate for a tarpaulin. McCovey regarded this slight as he did many other inconveniences: he shrugged it off. When somebody asked McCovey if he'd like to punch McCabe, he responded, "How can I hit him? I don't even know who he is."

4

Learning Lessons

He really was my mentor as far as hitting.

—Willie McCovey on Ted Williams

Despite Willie McCovey's struggles, he was taking shape as a hitter. His genesis accelerated during his first Major League spring training with the Giants, months before he captured his Rookie of the Year Award.

While training in Scottsdale from 1959 to 1965, the Boston Red Sox were a frequent Cactus League opponent for the Giants, who made their preseason home in neighboring Phoenix. Whether he was a bashful youth or a bold veteran, McCovey refrained from batting cage chitchat. "When I showed up at the ballpark and went on the field, I had my game face on," he said.

McCovey made an exception in the spring of '59 for a particularly garrulous member of the Red Sox: the one and only Ted Williams.

One can imagine that their conversations were one-sided yet not imbalanced, since they complemented each other nicely—one speaking, the other listening. Williams surely did virtually all the talking, which should have been expected from the man widely considered the greatest hitter who ever lived—and who was known to freely share his philosophies of how a big leaguer should comport himself in the batter's box. McCovey absorbed every word uttered by this more accomplished and experienced version of himself: a slender left-handed batter with remarkable power and a slightly uppercutting swing. "For some reason, he kind of took a liking to me," McCovey said. "We were always kind of the same in stature."

One can guess that McCovey had to stifle a chuckle more than once at Williams's colorful language. McCovey's parents did not tolerate cursing in their household, and he would have laughed inwardly if he imagined how shocked and horrified they would have been to hear Williams's profanity. "The Splendid Splinter" may have been crude, but he was anything but cruel. His salty language simply added spice to his message. Most likely, McCovey occasionally nodded to let Williams know that he was listening. McCovey was so quiet and transfixed, you couldn't really tell.

McCovey attributed his knack for refusing to chase bad pitches to Williams, a six-time American League batting champion who hit .344 lifetime.

"I learned from Ted Williams about getting a good pitch to hit," McCovey said. "He was really my mentor as far as hitting. I talked to Ted a lot."

Selecting the right bat was an endless topic of fascination for Williams and McCovey. Initially, McCovey used a 34½-inch model that varied in weight between 32 and 33 ounces. "Ted said that it's best to have a bat too light than to have one too heavy," McCovey said. "That's when I went down from 34 ounces to about 33, 32. As I got older, though, I went back up."

At that point, McCovey increased the length of his bat to 35 inches. "When I look back at it, I kind of hate that I did that," said McCovey. "You'd be amazed how much that little half-inch difference makes. It doesn't sound like much, but it is. It's hard to get to that inside pitch. I have long arms anyway. So why do I need a long bat?"

Jeff Torborg, a Dodgers catcher during the 1960s, insisted that nothing was wrong with McCovey's plate coverage. "The sweet spot of his bat might be two, three inches out of the strike zone. That's how much extension he got," Torborg said. By the time McCovey began flourishing in the mid-1960s, he was like most players—making constant adjustments, using whatever lumber felt good at the time.

Williams's other piece of advice for McCovey was to swing a weighted bat during the off-season. For McCovey, the resulting buildup of muscle helped his arms look a little less spindly and increased his bat speed. For Williams, this enabled him to get in a baseball-related workout while leaving him ample time to indulge in his off-season passion: fishing.

Though Williams retired as an active player in 1960, twenty years before McCovey, their career paths intersected on multiple occasions. Could either man have known that both would finish their illustrious careers with 521 home runs? That figure ranked third all-time when Williams retired; it tied for eighth when McCovey stopped playing.

The intentional walk was virtually unheard of in the middle of the twentieth century, but these two sluggers forced opposing managers to employ it. McCovey set a Major League record with 45 intentional walks in 1969, when he captured the National League's Most Valuable Player Award. That broke Williams's mark of 33, which he established in 1957.

Then there was The Shift. It was routinely used for several seasons, even when ordinary hitters were at the plate, before rules changes outlawed it in 2023. It was viewed as an act of desperation when Williams, McCovey, and another left-handed-batting, pull-hitting power threat, Braves star Eddie Mathews, confronted it. Since Williams was a pull hitter, Cleveland skipper Lou Boudreau positioned five fielders on the first base half of the diamond in an effort to neutralize him during the 1946 season. Cincinnati manager Dave Bristol dusted off the strategy against McCovey during the aforementioned 1969 campaign.

Finally, due to fortunate timing and longevity, each man performed in the Majors during four calendar decades. For Williams, it was a remarkable achievement, given his extensive military service.

Common sense dictated that the Giants should have fielded trade proposals involving McCovey as routinely as if they were ground balls hit during infield practice. As the 1960s began, the Giants insisted that McCovey was integral to their plans as a first baseman. Yet each season ended with Orlando Cepeda as the position's primary occupant.

Fresh off his fabulous Rookie of the Year campaign, McCovey was the Giants' 1960 Opening Day first baseman in the Candlestick Park inaugural against St. Louis. That was no surprise, since first base was the only position that McCovey ever had played. Cepeda started in right field. It seemed appropriate—a new lineup settling into a new home. Except that by July, McCovey was languishing in Triple-A. And despite playing exclusively left field through San Francisco's first 57 games, Cepeda ultimately made 61 starts at first base. The Giants showed no inclination to give McCovey the first base job and allow him to grow into it.

The 1961 season began with Alvin Dark, the Giants' new manager, promising to give McCovey more playing time at first base. Dark's resolve became a tad flimsy when McCovey's batting average dipped below .200 in each of the season's first two months. McCovey recorded one of his better months of the season in June (.325 batting average, 5 home runs, 15 RBIs) but started only 28 games from July 1 through the end of the season. This coincided with Cepeda's blossoming into one of the game's elite sluggers. "The Baby Bull" reached career bests in homers, with an NL-high 46, and RBIs, with a Major League–leading 142.

McCovey continued to weather impatience from fans and reporters. Why, asked the skeptics, can't he hit more often, as he did during his rookie season? Cepeda's learning the outfield; shouldn't McCovey do the same thing so Orlando can reclaim first base full time? Some observers believed that no matter what McCovey did, he never would possess a big leaguer's panache because he moved so awkwardly.

Through it all, McCovey and Cepeda remained close friends. They lived in neighboring apartment buildings on Pacheco Street and would take turns driving as they rode to Candlestick Park together. On nights off, they'd sample San Francisco's lively jazz scene, visiting clubs such as the Jazz Workshop, the Blackhawk, and Basin Street West to check out Oscar Peterson, Dizzy Gillespie, Mongo Santamaria, Cal Tjader, Miles Davis, Sonny Rollins, and others. "The big ones," Cepeda said.

McCovey recalled meeting Count Basie, the legendary pianist, bandleader, and composer. He also had some less cheerful memories that lasted more than a half century. Because McCovey was so quiet and docile, some reporters thought they could generate news by attributing remarks to him that he didn't utter. "They tried to make me and Cepeda enemies," McCovey said. "They tried to make me and Mays enemies." Through time, McCovey would learn which members of the media he could and couldn't trust.

Meanwhile, the McCovey-Cepeda brotherhood went only so far. Cepeda wouldn't budge from first base. And Giants management refused to exercise its prerogative to make him do so.

"When Willie McCovey came up, everybody knew he was going to be great," Cepeda said. "He came out of the minors strong but then he started struggling, especially against left-handed pitchers. They wanted both of us in the lineup every day, but I wasn't crazy about playing in the outfield. I know I could have played left field, but I was only 21 at that time and a little stubborn. I was proud and felt like I deserved playing at first, so it got in my head a little bit. But it never affected my hitting. Rigney told some reporters I was a better athlete than Willie and that's why I could play the outfield. So, I told him I'm your first baseman and not a left fielder. McCovey got sent back to the minors in 1960, so I got my job back for a while until he came back. Then in 1962, Al Dark moved McCovey to left field and I was back at first base where I belonged."

A latter-day comparison to McCovey would be another first baseman, Brandon Belt, who helped the Giants win World Series titles in 2012 and 2014 and proved instrumental to their franchise-best 107-win season in 2021. Belt's contributions to numerous victories weren't enough for a lot of fans—and even for some people within the Giants organization. He never batted .300, never drove in 100 runs, and didn't exceed 20 home runs until 2021, his 11th season. Even Belt's greatest moment as a Giant went relatively unnoticed. His 18th-inning home run at Washington in Game 2 of the 2014 NL Division Series gave the Giants a 2–1 win. But though the game ended before bedtime for most fans on the West Coast, many others likely lacked the stamina to stick with a 6-hour, 23-minute marathon all the way to the end.

Belt went on binges when he appeared poised to metamorphose into one of the league's top performers. Then came a slump or, worse yet, one of four concussions that would sideline him and impede his progress.

McCovey never endured that kind of physical misfortune, though his head must have been spinning at times. Manager Alvin Dark also had to find playing time for talented outfielders Felipe Alou and Harvey Kuenn, the 1959 AL batting champion with Detroit who was acquired from Cleveland on December 3, 1960, for left-hander Johnny Antonelli and outfielder Willie Kirkland. If both Alou and Kuenn started, Cepeda shifted to first base and McCovey was benched.

Here's how Dark made it work in 1961, with each player's number of starts listed by position:

Cepeda: 75 first base, 59 left field, 17 right field
Kuenn: 64 left field, 29 third base, 27 right field

Alou: 78 right field, 19 left field, 2 center field

McCovey: 79 first base

No wonder other ballclubs coveted McCovey. He appeared expendable. Then as now, genuine power hitters were a rare commodity. Despite McCovey's fluctuations in performance, the baseball world noticed his potential for greatness. Maybe that's why the Giants stubbornly held onto him. Besides, as general manager Chub Feeney pointed out, the Giants had lost enough Major League personnel due to the needs of the New York and Houston expansion clubs, not to mention the needs of Uncle Sam. Said Feeney shortly before the 1961 winter meetings, "We have already lost seven of the 25 players we carried last season to the Mets, Colts or U.S. Army, and we're not going to rush into any deal to part with more of our 1961 players." Then again, perhaps McCovey wasn't as untouchable as the Giants led the public to believe.

Early in the 1962 season, New York–based baseball columnist Milton Gross reported that the Giants had a deal in place during the previous off-season that would have sent McCovey to the St. Louis Cardinals for second baseman Julian Javier. This proposed swap was intriguing on several levels.

Cardinals first baseman Bill White, the future National League president who would finish his playing career in 1969 as an eight-time All-Star first baseman, would have had to move to the outfield with McCovey on board in St. Louis.

White broke into the Majors with the Giants in 1956 and spent a year in the military before rejoining the ballclub during their inaugural season in San Francisco in 1958. He went to St. Louis in a four-player deal that brought valuable righty Sam Jones to the Giants.

Second base, a position that remained a trouble spot for the Giants through most of the 1960s, was an issue at this time because they lost Joe Amalfitano to Houston in the expansion draft following the '61 season. It's anybody's guess as to whether Javier would have propelled the Giants to greater heights. But he did make the All-Star team in 1963 and '68. In between, he finished ninth in the National League's 1967 MVP voting.

Figuring that the Giants needed Javier more than McCovey due to Cepeda's massive presence, Dark gave San Francisco general manager Chub Feeney his support for the deal. But Horace Stoneham, Feeney's uncle, who also happened to be the Giants' owner, blocked the trade. Visions of McCovey bashing homer after homer over the low right-field roof at St. Louis' Sportsman's Park evaporated from the dreams of Cardinals management. Stoneham's reasoning was simple, according to Gross. Referring to White, Stoneham said, "We've got one of our guys over there knocking our brains out. How would it look if there were two?"

Nevertheless, the Giants appeared to have little or no use for McCovey at times. Dark announced before spring training began in 1962 that McCovey would play left field. That doomed McCovey to a reserve role, due largely to Kuenn's steady presence. Moreover, McCovey would need ample on-the-job training in left, which the Giants could not afford to provide if they were to meet their expectations of contending for the pennant again.

In fact, McCovey received a career-low 262 plate appearances in 1962 while appearing in just 91 games. Yet he remained a legitimate force by making the most of his scant opportunities. He hit 20 homers, an average of 1 every 11.45 at bats.

Being a Giant meant being capable of supplying this kind of pop. On April 16, for example, they manhandled the archrival Dodgers, 19–8. It was the Giants' seventh game of the '62 campaign and the first of thousands that ten-year-old Jon Miller of Hayward, California, witnessed in person.

As Miller, the Giants' heralded broadcaster, recalled that night, he sounded as if he already had begun studying depth charts to prepare for calling a game. "Think of the talent on the bench!" he exclaimed. In fact, the Giants' late-inning substitutes included McCovey, a future Hall of Famer; Matty Alou, a future batting champion; and Manny Mota, one of the finest pinch hitters ever. Also on the Giants' roster was future All-Star catcher Tom Haller.

McCovey may not have been essential to the team's success that year, but he certainly was involved in it. On May 10, he clobbered a 3-run, 5th-inning homer off Bob Gibson to support Billy O'Dell in a 6–0 decision. Then, before a standing-room-only crowd in the Giants' first game at the Polo Grounds since they left New York, McCovey upstaged Mays, the darling of Manhattan, by homering twice in a 9–6 San Francisco conquest. Mays homered off future Giants manager Roger Craig in the

5th inning, but McCovey belted 2 homers off Craig, yanking 1 to right in the 1st inning before stroking 1 to left in the third. In the opener of a July 4 doubleheader against the Mets, McCovey drove in 7 runs with 2 home runs and 2 sacrifice flies in a 3-for-3 performance as San Francisco outdistanced the Mets, 11–4.

McCovey's next addition to his personal highlight collection no doubt can be termed as one of the biggest moments of his career. It was August 11, 1962, and 41,268 spectators jammed Candlestick for the second of a 3-game series against the first-place Dodgers. One night earlier, the Giants thumped the Dodgers, 11–2. But Los Angeles still led the second-place Giants by 4½ games in the NL standings. Many "must-win" moments arise during the course of a pennant race. For the Giants, this was one of them.

The game would have delighted any baseball purist. San Francisco left-hander Billy Pierce drew upon his veteran craftiness and subdued the Dodgers with finesse. Los Angeles right-hander Don Drysdale avoided such subtlety. He was the quintessential power pitcher, seeking to intimidate everyone he faced with hard stuff. That year's eventual NL Cy Young Award winner entered the game with a 21-4 record, proving that his approach was working nicely. But he wasn't invincible.

Tommy Davis, a leading Giants nemesis, ambushed Pierce with a 3-run, 1st-inning homer. The Giants narrowed their deficit to 3–2 in the 5th when Willie Mays lashed a lead-off double and scored on Felipe Alou's 1-out single, which preceded Jim Davenport's 2-out RBI double. The Dodgers still led by a run when McCovey was announced as the pinch hitter for Pierce with 2 on and 2 out in the 6th.

Drysdale and McCovey arm-wrestled each other to a 3–2 count. The pro-Giants patrons clapped their hands rhythmically, hoping for a big moment. It came with McCovey's next swing. He propelled the ball over the right-field barrier, giving the Giants a 5–3 advantage. Mind you, this was McCovey's first plate appearance since August 4. Pinch-hitting is a challenging task for batters receiving regular activity. For players relegated to spot duty such as McCovey, it's virtually impossible. A week had passed since McCovey had faced big league pitching, and he still managed to excel. Then again, McCovey rarely, if ever, looked overmatched as a hitter.

Giants broadcaster Russ Hodges instantly knew that this was no ordinary home run. It was an act that was destined to live forever in Giants-Dodgers lore, provided by a man who ascended to the summit of his skill. "That's one of the big thrills in the history of Candlestick Park—to see Willie McCovey put the Giants ahead, 5–3," Hodges said on the broadcast as the crowd continued to roar in the background. Fans were still buzzing after the inning ended.

The Giants held on to win, 5–4. They subdued Los Angeles again the next day, completing a 3-game sweep that trimmed the Dodgers' lead in the NL standings to 2½ games. But McCovey had scant impact on the race he intensified, at least immediately. He started 5 games during the rest of August. But he made 18 starts in September, and given the fury of the pennant race, every big game he had was hailed as significant.

Reigning NL champion Cincinnati entered the home stretch believing it had a chance to overtake the Giants and Dodgers. McCovey helped cool the Reds' hopes, however. He homered and drove in 4 runs in a 10–2 rout over Cincinnati on August 31, then drove in a pair of runs on September 2 as the Giants outlasted the Reds, 6–4. Before these contests, the third-place Reds (82-53) trailed the second-place Giants (84-49) by 3 games and the front-running Dodgers (87-47) by 5½. After the McCovey-led wins, though, the Reds trailed the Giants by 4 games and the Dodgers by 7½. Cincinnati did not come closer than 3½ games behind Los Angeles thereafter.

Meanwhile, the Giants maintained pressure on Los Angeles by winning 3 of 4 at Dodger Stadium in a September 3–6 series. McCovey started in left field and went 0-for-4 as the Giants took the opener, 7–3. But he made his presence felt in the finale by singling home a 1st-inning run and doubling and scoring in the 3rd inning to highlight a 3-for-4 effort. The Giants' 9–6 conquest trimmed the Dodgers' lead to 1½ games.

The road between mid-September and game 162 seemed to be paved with quicksand. A 7-game winning streak left the Giants only a ½ game behind the Dodgers on September 11. Then came an 11-game, four-city sojourn, which began with 6 consecutive losses. The Dodgers' lead swelled to 4 games before the Giants returned from their trip 3 games back with 6 to go on September 25.

It was at that point that the Dodgers forgot how to hit. Following a 7-game winning streak, they dropped 10 of their final 13 decisions, including 8 games in which they scored 2 runs or fewer. An oft-told anecdote from that juncture features ex-Giants infielder Joe Amalfitano, who played for the Houston Colt .45s but retained a silent, tempered fondness for his former team. The season's final weekend was at hand, and Amalfitano, who was in San Francisco with the Colt .45s, felt compelled to offer Willie Mays some encouragement after Houston took 2 of 3 games from the Dodgers. Said Amalfitano, "Can you score a run?" Mays seemed nonplussed by the question. "I think we can," Mays replied. Amalfitano elaborated, "Then you've got the pennant. Those Dodgers are never going to score another run."

The Friday night Colts-Giants series opener at Candlestick was rained out, forcing a Saturday doubleheader. McCovey contributed handsomely to the Giants' 11–5 triumph in the first game, collecting his 20th homer and scoring 3 runs in a 2-for-3 afternoon. But Houston won the nightcap, 4–2, leaving San Francisco 1 game behind Los Angeles. Meanwhile, St. Louis smothered the Dodgers in 10 innings on Friday, 3–2, then blanked them on Saturday, 2–0. For a 3-game playoff to ensue, the Giants had to win their regular-season finale, then hope that St. Louis could stop the Dodgers again.

Everything went the Giants' way at Candlestick. Mays's 8th-inning homer lifted them to a 2–1 triumph minutes before the Cardinals sealed their 1–0 victory over the punchless Dodgers. Houston started Dick Farrell, a power-pitching right-hander, which may have explained why Giants manager Alvin Dark played McCovey at first base instead of Cepeda. "The Baby Bull" was unhappy about his benching, but the passage of the years mellowed his attitude toward Dark. "He had his hands full, trying to play me and Willie at the same time," Cepeda said.

In the tiebreaker series, McCovey performed sparingly but effectively, as he had done all year. After sitting out Game 1, which the Giants captured, 8–0, he contributed an RBI single in the 6th inning of Game 2, a 4-run outburst that gave San Francisco an apparently insurmountable 5–0 edge at Los Angeles. Then the Dodgers emerged from their stupor of 33 consecutive scoreless innings by scoring 7 runs in their half of the 6th en route to an 8–7 victory. McCovey was back on the bench for Game 3, though Dark called upon him when necessary. Batting for Chuck Hiller, he coaxed a 9th-inning walk from Dodgers reliever Ed Roebuck with a runner on first base and one out. The free pass helped generate the Giants' 4-run surge at Dodger Stadium that turned a 4–2 deficit into a 6–4 win that put them in the World Series against the New York Yankees.

McCovey was beyond euphoric during the postgame celebration. According to David Plaut, whose book *Chasing October* provided a superb account of the 1962 season from the Giants' and Dodgers' perspectives, a television camera caught McCovey bellowing, "This is the greatest day of my life!"

He nearly found more precious joy a few weeks later.

5

"The Day I Hit the Line Drive"

He said later that it was one of the hardest balls
he had ever hit.

—Yankees second baseman Bobby Richardson

It's legitimate to speculate that Willie McCovey's eventual popularity began
to grow the instant that his 1962 World Series–ending line drive settled into
the glove of Yankees second baseman Bobby Richardson. Shortly after the
Series, Peanuts cartoonist Charles Schulz captured the feelings of Yankee
haters everywhere by depicting Charlie Brown and Linus bearing long faces
and a gloomy silence. Charlie Brown suddenly wails, "Why couldn't McCovey
have hit the ball just three feet higher?" That was followed a few days later with
an identical scene—except this time, Charlie Brown asks the baseball gods,
"Or why couldn't McCovey have hit the ball just two feet higher?" Schulz
wasn't at all disparaging McCovey; he was just bemoaning the Giants' luck.
Indeed, McCovey should have been saluted for his efforts, never cursed. His
smash to Richardson was an obviously gallant game-winning attempt. Asked
two months after Game 7 to summarize his lingering emotions, he said, "I
just feel proud." That's how professionals should feel about their handiwork,
regardless of their craft. McCovey repeated that word—*proud*—to express
his feelings about the franchise's Major League–high 10,000th victory in 2005
and about his records for home runs (236) and games played (1,086) at Candlestick Park. The latter figure doesn't count four postseason games—most
notably the October 16, 1962, contest that decided the Fall Classic.

McCovey derived a demitasse of satisfaction from frustration. When he
encountered Richardson in July 2007 at a forty-five-year reunion in San

THE DAY I HIT THE LINE DRIVE

Francisco of Giants and Yankees who participated in the '62 World Series, McCovey couldn't resist throwing a friendly little verbal jab. As Richardson related, McCovey approached him and said, "I'll bet your hand is still hurting." That, of course, referred to McCovey's Series-ending line drive. The play sealed New York's 1–0 victory in Game 7 as well as its winning 4–3 margin in the Series. Prolonged as it was by three days of rain on the West Coast following a rainout in New York, the Series commanded the attention of the entire Bay Area. As a result, McCovey was instantly recognized when he tried to relax after Game 7 at Fack's, a popular San Francisco nightclub where Duke Ellington's band was performing. Noticing McCovey, the band broke into one of Ellington's hits, "I Got It Bad (and That Ain't Good)." Except the musicians, in McCovey's honor, changed the lyrics to, "You Hit It Good (And That Ain't Bad)."

As was the case following the Giants' scheduled regular-season finale, a 2–1 victory over Houston that sent them into the playoff against the Dodgers, along with the playoff triumph itself, the Giants lacked time to savor their success. They had to meet their next challenge without a scheduled day off that would allow them to gain perspective or simply take a deep breath. And so it was that they opened the World Series against the Yankees at Candlestick Park scant hours after washing off the champagne that they spilled all over one another in their cramped Dodger Stadium clubhouse after eliminating Los Angeles. McCovey didn't play in San Francisco's 6–2, Game 1 loss to the Yankees, which was no surprise, given left-hander Whitey Ford's presence on the mound for New York and Giants manager Alvin Dark's well-known scorn for McCovey's efforts to hit southpaws. Nor would McCovey play in Ford's two other starts in the '62 Series, Games 4 and 6. But Dark knew that Game 2 would be much different. The differences led to McCovey's replacing Orlando Cepeda at first base. The Giants would confront Ralph Terry, the American League's leading regular-season winner with 23 victories. Terry also topped the Majors with 40 home runs allowed. Those two statistics weren't altogether contradictory. Obviously, pitchers thrive by throwing strikes—or, at the very least, pitches that resemble strikes. When any of those deliveries remains hittable for a split second too long, the offensive potential improves for the batters, particularly free swingers like the '62

Giants. McCovey maximized all theoretical advantages. Home field, for one. McCovey clobbered 12 homers in just 108 regular-season plate appearances at Candlestick. Dark also reasoned that favorable platoon matchups could help the Giants. That meant employing as many left-handed batters, such as McCovey, as possible against the right-handed Terry. Lefties batted .249 off Terry in the regular season compared to .218 for righties. Not only was Cepeda benched, but so was left fielder Harvey Kuenn, a righty swinger who owned a .446 lifetime batting average against Terry but was 0-for-5 in Game 1. Left-handed-batting Matty Alou started in left field, though Cepeda outhomered him 35–3 during the regular season. The moves proved effective, considering Alou drove in San Francisco's initial run with a 1st-inning groundout and McCovey lined a home run to lead off the 7th as the Giants captured Game 2, 2–0. Thus it was that McCovey, not more fabled sluggers such as Willie Mays or Cepeda, smacked San Francisco's first Series homer.

As always, McCovey rounded the bases without histrionics, a sobriety that typified that era's power hitters. His gait was at once lumbering and graceful—like a pro football tight end who possesses athleticism to match his size. Outwardly, nothing about McCovey's running out a homer looked extraordinary. A ten-year-old boy growing up in Alhambra, California, named Mike Krukow would have begged to differ. Krukow, who would become an All-Star right-hander and later a hugely popular Giants broadcaster, reveled in McCovey's tendency to keep his arms cocked as he ran. Krukow considered this trait a primary element in McCovey's ensemble of baseball style, which included his smooth footwork and sidearm throws at first base. "The guy who had the coolest home-run trot was Willie McCovey," Krukow said. "We knew Willie McCovey's trot, with the high elbow swing. It was awesome. That was the best trot ever." He and his buddy, David Munson, delighted in imitating McCovey when they played "Home Run Derby" in a small vacant lot separating a pair of houses. To avoid causing damage to either residence, they had to hit the ball to straightaway center field. Only then were Krukow and Munson free to break into "The Trot"—their pet name for a McCovey home run jog. McCovey's round-tripper showcased his hitting form. It was a titanic drive that cleared the fence easily and quickly. Sitting in Candlestick Park's right-field bleachers, twelve-year-old San Francisco native Steve

Mesenburg was briefly terrified as he considered the ball's possible path. "He hit it right in my lap, almost," Mesenburg said. "I'll never forget that ball coming at me." Fortunately for Mesenburg, McCovey connected so fiercely with Terry's first-pitch toss that the drive hooked away from the packed section of backless seats, enabling dozens of souvenir-hungry fans—largely kids—to pursue the ball.

The Series shifted to New York, where a throng of 71,434 filled Yankee Stadium for Game 3. It was the largest postseason audience in the Bronx since the Yankees hosted 71,563 in Game 4 of the 1958 Fall Classic, 8 home Series games earlier. McCovey started in right field, a position he played only 12 times during the regular season, and went 0-for-3 with a walk. Dark reasoned that left field was the more challenging of the two corner outfield spots at Yankee Stadium due to the sun's glare in left and the huge amount of outfield acreage that had to be covered there. Felipe Alou, San Francisco's everyday right fielder, moved to left. Both he and McCovey committed 7th-inning misplays that helped the Yankees score their only runs in a 3–2 victory. Alou's fielding error enabled Tom Tresh and Mickey Mantle to advance to third and second base, respectively. Roger Maris singled for the inning's third consecutive hit, scoring Tresh and Mantle. McCovey was charged with an error that enabled Maris to reach second base. Maris later scored when second baseman Chuck Hiller failed to turn a double play on Clete Boyer's grounder, a lapse that probably spared McCovey excessive criticism for his defense. Giants fans probably were more concerned with their ballclub's struggles to score after amassing 878 regular-season runs—more than any team would tally in a season from 1963 to 1988.

Hiller roped the first World Series grand slam by a National Leaguer in San Francisco's 7–3 Game 4 win. McCovey was back in his comfort zone in Game 5, starting at first base and batting fifth behind cleanup hitter Mays. But the Yankees won, 5–3, behind Terry's complete-game effort. McCovey contributed by singling to lead off the 9th inning and scoring on Tom Haller's 1-out double. But Ed Bailey, representing the potential tying run, ended the game by lining out to right field.

Back in San Francisco, the teams remained idle for four days while a major rainstorm stayed over Northern California. Cepeda took over at first base for Game 6, batting fifth, and responded with perhaps the best offensive performance of any Giant in this World Series. He went 3-for-4 with an RBI double and a run-scoring single as the Giants triumphed, 5–2. But Dark did not overlook McCovey when it counted most—in Game 7, when the Giants and Yankees would engage in a classic confrontation to determine baseball's championship. In selecting his lineup, Dark wouldn't let himself ponder whether Cepeda *or* McCovey should play. Opting for an offense-first mentality behind right-hander Jack Sanford, who finished 24–7 in the regular season and blanked the Yankees on 3 hits in Game 2, Dark used his biggest bats in a right-left-right combination, with center fielder Mays batting third, left fielder McCovey hitting fourth, and first baseman Cepeda occupying the fifth spot. McCovey thus set a record by starting games at three different positions in one Series. And McCovey's critics were forced to admit that having him in the lineup gave the Giants their best chance of winning. Oddly, the trio of future Hall of Famers hit in that sequence only 16 times during the regular season—despite being the Major Leagues' only threesome to each record an OPS+ of 160 or higher since Ed Delahanty, Sam Thompson, and Jack Clements of the Philadelphia Phillies in 1895.

All year long, the Giants won when they absolutely needed to—after ceding first place to the Dodgers, in Game 3 of the playoff at Los Angeles, and following defeats in Games 1, 3, and 5 of the World Series, which was tied at 3 games apiece. But if anybody could rival the Giants' motivation, it was Terry. Since October 10, 1960, he had shouldered the weight of yielding Bill Mazeroski's Series-winning home run in Game 7 at Pittsburgh. His opportunity for redemption was at hand. "If I lost that game," Terry said, referring to the Game 7 showdown against San Francisco, "I'd have thought about losing my identity." Actually, Terry already had responded admirably to the heartache Mazeroski caused. He finished 16–3 with a 3.15 ERA in 1961 before putting together his big '62 season. Moreover, Terry pitched under execrable circumstances in the '60 Series. He drained his energy by warming up five times in the bullpen before entering the game to retire Don Hoak on a fly ball to end Pittsburgh's 5-run 8th inning. Terry didn't complain about being "dry-humped"—relievers' parlance for warming up without pitching in the game. "Seventh game, you can't mess around," Terry said, citing the need to be ready. But he did take issue with what he considered to be inconsistencies in the condition of the mounds at Pittsburgh's Forbes Field. Terry called New York's bullpen mound a "piss-ant mound—real tiny but very steep." By contrast, Terry said, the game mound at Forbes Field was high but flat. "My front foot hit the ground early. Everything was shoulder-high," Terry said. "I tried to bounce it but I couldn't get it down after pitching so much on that steep bullpen mound." Mazeroski capitalized on Terry's lack of command by driving a 1–0 pitch over the left-field wall.

A little more than a year after the '62 Series, the world would endure an epochal event with President John F. Kennedy's assassination. For now, and for Bay Area Giants fans, Game 7 between the Giants and Yankees was epochal enough, as far as providing people with a "where-were-you-when" experience. Decades later, Al Klein would coach Menlo School to the Division II California state high school basketball championship. On this day, however, Klein was all about baseball. He sat in the back of his World Geography class at Menlo-Atherton High School, the better to listen to the game broadcast on his pocket-sized transistor radio and conceal his earpiece. Eleven-year-old Jon Miller, a sixth grader at Hillcrest Elementary School, followed the action despite being in transit. "I left school early because of a dentist's appointment and he had the game on the radio," the future Giants broadcaster said. Barry Tompkins, a San Francisco native who was raised in the Mission District, prowled the outer perimeters of Candlestick Park until he found somebody who had a single ticket available for sale. "I was in the absolute worst seat—left field, upper deck, top corner," recalled Tompkins, who a little less than a decade later became the sports anchorman for KPIX, San Francisco's CBS television affiliate. He went from there to Showtime, where he gained renown as a top boxing announcer.

Terry gave these youths and other Giants fans virtually nothing to cheer about while taking a 1–0 lead and a 2-hitter into the 9th inning. He yielded only a 2-out, 6th-inning single to Sanford, his mound opponent for the third time in the Series, and a 2-out triple to McCovey in the 7th. Cepeda ended the threat by striking out. The Yankees scored the game's lone run in the 5th. Moose Skowron and Clete Boyer singled before Terry walked to load the bases with nobody out. Tony Kubek's grounder resulted in a double play that scored Skowron. After the game, Sanford tortured himself by mentally rewinding to the inning's biggest lapse. "That walk to Terry did it," Sanford said, well aware of the pitfalls of issuing a free pass to the opposing pitcher.

The Giants' final chance came down to the most famous plate appearance of Willie Lee McCovey's career. First came the setup, launched by pinch hitter Matty Alou's bunt single. "I knew he was going to bunt, but he laid down what I thought was a perfect bunt, right between the pitcher and first base," Richardson said. Playing for the tying run, Dark ordered a sacrifice bunt. But Felipe Alou and Chuck Hiller both struck out after fouling off bunt attempts. Up came Willie Mays, who was contemplating anything but trying to prolong the inning with a dinky single. Digging into the right-handed batter's box, Mays looked almost regal, as if the rest of the world should halt its trivial activities while he established his foothold. His strategy was simple and specific. So was Terry's.

> MAYS: I was going for the bomb. We needed a home run. I was going for it. But I was a little behind the pitch.
> TERRY: Try to pitch him inside, work left to right. Ball one, ball two. They looked like brushback pitches. Then go low and away. It was pretty obvious what I was trying to do.

Mays lashed the third pitch he saw from Terry into the right-field corner, where the ball could have been expected to carom away from Roger Maris. But the recent downpours rendered the earth soggy instead of springy, enabling Maris to pounce on the ball and fling it to Richardson, the cutoff man. He, in turn, fired a throw to catcher Elston Howard that forced Alou to halt at third base as Mays pulled in standing up with a double. Scattered groups of revisionist historians insist that Giants third base coach Whitey Lockman should have sent Alou home, but that would have been sheer lunacy. A wire-service photograph, providing a wide-angle perspective from Candlestick's upper deck, clearly shows Richardson taking Maris's throw with Alou barely having rounded third base. Richardson's one-hop relay to catcher Elston Howard would have beaten Alou by an embarrassingly huge margin had he continued home. Had it not been for all that rain drenching the field, the ball would have skittered away from Maris and Alou indeed would have scored easily, with Mays proceeding to third base.

The atmosphere at Candlestick was sheer bedlam in the stands and practiced calm on the field—including second base, where Mays, Yankees shortstop Tony Kubek, and Richardson convened. Said Richardson, "I went over to second base and Kubek was there and Willie Mays was there and I remember Tony said to me, 'I sure hope McCovey doesn't hit the ball to you.' I said, 'Why?' And he said, 'Because you've already made one error in this Series. I'd hate to see you blow it now.' Mays laughed a little bit and I went back to my position."

At the same time, Yankees manager Ralph Houk strolled to the pitcher's mound to chat with Terry. Though right-handers Bill Stafford and Bud Daley had been warming up since the 7th inning, Terry was Houk's man. As Terry related, Houk laughed as he reached the mound and said, "I don't know what the hell I'm doing out here." Houk then ran through the managerial checklist.

"How do you feel?" he asked Terry.

"I feel all right," Terry responded.

"How's your control?" questioned Houk.

Replied Terry, who went to only one 3-ball count all afternoon, "I think it's all right."

Howard agreed.

Then came the only question that meant anything at this juncture, this moment, this instant, with Mays on second base, Alou on third, 2 outs and the World Series on the line: "Walk McCovey or pitch to him?"

Nearly sixty years later, Terry recalled the logic he ultimately employed with stunning clarity: "It's hard at Candlestick to adjust to the strike zone. One curveball breaks a foot, another two or three inches. My thing was, you're in a National League ballpark and it's the seventh game of the World Series with a National League umpire [Stan Landes] behind the plate. If it's a close call, you're probably not going to get it. And, like Casey Stengel used to say, never bring in a reliever with the bases loaded. With a base open, you can pitch around the hitter. So now I say, 'Let me go after him—low and away, high and tight. If we get behind in the count, then we can put him on.' That was the plan."

Incredulity reigned among the Giants. "Nobody in the world could figure out why Ralph Houk pitched to McCovey," right-hander Bob Bolin said. Especially since McCovey had tripled to center field off Terry just two innings earlier. That hit should have scored a run. But Yankees left fielder Tom Tresh dashed to his right to snare a searing drive by Mays that appeared destined for extra bases. Observers also recalled McCovey's Game 2 homer off Terry. Said McCovey, "I had hit Terry pretty good, and for just that reason alone I thought they might put me on, but they elected to pitch to me. I was surprised that they did with first base open and a righthand hitter coming up, even though the righthand hitter was Cepeda. In a way it shows just how much they respected him." One day after his Game 6 offensive outburst, Cepeda was 0-for-3 with 2 strikeouts against Terry. However, that bothered "The Baby Bull" not one iota. "I was ready," Cepeda said.

So was McCovey, who jumped on a first-pitch curveball designed to act as a changeup. He hit a vicious line drive down the right-field line that hooked foul. Richardson was suitably impressed with McCovey's bat speed. Deepening the what-might-have-been heartbreak for the Giants and their fans, Richardson recalled repositioning himself for the second pitch. "I think I moved over a little bit," Richardson said, influenced by McCovey's ability to pull the ball. "He said later that I was playing out of position. Ralph Terry even told me he started to pitch and looked around to see where I was playing and he felt I was playing him too far in the hole and he took one step toward me, and then he said, 'Well, he's played 1,400 games there, maybe he knows something I don't.' And he didn't come out my way." Terry indeed figured that Richardson knew what he was doing. "He played McCovey way over to pull in the hole, just like they do now. A little too far," Terry said. "I'd like to move him back. But we played together since we were 18 years old. And you don't move a five-time Gold Glover."

McCovey swung and connected, and the result came as quickly as a match being blown out at Candlestick. "I doubt that the crowd noise even got to a roar, because it was over before the roar came," Tompkins said. Referring to the winner's share of $12,000 per man and the loser's share of $8,000, Bolin remarked, "When we jumped up, we thought we had won; by the time my rear end hit the bench, we lost $4,000 apiece." The sportsmanlike Cepeda felt compelled to cross the tunnel leading to the clubhouses and congratulate the Yankees. Referring to their performance throughout the Series, Cepeda said, "The Yankees played perfectly. They didn't make any mental mistakes." New York's efficiency, he added, seemed to quicken the game's pace, particularly its conclusion: "It's amazing how fast things happened. You didn't have time to think."

Richardson certainly knew what he was doing in handling McCovey's liner. "As you know, the ball was hit hard and basically right to me. One step to the left. It was an easy play," he said. The catch's most challenging aspect was the considerable amount of topspin that McCovey imparted upon the ball with his quick uppercutting swing. The ball changed eye levels so suddenly that Richardson had to reach for the ball with his palms facing downward, as if he were trapping a butterfly. "I remember seeing Mickey Mantle hit balls like that," Richardson said. "They would come down in a hurry. When the ball left the bat it looked like a ball that was in the outfield. It looked like it was going to be over my head. But it had the topspin you're talking about. It came down in a hurry. And that's what made it a little difficult play."

That provided no consolation for McCovey as photographers trapped him sitting in front of his dressing stall, cupping his head in his left hand and wearing a look of profound gloom. "I don't think anybody could have felt as bad as I did," he said. "Not only did I have a whole team on my shoulders in that at-bat, I had a whole city." Asked later if that was as hard as he could hit a ball, McCovey said, "I wouldn't say that." He politely added, "Well, I guess *you* could say that. I could have hit it in a different direction, that's for sure." He would forever refer to October 16, 1962, as "the day I hit the line drive."

If the atmosphere in the Giants' clubhouse wasn't thoroughly funereal, it's because they believed they possessed the talent to return to the World Series relatively quickly. In fact, San Francisco recorded the National League's best record in the 1960s (902-704). But the Giants didn't reach the postseason again until 1971 and had to wait until 1989 to win a spot in the World Series. They wouldn't win a World Series until 2010.

McCovey pointed an accusing finger at club management. "We always needed that one player to get over the hump, and Horace Stoneham just would never do it," he said, referring to the Giants' owner at the time. "He would never go out and get that one player we needed down the stretch, ever. He always thought we could win with what we had." Asked if the missing link was usually a position player or pitcher, McCovey said, "Either. Usually it was a pitcher. Because we always had the hitting."

6

Domination of Don

McCovey? I wish he'd quit.

—Dodgers pitcher Don Drysdale

Goofy as Casey Stengel occasionally sounded, he never prompted doubts about his baseball acumen. He was the individual most responsible for developing Yogi Berra's diverse baseball skills, playing the future Hall of Famer at the outfield corners as well as at catcher. Stengel's ability to derive maximum effectiveness from his bench and bullpen was peerless. The seven World Series titles that he won with the New York Yankees, including five consecutive from 1949 to 1953, stand as proof of his baseball wizardry. So when Stengel loudly delivered his opinion of Willie McCovey after the Giants slugger homered in San Francisco's 2–0 victory over New York in Game 2 of the 1962 World Series, the "Ol' Perfessor's" judgment was duly noted by a hospitality suite full of thirsty sportswriters, which happened to be the scene of Stengel's declaration.

"I'll give any of you $250,000 for him," Stengel said. "Right this minute, too." As manager of the New York Mets, Stengel lacked the authority to engineer such a transaction. The writers, lacking affiliation with any professional baseball organization, had even less influence than Stengel, who at least could recommend acquiring McCovey to the Mets. What should have made an impression upon McCovey's detractors—some of whom probably heard Stengel having his say—is that the twenty-four-year-old's budding greatness was so obvious and valuable to a talent evaluator of Stengel's caliber. For example, McCovey's dominance of Don Drysdale, a subject of curiosity to much of baseball's cognoscenti, should have demanded nothing more than this simple explanation: Hall of Fame players do Hall of Fame things.

McCovey, a Hall of Fame hitter, towered over Drysdale, a Hall of Fame pitcher, during many of the 11 seasons they spent in the Major Leagues together (1959–69). McCovey built a commanding statistical advantage against Drysdale at the outset of his career, batting .543 (19-for-35) with 7 home runs off him from 1959 to 1962. Maintaining that kind of pace for much longer than that would have been virtually impossible for McCovey, and in fact, he finished with a .336 lifetime batting average off Drysdale (43-for-128) with 12 home runs—his highest total against any pitcher. But first impressions tend to linger. Thus, fellow big leaguers accepted McCovey's battering of Drysdale as a basic fact.

> Larry Dierker: Lifetime versus McCovey: .296 (21-for-71), 3 home runs. "I wasn't surprised to see that he hit me well. But he hit Drysdale harder. He probably hit most of us pretty hard."
>
> Jim Maloney: Lifetime versus McCovey: .324 (22-for-68), 5 homers. "I don't think Drysdale could get him out."
>
> Joe Amalfitano, infielder: "One game, Drysdale threw McCovey a sinker and he hit it to the back wall of the left-field bullpen at Dodger Stadium."
>
> Jeff Torborg, Dodgers catcher: "Drysdale had trouble with him. We tried to pitch him inside, but if he took it, we'd be in trouble. Because then we had to go back outside. And he had such long arms."
>
> Juan Marichal, Giants teammate: "Oh my God. He hit Drysdale like he owned him."
>
> Hal Lanier, Giants teammate: "It's unbelievable what Willie did against Drysdale. I can't remember in the eight years I played with the Giants that I saw anybody knock Willie McCovey down. They might have hit him not on purpose, but I never saw any pitcher throw at him like they did Mays."

Intimidation was part of each man's game. Drysdale had a lot going for him in this regard. The pitchers' mound accented Drysdale's 6-foot-5 stature, giving him the appearance of being master of all that he surveyed. Drysdale threw right-handed and employed a low, sidearm release point, which made standing in the batter's box against him a fearful challenge for right-handed hitters.

Left-handed hitters such as McCovey were afforded clearer views of Drysdale's pitches, which didn't look as if they were boring in at their heads. Not that it made any difference to McCovey, who seemed impervious to mind games. If Drysdale dented McCovey's equilibrium at all, the slugger didn't show it.

"Sometimes [pitchers] were probably saying, 'You couldn't intimidate him,'" Cubs outfielder Billy Williams said of McCovey, his friend and fellow Mobile, Alabama, native. "He was a big guy. Matter of fact, you didn't want to intimidate him. You didn't want to make him mad on a baseball field. He looked like he would pinch your head off. He was such a big guy."

Said McCovey in 1963, "Why I hit [Drysdale] consistently is hard to explain. I regard him as the best pitcher in the National League. Right-handers claim they have trouble picking up the ball when it comes out of his sidearm or three-quarters delivery. I don't have any trouble seeing the ball. Maybe that's it."

Early in his career, McCovey resented any implication that his prowess revolved solely around facing Drysdale. "I am tired of people saying my output is against one pitcher," he grumbled in another 1963 interview. By the end of the '63 campaign, nobody would dare suggest such a thing. That was the year when McCovey established himself as a truly formidable hitter, clobbering 44 home runs to tie Hank Aaron for the National League lead. McCovey's success against Drysdale, it turned out, was simply an indication of his capabilities. Giants fans certainly had learned to appreciate McCovey after years of mostly supporting Orlando Cepeda over him. In fact, shortly before the end of the 1963 season, on September 22, the San Francisco Chronicle felt compelled to honor McCovey with the Candlestick Award. Mrs. Charles de Young Thieriot, wife of the Chronicle's editor and publisher, shook hands with McCovey as she gave him a brass candlestick holder. The inscription read, "To Willie McCovey, whose deeds have been an inspiration to our fair city." McCovey proceeded to record his first of three career 3-homer games in the Giants' 13–4 pasting of the New York Mets that afternoon.

Suddenly, stationing McCovey in the outfield wasn't a big issue anymore, especially as long as he kept hitting home runs at a league-leading pace. Giants manager Alvin Dark admitted that he played McCovey in the outfield in spring training of 1962 to showcase him for a trade. Eventually, McCovey proved that he may have had some shortcomings as an outfielder but wasn't a liability. Indeed, McCovey received widespread credit for preserving Juan Marichal's June 15, 1963, no-hitter against Houston with a 7th-inning grab of Carl Warwick's twisting line drive. "He's done a great job for us," Dark said. "I won't say that he's a great outfielder, but I will say that he's an adequate outfielder."

With McCovey's hitting, at least two factors were at work. First, Dark finally gave McCovey, who was beginning his fourth full big league season, a chance to play every day. McCovey started 145 games, including 130 in left field. Moreover, Dark no longer benched McCovey against all left-handed starting pitchers. McCovey nearly matched his total number of plate appearances against lefties in 1963 (175) that he accumulated from 1959 to 1962 (207). "I don't hit left-handers as consistently as right-handers," said McCovey, who batted .222 against lefties in 1963. "Does this make me different from any other left-handed hitter?"

Secondly, simply stated, McCovey was improving as a hitter. Maloney understood what he was seeing while spending eleven years of his twelve-year pitching career with Cincinnati, confronting McCovey in the National League. "At fantasy camps, they always ask you, 'Who was the toughest hitter you faced?' And I always say that the two toughest hitters with power that I faced in my career were Willie McCovey and Willie Stargell," Maloney said. "McCovey, when he first came up, you could start him with a fastball at the belt, the next one at the shoulder, then throw the next one eye-high and he'd chase. That's called 'going up the ladder' and you could get him out pretty easily. Then he learned the strike zone. He wouldn't chase those balls anymore. And he became a really tough out for me."

During the 1968 season, when Charlie Fox was two years away from becoming the Giants' manager and serving the team as a coach, he summarized McCovey's improved technique. "When Willie learned to handle this pitch," said Fox, tracing a straight line with his right hand across his chest, "he became a hitter, not solely a slugger." The club record 24-game hitting streak McCovey maintained from June 25, 1963, through July 19, 1963, reflected his maturity at the plate.

McCovey put the power in the term *power hitter*. Cincinnati Reds pitching coach Mel Harder paid McCovey a high compliment during the 1968 season—exceedingly lofty praise, considering Harder had been involved in professional baseball for more than forty years: "When it comes to sheer strength, I'd have to rate McCovey with [Babe] Ruth, [Lou] Gehrig, [Jimmie] Foxx and [Hank] Greenberg." If you're counting, that quartet combined for 2,072 home runs—an average of 518 per man. That's suitable company for McCovey, given his career total of 521 homers.

Dodgers manager Walter Alston echoed Harder after McCovey, coping with blurred vision, a jammed right shoulder, and a sore right knee, homered twice in San Francisco's 5–4 win at Los Angeles on May 16, 1970: "For pure strength, McCovey is the strongest man in the National League."

Opponents tried everything against McCovey. Alston tried faking an intentional walk—with the catcher jumping behind the hitter to take a third strike. "We tried it and McCovey almost killed Wes Parker at first base," Torborg said. "He hit a *rocket*. He hit it so hard, I don't know how Wes held onto it. Maybe it caught him. We got an out, but we almost lost Wes. McCovey could generate so much bat speed. The ball would just shoot out of there."

Cincinnati's Pete Rose recalled being stationed at second base when he and his fellow infielders were ordered to play in. For Rose, that was uncomfortably close to the pull-hitting McCovey. "We had the infield pulled in to the edge of the grass—I don't know why—and he hit a f**king rocket that almost took my f**king hand off," Rose said. "The worst thing you want is to have the infield pulled in with Willie McCovey hitting. Especially on the right side. That's the way you get harelipped."

Giants right-hander Jim Barr recalled when McCovey hit a ball that barely cleared the infield—and yet his hitting prowess was very much evident. Barr was pitching against San Diego in a Cactus League exhibition game at Phoenix Municipal Stadium during one of McCovey's three seasons with the Padres. "He hit his typical high shot," Barr said. "Just about the time it got over the second baseman's head, you hear this 'brrrrrrrrrrrrrrah' and the ball falls to the ground, halfway between the right fielder and second baseman. I thought, 'Wow! What was that?' They throw the ball back; I look at it and almost half of the cover is unstitched and flapping around. I'm standing there, getting ready to look in for the sign and I'm thinking to myself, 'You gotta be kidding me. Am I the only guy that saw this? None of the umpires is going to check the ball?' Then Joe West asked to look at it and he threw it out."

If anybody could have given such a hobbled baseball some legs, it would have been McCovey, who darn near hit the cover off the ball. Had McCovey not pulverized the ball instantly, Barr said, "It would have been a home run, easy. As soon as it was hit I turned around to see how far it would go."

McCovey provided relatively few classic moments in 1964, due largely to aching feet. Described most often as fallen arches, they forced McCovey to wear cumbersome insoles in his cleats for the rest of his career. By any name or definition, the injury hampered McCovey's performance dramatically. His batting average plummeted from .280 in 1963 to .220 in '64, while his home run total dwindled from 44 to 18. Some observers suggested that the death of McCovey's father on January 18 at age seventy-three weakened his competitive spirit. But his niece, Angelia, insisted this wasn't so. "Even if he felt that way, he would never use it as an excuse," she said. Then came 1965—and with it, a six-year run of sustained excellence in which no pitcher could stop McCovey, nor could any injury fell him.

7

The Peak Years

Big Mac didn't have any real weakness. He had a good, low
swing, but he also could hit the ball chest-high. And he hit it
hard. He was probably the toughest out in that lineup.

—Hall of Fame outfielder Frank Robinson

The San Francisco Giants' roster featured an excess of first basemen as the
1966 season approached. That is, if you can call one man an excess. The sur-
plus consisted of either Willie McCovey or Orlando Cepeda, depending
on your point of view.

Before '65, the notion of trading Cepeda would have bordered on the
unthinkable. His career remained on a Hall of Fame trajectory during his
first seven seasons, all of which he spent with the Giants. Cepeda ranked
among baseball's most productive hitters during that span, averaging an
annual slash line of .309/.354/.537 to go with 32 home runs and 107 RBIS
per year. Then the Giants endured a wholly frustrating 1965 season, finishing
2 games behind the National League pennant-winning Dodgers despite
recording a 14-game winning streak from September 4 to 16. Los Angeles
trumped the Giants by winning 13 in a row from September 16 to 30. To
upgrade themselves and leapfrog the Dodgers in the standings, the Giants
would have to trade either McCovey or Cepeda, according to conventional
wisdom. That is, unless one of them could be entrusted with left field while
the other would patrol first base.

McCovey would have been the likeliest commodity available for trade a few
short years earlier. His value dwindled in the estimation of some observers
in 1964, when he batted .220 and hit 18 home runs. Then it became known

that McCovey played 130 games on sore feet. Arch supports helped only nominally. Despite the lingering pain, McCovey slugged 39 home runs in 1965, second among National Leaguers to Willie Mays's 52. Meanwhile, a right knee injury limited Cepeda to 33 games and a .176 batting average. Following the 1965 season, trade rumors involving Cepeda were rampant. Once he proved he was healthy, a deal would be done. But Giants owner Horace Stoneham wouldn't acknowledge after the '65 season that rumors of a swap involving the still-formidable Cepeda were legitimate.

"We have no intentions of trading Orlando," Stoneham told reporters. "We have no plans to make a deal for him and haven't attempted to make one. First off, if his leg is sound and he is in shape to play next spring, we want him ourselves. Second, if he isn't able to play for us, nobody would want him." Though Stoneham was a rarity among owners by making his own deals instead of entrusting that responsibility to baseball operations executives, Giants general manager Chub Feeney felt empowered enough to keep thoughts of a Cepeda trade alive: "I think if we were offered somebody really outstanding, Mr. Stoneham might reconsider."

During the calm of the off-season, Stoneham's sentiment could have been sincere. But the Giants had just entered their rut of five consecutive second-place finishes, though they didn't know it yet. San Francisco needed a left-handed pitching complement to Juan Marichal and Gaylord Perry as well as depth behind the pair of magnificent right-handers. Trade speculation remained active, and it focused on the following:

Mike Cuellar, Astros: Nobody sensed at this point that Cuellar ultimately would win the 1969 American League Cy Young Award and earn a spot on four All-Star teams with Baltimore. He had played for five organizations since 1957, none of which came close to helping him realize his potential.

Dick Ellsworth, Cubs: Finished 14-15 with a 3.81 record a year earlier, which was pretty decent for an eighth-place club in a ten-team league. Posted a 2.11 ERA in 1963, second in the NL behind Sandy Koufax's 1.88 for the Dodgers. Soft-tossing lefty who owned a 3-6 record with a 4.18 ERA at Candlestick at that juncture of his career.

Jim O'Toole, Reds: Ranked among the NL's top lefties from 1961 to 1964, when he was 70-43 and made the 1963 All-Star team. Injuries limited him to a 3-10 record with a 5.93 ERA in 1965. Was 4-7 with a 3.32 ERA in 13 career games (12 starts) at Candlestick.

Ray Sadecki, Cardinals: Despite being only a season removed from winning 20 games in 1964, Sadecki did not remind observers of a 20-game winner, particularly with his 6–15 record and 5.21 ERA in 1965. That season elevated his career ERA and his lifetime WHIP to 1.423. He was 3-5 with a 2.82 ERA at Candlestick as of this off-season. In short, nobody fit the description of the "really outstanding" pitcher the Giants would want in exchange for Cepeda.

The Giants occupied first place in the NL during the season's early weeks, though they knew that the National League would be as hypercompetitive as ever. San Francisco owned a 2½-game lead over second-place Pittsburgh after a 3-game sweep at St. Louis that concluded with a 10–5 decision on May 8. The Giants used the series to showcase Cepeda, who responded by going 3-for-8 with a grand slam, a double, and 6 RBIs. The Giants left town while leaving Cepeda with the Cardinals, who parted with Sadecki to get him. "It was very emotional," Cepeda said. "I cried. But it was one of the best things that ever happened to me." That became obvious in 1967, when Cepeda batted .325 with 25 homers and 111 RBIs. Thus he propelled St. Louis to a 7-game World Series conquest over Boston and won the NL Most Valuable Player Award. How valuable was valuable? According to legend, a packed Cardinals team bus, minus Cepeda, was about to leave the ballclub's hotel for New York's Shea Stadium one afternoon. The scheduled departure time came and went. St. Louis manager Red Schoendienst ordered the bus driver to head for Shea. That's when right-hander Bob Gibson, a commanding presence if there ever was one, exercised his influence. "This bus doesn't leave until Orlando Cepeda's on it," Gibson said. Schoendienst declined to utter a single word of protest. Cepeda soon arrived, and the Cardinals' world was back on its axis.

For the Giants, the trade's immediate postscript could best be summarized as a nightmare. They finished 1½ games behind Los Angeles, the slimmest margin during their streak of second-place finishes. The designated scape-goat for 1966 was none other than Sadecki, who went 3-7 with a 5.40 ERA in 26 games (19 starts) for San Francisco. He frustrated the Giants coming and going, beating them 5–1 with a complete-game 5-hitter on April 29 while still a member of the Cardinals. "All I had to do was to win five ballgames, and we would have won the pennant," said Sadecki. McCovey's most memorable contribution to the pennant race resulted in one of the biggest clutch hits of his career. With the Giants needing to sweep a Sunday doubleheader at Pittsburgh to maintain their hopes of facing the Dodgers in a 1-game playoff for the pennant, manager Herman Franks actually benched McCovey in the season finale. Pittsburgh's starting pitcher was left-hander Bob Veale, among the toughest hurlers for McCovey to face up to that point in his career. Veale departed after 10 innings with the score tied, 3–3, freeing McCovey to clob-ber a 2-run, pinch-hit, tiebreaking homer off Steve Blass in the 11th inning to lead the Giants to a 7–3 win. But Dodgers great Sandy Koufax outlasted the Phillies, 4–3, in the second game of a doubleheader at Philadelphia, thus clinching the pennant for Los Angeles.

Given the respective career paths McCovey and Cepeda took, there's no doubt that the Giants kept the right player.

Cepeda's departure guaranteed that McCovey would play first base every day, enabling him to sustain his six-season run (1965–70) as the Major League's preeminent offensive force. During that span, he totaled 226 home runs, an average of 38 per season. Only Atlanta's Hank Aaron matched that output. McCovey topped the Majors with 636 RBIs, a .405 on-base per-centage and a .578 slugging percentage in the same period. He also batted an authoritative .291.

But the Giants squandered the opportunity to field an otherworldly lineup with McCovey *and* Cepeda in it. As it was, Cepeda and McCovey started only 430 games together—with Mays—out of a possible total of approximately 900. "I would have found room for both of them somehow," said shortstop Hal Lanier, who managed the Houston Astros from 1986 to 1988.

Having first base all to himself enabled McCovey to flourish. A growing number of ballparks became sites for his Bunyanesque deeds. The most noteworthy clout occurred on September 4, 1966, at St. Louis off left-hander

Al Jackson. Lanier remembered seeing Cardinals right fielder Mike Shannon running toward the infield immediately after McCovey made contact. "I wanted to see how far that ball was going to travel," Shannon explained. Cardinals catcher Tim McCarver had a front-row seat. The ball instantly vanished and may have joined pedestrians outside the ballpark. "Hanging breaking ball," said McCarver, recalling the event with clarity. "The ballpark [Busch Stadium] was in the process of being built. The final touches were being put on the ballpark. The part that hadn't been finished was in right-center field, next to where the scoreboard would be. And Willie hit it next to where the scoreboard would be. It was a monumental pop." Deadpanned McCarver, "I was impressed." Hall of Fame right-hander Bob Gibson was another Cardinal impressed by McCovey, who he called "the scariest hitter in baseball." Said McCarver, "Bob had respect for anybody with talent and anybody who worked hard. He was not one to win friends easily when they played in a different uniform. But Willie McCovey was an exception. Willie Stargell was an exception. With 'Stretch,' we liked the way that he was playful. As an example, he picked up my bat one day and said in his very slow demeanor, 'Tee-im, this is a baby bat. I pick my teeth with bats this small.' One day, Bob was going to throw between starts and I was out to catch him. And we were walking to the bullpen, and Willie had my bat in his mouth, serving as the toothpick. And we laughed. That was one of the funniest things we'd seen." The previous version of Busch Stadium featured a low-hanging right-field roof that batters cleared with regularity. Russ Hodges, the Giants' superb play-by-play announcer, found a colorful way to describe a 3-run homer McCovey hit off Gibson at St. Louis on May 10, 1962, that Busch couldn't contain: "That one went clear over the right-field roof and disappeared down the street on its way to a hamburger joint."

McCovey's home run collection prompted Hodges's sincere admiration. Said Jon Miller, "He would say, 'Every ballpark the Giants go into, people will point to a certain spot and say, that's where McCovey hit the longest home run in the history of this ballpark.'"

Pittsburgh's Forbes Field provided the backdrop for another of McCovey's epic wallops. Center field was so deep—the wall stood 457 feet from home plate—that the batting cage was stashed there, even during ball games. After all, who could hit it out there? But Pittsburgh right-hander Steve Blass recalled a McCovey drive that cleared the batting cage and the wall before bouncing onto the adjacent Schenley Park golf course. "It disrupted a foursome," Blass said. Suffice it to say that McCovey felt comfortable against Blass, who ranked among Pittsburgh's top starters. McCovey batted .410 (16-for-39) lifetime off Blass. "His swing was so powerful that he didn't have to overswing, which enabled him to be more selective. I was just intimidated. I almost remember the breeze from his swing when I was on the mound. That whole lineup was intimidating. But he was the guy who was in the center of that universe," Blass said.

Other vintage ballparks where McCovey left his mark included Philadelphia's Connie Mack Stadium and Cincinnati's Crosley Field. On May 22, 1967, at Connie Mack, McCovey hammered a Jim Bunning slider approximately five hundred feet to become the only player besides Philadelphia's Wes Covington to hit a home run between the clock that sat midway on the top of the sixty-four-foot-high scoreboard and the center-field light tower. As for the Crosley clout, eyewitnesses vow that they saw McCovey redirect a pitch and send a ball through a parking lot and over railroad tracks before it came to rest on I-75.

Sometimes the legend McCovey encountered was a person, not a place. For instance, McCovey homered just once in 48 career plate appearances against Sandy Koufax. That was understandable, given the lefty-on-lefty matchup that favored Koufax. But had it not been for a late Los Angeles rally in that game, McCovey's round-tripper would have gone down as a stirring moment in Giants-Dodgers lore. It was an exceptional night for baseball: August 31, 1959, almost a month to the day following McCovey's Major League debut. A crowd of 60,194 at the LA Coliseum watched Koufax and Jack Sanford pitch to a 1–1 tie before McCovey's 5th-inning homer put the Giants ahead, 2–1. But the Dodgers pulled even in the 8th inning before Wally Moon's 3-run homer won it in the 9th for the Dodgers and Koufax, who struck out 18 in a marvelous complete-game effort. Years later, McCovey named Koufax as the best pitcher he ever faced. "I don't think there ever will be another pitcher like Sandy," said McCovey, who batted .143 (6-for-42) lifetime off his remarkable rival. "He really had only two good pitches. His fastball was exceptional and his curveball even more so."

As the all-time leader in home runs at Candlestick Park with 236, McCovey could have been expected to hit some mammoth homers at the Giants' windswept yard. For visual effect, few could match a drive that longtime National League umpire Eddie Montague vowed that he witnessed while selling concessions in the outfield seats. Montague, a San Francisco native whose father, Eddie Sr., signed Willie Mays, insisted that he saw McCovey knock the leading *L* out of *Los Angeles* on Candlestick's scoreboard. Said 6-time 20-game winner Ferguson Jenkins, "He didn't miss fastballs. If you hung a pitch, like a curveball or a slider, you got punished. In San Francisco, he hit a ball off me that went over the players' parking lot into the fans' parking lot, which probably was 500 feet." Echoed Don Sutton, another Hall of Fame right-hander, "He hit a particular home run off me that you could have chopped into 25 singles."

A McCovey home run that wasn't, so to speak, enabled history to unfold. On July 2, 1963, the Giants edged the Milwaukee Braves in 16 innings, 1–0, with the two masterly starters, San Francisco's Juan Marichal and Milwaukee's Warren Spahn, going all the way. Willie Mays's homer with 1 out in the 16th won it. But the game nearly ended with 1 out in the 9th when McCovey hit one impossibly high, impossibly far, and impossible to definitively judge. Most observers thought the ball was fair. However, home plate umpire Chris Pelekoudas ruled it foul. "I followed the ball all the way, but apparently the umpire didn't," McCovey said. "It's a shame to hit a ball like that and lose what it means. It made me mad because I couldn't do anything about it. As hard as I hit the ball, it didn't have a chance to curve foul." Such displays explained why, in a 1965 poll of big league managers and coaches coinciding with the opening of Houston's Astrodome that year, McCovey was chosen as the hitter most likely to scrape the Dome's ceiling (height: 208 feet) with a pop-up. "You knew everything he hit on the ground was going to be hard," Dodgers second baseman Jim Lefebvre said. "Anything in the air at Candlestick, you had no idea where the ball was going to go because he hit them so damned high. When he popped up, he *popped* up. You'd be chasing that thing all over the place." McCovey's choice to be the likeliest Dome denter was his more powerfully prolific teammate, Mays. "Willie Mays can hit a ball as far as anybody. He has a natural long-ball hitter's swing," McCovey said. "I'm bigger and heavier, but I'm not sure size is everything. I'm also younger, but Mays is every bit as strong. He has hit longer balls in batting practice than I ever dreamed of hitting 'em."

8

Eclipsing a Legend

I am aware I am the number-one San Francisco Giant.

—Willie McCovey

The question must have resembled a hanging curveball to Willie McCovey: He instantly realized he could crush it. *You're in the Hall of Fame, you had a fabulous career, but did you ever feel like you were under Willie's shadow?* McCovey paused an extra half beat before responding, which had a comic effect. "Well, I was," he said, prompting laughter from a pair of reporters. "Everybody knows that."

The shade created by Willie Mays's shadow was not an uncomfortable habitat for McCovey. Rather, it afforded McCovey a cool, calm place from where he could operate. He combined with Mays, widely considered the finest player ever, to form a duo that's virtually unmatched in the annals of slugging. "I had probably the greatest seat in baseball for 14 years, hitting fourth behind Willie Mays and watching him from the on-deck circle," McCovey often said.

McCovey spent the second half of the 1960s gradually yet inexorably replacing Mays as the team's top man. "Yes, I am aware I am the number-one Giant," McCovey said before the 1969 season. How Mays felt about the change in status is unclear. At times, he could be gracious in his praise of McCovey. Here's one example: "Stretch is the strongest man in baseball. Guys like Frank Howard and Harmon Killebrew can hit them far, but they're pull hitters. Stretch can hit them deep to any part of the ballpark." Yet when both visited spring training simultaneously in their roles as club advisors, they rarely mixed. Mays declined to attend McCovey's Hall of Fame induction ceremony in Cooperstown, New York, in 1986. And in 2003, when speaking during the dedication ceremony for McCovey's statue outside then Pacific Bell / SBC Park, Mays regaled listeners with a bizarre tale about a visit to the dentist instead of sticking to the easy, obligatory happy talk about McCovey that the occasion called for.

Overall, though, McCovey and Mays seemed to have avoided any serious enmity. They were roommates on road trips briefly during the early 1960s. McCovey considered it an honor. "Everybody looked up to Willie," said McCovey, who was nearly seven years younger than Mays. "You know that. Why wouldn't you, as a young kid?" During that period, McCovey served as something of a security blanket for Mays in certain social situations. Said McCovey, "Mays was the type of guy, I don't know what it was about him, but anywhere he went he felt he had to take somebody with him. And that somebody was usually me. Even on a couple of his dates he brought me along. There was one girl he was going with in Philadelphia, they were pretty close, and I kind of started going out with the sister, but that didn't work out too well." And if a picture is worth a thousand words, then a particular shot taken by renowned sports photographer Neil Leifer nicely captured the McCovey-Mays relationship, at least in its early stages. The black-and-white photo shows Mays laughing heartily at something McCovey's saying as they dress for a game at Philadelphia's Connie Mack Stadium.

Once formed, such bonds tend to remain at least partially intact. During spring training of 2010, Mays was at Giants camp in Scottsdale, sitting in the clubhouse as he received help sorting boxes of copies of James S. Hirsch's recently released biography of him. Nothing else of great importance was transpiring, so McCovey, who also was in the clubhouse after watching batting practice through the late morning and early afternoon, decided to leave. The steel canes supporting him went *clankety-clank* as he walked toward the parking lot. The noise receded, suddenly stopped, then grew in volume as McCovey returned to the clubhouse. When he arrived, he approached Mays wearing a broad smile that belied his voice's demanding tone. "Hey, Buck!" said McCovey, addressing Mays by the nickname that teammates reserved for him during his playing career. "Where's my *book*?" Suddenly it was the early '60s again. Needless to say, McCovey got his copy.

McCovey and Mays differed in one significant aspect: management style. Asked to cite a Mays characteristic that the public didn't know about but should, several players issued identical responses: he was a great team leader. This prompted managers such as Alvin Dark and Herman Franks to appoint Mays as, for all intents and purposes, an assistant manager who was more than capable of running the ballclub on the field—by positioning teammates, for instance. Chicago Cubs star Billy Williams insisted that, in an effort to break a Giants losing streak, Mays called pitches for the batterymen while playing center field. When asked about this, Mays replied, "Naw, naw, naw, naw," before giggling and walking away. The giggle said it all.

What wasn't in doubt was the exacting approach Mays took toward each of Juan Marichal's starts. The Hall of Fame right-hander recalled that before his outings, he and Mays discussed how he planned to approach each opposing hitter. Marichal called it the "three-minute meeting." Mays also conducted these strategy sessions with Gaylord Perry, San Francisco's only other starting pitcher who could be trusted to locate his pitches consistently. Marichal said that the Giants' starting catcher du jour also participated in the meetings. But Mays countered, "Naw, man. We didn't need a catcher." By knowing how each batter would be pitched, Mays could estimate where each ball would be hit. And, as mentioned previously, he positioned the other outfielders accordingly. "He played the hitters so well," Marichal said. "If you made a mistake, right away he'd come and tell you. 'You were supposed to pitch him away, and you threw him a breaking ball, and he pulled the ball and got a hit.' That's *your* mistake. When you were on that mound, you tried not to make any kind of mistake. Otherwise you were going to hear from Willie."

If this sounds a tad harsh, bear in mind that Mays served in the army, where the chain of command is regimented and inflexible. McCovey, by contrast, could be termed a little on the warm and fuzzy side, more likely to make his point by having a quiet conversation instead of issuing an order. "He always took time to talk to young players around the batting cage. That's one thing I liked about Willie," said Pete Rose, baseball's all-time hits leader. In this sense, McCovey was "paying it forward," bestowing advice on younger players as Ted Williams and Stan Musial did with him. One way or another, McCovey's soft drawl was the voice of experience. In 1967 he soothed an upset Ollie Brown after the Giants demoted the outfield prospect to Triple-A. Being sent to the minors in 1960, one season after winning the NL Rookie of the Year Award, enabled McCovey to empathize with Brown. Before a 1971 game at Chicago's Wrigley Field, McCovey gave rookie pitcher Steve Stone a brief and necessary seminar on power hitting. Recalled Stone, "We walked out on the field and the wind was blowing straight in. I said to Willie, 'Nobody's hitting one out of here today.' And he said to me, 'Steve, when the big guys hit them, they go out of anywhere.' That's kind of his philosophy, and it's a good philosophy, because he was one of the big guys and he could hit it out of anywhere."

What led McCovey, for whom silence came naturally on most occasions, to speak so freely and easily with teammates at other times? "Mac had this general niceness about him where he seemed to have time for just about anybody," Stone said, praising McCovey's "overall understanding of the human condition." Stone added, "I don't think he ever forgot what it was like to be a kid growing up, loving baseball. He never got that big-league [to] where [he would say], 'I don't have time for you.' I found him to be surprisingly funny. He was just one of those guys that made you feel good to be around him. That couldn't be said about a lot of other people."

Right-hander John D'Acquisto thrived on McCovey's "general niceness" that Stone mentioned. "He was my big brother," D'Acquisto said of McCovey. "There's not much more I can say about him except that he was the best. He showed me how to be a big leaguer in the proper sense of the matter. I learned from the best in the business. How to behave. How to be cordial. How to be polite. Don't make any enemies. Tip well. Be nice to your girlfriends and treat them with respect. I was 18 and out of the house so I really didn't have my dad to help me along at that point. I was learning on my own. So Mac kind of turned into my dad. He taught me the things I should know as a young man growing up in the big leagues. Because he knew that I was going to be there a lot faster than people anticipated. He was responsible for molding me into the person I am today in more ways than one. Along with my parents, of course. But he took it from 18 years old on. He was the gentle Giant. He was massive in size. And yet he talked so softly and so logically. Willie Mac was a very special human being who lit up a lot of people's lives."

The seismic trade of Mays to the New York Mets on May 11, 1972, forced by the financial woes of Giants owner Horace Stoneham, quickly transformed McCovey into The Man on San Francisco's roster. "Willie Mac was one of those kind of guys who, when he was around, you don't horse around," right-hander Jim Barr said. "You could have fun with him, laugh and stuff like that. But don't do too many things that might be considered out of line when he's around because he's gonna let you know about it. He just had that presence that, just sitting there, he didn't have to say anything or anything like that. Just the fact that he was there, guys kind of watched what they said and watched what they did. Basically all he had to do was just look at you. He didn't have to say anything. You know—'Okay, I think we better calm this down right now.' That was Mac. When it was getting closer to game time, don't go messing around Mac. He's getting dressed. He was perfect. He would get his socks on just perfect, his shirt was tucked in just perfect. He knew that was him as a baseball player and that's what he was going to do every day. Every game was a big event for him. You could tell by the way he would get ready."

McCovey demonstrated his readiness with his hitting proficiency that he shared with Mays. They hit 801 home runs from 1959 to 1972 while playing together for the Giants, according to the Elias Sports Bureau. Among teammate duos, they're exceeded only by Hank Aaron and Eddie Mathews of the Braves (863; 1954–66) and Babe Ruth and Lou Gehrig of the Yankees (859; 1923–34). Predictably, the list of teammate twosomes homering in the same game looks similar. Aaron and Mathews top the chart at 75, followed by Ruth and Gehrig at 73 and Mays and McCovey at 68. It's worth noting that the formidable Dodger pair of Gil Hodges and Duke Snider are close behind with 67, as are Cubs greats Ron Santo and Billy Williams, McCovey's longtime buddy and fellow Mobile, Alabama, native. They're at 64.

Except for left-handed swingers Ruth and Gehrig, they're all ideal complements, one batting right-handed and the other left-handed. Through the 1960s, though, Mays and McCovey remained the National League's classic couple. Each led the league in homers three times during the decade, with Mays capturing the crown in 1962, '64, and '65, while McCovey topped the chart in 1963 (tied at 44 homers alongside Aaron), '68, and '69. To fans, Mays was the métier of ballplayers, and deservedly so. But among peers, McCovey commanded equal respect.

"Willie McCovey was the most underrated superstar in that magical era," said former infielder Jim Lefebvre, who began his eight big league seasons with the Dodgers in 1965 as the National League Rookie of the Year. "McCovey was always the guy who we feared the most. If you needed a base hit to tie the game up, if you needed a two-run double off the wall to tie the score or if you needed a three-run homer to win the game, he was the guy who was gonna do it. Willie Mays was on a different planet. We all know that. But McCovey was right behind him. We talk about great players—who do you think was better? Willie Mays. Roberto Clemente. Hank Aaron. Frank Robinson. You can go on and on and on about all the great players in the game. Well, McCovey should be mentioned with those guys, too, as far as I'm concerned."

McCovey thrived despite undergoing knee and ankle surgery in 1959 for injuries he sustained a season earlier with Dallas in the Double-A Texas League. "Those were the first of many [surgeries]," he said without remorse. The Giants had moved from New York to San Francisco, but their top doctors remained in Manhattan. So McCovey headed for the Big Apple to undergo his operation. One of the veteran Giants volunteered to house McCovey throughout his stay in New York. Who? None other than Mays, of course. "I knew Willie before I came up to the Majors," McCovey said. "A lot of people don't know, but I stayed at Willie's place in New York when I was just a teenager. I had to go back and see the doctor in a week or so after my surgery. So rather than come all the way back out to Mobile or stay in a hotel, Willie suggested I stay with him in his apartment."

McCovey appreciated the hospitality and admitted feeling in awe of his host. However, he had to remain patient while Mays engaged in his favorite form of entertainment: billiards, which he played with one of his closest off-the-field friends, Dodgers infielder Junior Gilliam, during McCovey's visit. "Willie would take me to the pool hall, and I would watch them," McCovey said. "I wasn't a good pool player. But they were."

Spending time with Mays gave McCovey an introductory lesson in handling celebrity. Said McCovey, "Willie was everything in New York at the time. He was Mr. New York. You got a lot of attention when you went out." McCovey shared Mays's sense of style, at the ballpark and away from it. Both wore their Giants uniform as if it were a tuxedo. Former Giants infielder Joe Amalfitano pointed out that a full-length mirror occupied the dressing stall between theirs at Candlestick Park. "Those guys were entertainers," Amalfitano said. "They were very, very meticulous about how they put the uniform on." Accessorizing, apparently, was a high priority for them both. "We'd go on the road and those guys had separate suitcases for shoes," Amalfitano said. "They took great pride in looking good—in and out of uniform."

Until the 1970s, those road trips could last as long as three weeks. A journey out East during summer might cause McCovey or Mays to lose several pounds. To avoid the horrifying prospect of wearing a baggy home uniform, they hired a tailor to take an inch off the waist or perform whatever adjustments were necessary. Amalfitano recalled that McCovey demonstrated this kind of fussiness about his garb when they were Minor League teammates. "I can see Willie Mac tucking in that jersey just right," Amalfitano said. "He was *clean*. And those uniforms in the minor leagues were made by old Martha the tentmaker."

McCovey played a significant role in Mays's biggest day in the Major Leagues—his 4-homer game at Milwaukee on April 30, 1961—though it wasn't what either man would have hoped. On the previous night, McCovey ordered a plate of ribs via room service as a late-night snack. "They were famous in Milwaukee then," said McCovey, who had reason to celebrate. One day after Warren Spahn opened the series on April 28 by no-hitting the Giants, McCovey led the offense's return to normalcy by ripping 3 hits, including a pair of homers, and driving in 4 runs in 5 at bats as San Francisco prevailed, 7–3. Hence McCovey's triumphant nosh. Mays, who was McCovey's roommate on this trip, sampled a few bites of the ribs. That was enough to make him violently ill overnight. "There were doubts about whether he was going to play the next day, and because I was his roommate, it was going to be my fault," McCovey said.

Amalfitano didn't play, but he came to the rescue in more ways than one. First, he convinced Mays to at least take batting practice. "I asked him, 'What are you from 1 percent to 100 percent?' He said, 'Maybe 70.' I said, 'Well, your 70 is going to be better than whoever goes out there for their 100.'"

Amalfitano also suggested that Mays use a different bat: "He had a 35-inch, 33-ounce Adirondack bat that was too light for him. I used it in batting practice and I could try to get my hands going. When I hit it right in BP, the ball would come off that bat much better than it did off of mine. It had two or three knots in the barrel and a nice wide grain. I said, 'Willie, you oughta try this.'" Said McCovey, "All I know is, I was hitting behind him and I kept shaking his hand when he crossed home plate."

Mays proceeded to avoid McCovey's culinary tastes, though he felt free to help his younger teammate in various ways. Game 3 of the 1962 World Series was a prime example. McCovey's defensive skills as an outfielder were shaky at best. But manager Alvin Dark started him in right field because he wanted to maximize the Giants' offensive potential against Yankees starter Bill Stafford. Bobby Richardson, the Yankees' second batter of the game, lifted a fly ball between center field and right field. Either Mays or McCovey could have reached the ball in time to make the put-out. McCovey was startled when, out of the corner of his eye, he saw Mays stop pursuing the ball and silently fix his gaze upon him. Perhaps nobody in the massive Yankee Stadium crowd of 71,434 realized what was happening. But McCovey fully understood Mays's message. It was nonverbal communication, and Mays was clearly saying, "It's yours," wanting McCovey to bolster his confidence by handling an early play. McCovey indeed made the catch, though he committed a 7th-inning error that led to an unearned run.

Acknowledging McCovey's burgeoning offensive prowess toward the late '60s, Mays began employing an unusual baserunning gambit. He'd smoke a line drive toward an outfield gap, but instead of turning aggressively toward second base for an easy double, he'd halt at first base. Thus, opponents would be much more likely to pitch to McCovey rather than intentionally walk him with first base open. In fact, Mays hit 29 doubles in 1966, exceeding his career high by one. He followed that with 22, 20, 17, and 15, respectively, in the next four seasons. It's impossible to determine the effectiveness of Mays's stratagem without studying videos of his relevant plate appearances—a technologically impossible act. But at least the hint exists, in the form of Mays's diminishing doubles totals, that he tried on multiple occasions to preserve McCovey's potential as a home run threat.

Regardless of what transpired on the field between McCovey and Mays, their relationship was mutually comfortable.

To McCovey, Mays set himself apart in other ways. Before Mays migrated from San Francisco to Atherton, California, in the late '60s, McCovey paid occasional off-season visits to his incomparable teammate, who was inevitably lounging in his pajamas. Mays might motivate himself enough to shoot a game or two of pool. Then it was back to sleep. Not exactly the embodiment of high energy. Then Mays would report to spring training, and he was transformed into the nonpareil that everybody knew, already primed for opening day. "Mays was Mays," McCovey said. "Nobody was as good as Mays. He was amazing. He didn't do anything during the offseason. Then on the first day of spring training you would think it was midseason, the way he went out there and played. Everybody else was huffing and puffing, trying to get in shape."

McCovey found himself a step ahead of virtually everybody else in 1968. It was the "Year of the Pitcher" for nearly every batter except McCovey, who was on his way to leading the NL with 36 home runs and 105 RBIs. "It was just about then that I was really coming into my own," McCovey said—a curious remark, considering that he had averaged 35 homers and 93 RBIs per year while compiling a .937 OPS in the previous three seasons. Intent on supporting his friend and teammate, Mays lobbied influential members of the Baseball Writers' Association of America to persuade them to cast their National League Most Valuable Player votes for McCovey. "He's the best slugger right now," Mays said. "McCovey has been doing the job for us." During many other years, Mays's stumping might have succeeded. But not this year. Not with St. Louis' Bob Gibson forging a season for the ages with a 22-9 record, 13 shutouts, and his now legendary 1.12 ERA. Gibson won the MVP balloting with relative ease, garnering fourteen of twenty first-place votes. Cincinnati's Pete Rose, who led the Majors with 210 hits and a .335 batting average, captured the other six first-place votes and finished second. McCovey, the personification of power, settled for third place.

"So the next year, I decided to have a little better year," McCovey said. "I said, 'I'll show you.'"

9

Mr. MVP

He's going to have his best season.

—Giants hitting instructor Hank Sauer

Determined to reach his goal of improving upon an excellent 1968 season, Willie McCovey looked ready for the challenge as he reported to the Giants' spring training base at Casa Grande, Arizona, in February 1969. Hank Sauer sounded tempted to cast McCovey as Cassius, he of the "lean and hungry look" in Shakespeare's *Julius Caesar*, in an interview with the *San Francisco Examiner*.

"He's going to have his best season, a great year," said Sauer, the Giants' hitting instructor who led the National League with 37 homers for the Cubs in 1952. "He had a good season last year but he's headed for a better one. What I like about him this spring is the freedom he has around the shoulders. He's down to 215 [pounds] and a lot of that 10 pounds or so he has dropped since last season has come off his chest and shoulders. That's what happens to hitters. They put on weight around the shoulders and chest and their swings become restricted. They don't get the bat around as fast."

Having led the NL in home runs, RBIs, and slugging percentage in 1968, McCovey felt confident about his bat speed as he approached the new season. Health was another matter. He endured left knee discomfort despite excelling in '68, so he figured that shedding fifteen to twenty extra pounds would reduce the strain on his knees and increase the number of games he could play. In fact, he started 148 games at first base in 1969, second in his career only to the 150 he started in 1965. He hit his first homer of the year in the team's second game, a 10–2 loss to Atlanta. He homered again in back-to-back, 5–1 wins at San Diego on April 12–13. He went deep in the Giants' home opener on April 17 at Candlestick Park, a 5–4 San Francisco win over San Diego. Two days later, continuing to torment the expansion Padres, he recorded his first 2-homer game of the season. McCovey then sustained a balanced effort in an April 27 doubleheader against the Houston Astros at Candlestick, mashing go-ahead, 3-run homers in each game of a doubleheader sweep.

McCovey finished April with 8 home runs, tying a National League record shared by Chicago's Lee Walls (1958) and Los Angeles' Wally Moon (1961). McCovey clearly was benefiting from the relative absence of pain in his troublesome left knee. "It makes a big difference when you can play with nothing else on your mind," he said. Meanwhile, Baltimore's Frank Robinson bashed 9 homers to equal the AL mark set by Ken Williams of the St. Louis Browns in 1922. It was obvious that big league hitters felt emboldened by two changes meant to help them and reverse the steadily increasing dominance enjoyed by pitchers. The elevation of the pitcher's mound was lowered from 15 inches to 10 inches entering the '69 season. Hurlers looked a lot less imposing when throwing closer to ground level. Also, the strike zone shrank and now extended from the batters' armpits to the top of the knees. It previously extended from the top of the batter's shoulders to the knees. For good measure, expansion of the Major Leagues from 20 to 24 teams diluted pitching talent. By season's end, runs per game for each team would jump from 3.42 in 1968 to 4.07 in '69.

Though McCovey personified the offensive revival, he insisted that hitters had not totally wrested superiority from pitchers. "It still comes up just as fast as before and the curveball still curves," he said. "I know everyone is talking about how much easier it is for the hitters since they made the mound lower, but I for one don't think so. Even if we hitters have an edge, as everyone says, then it's about time, but it won't last. The good pitchers will make their adjustments and it will all even out."

As if to verify his remark, McCovey went homerless in 15 of his next 16 games after the Houston doubleheader. "They stopped pitching to me, and all of a sudden I found myself going for bad pitches," McCovey told *The Sporting News*. "I want to hit the ball when I'm up there at the plate and you can't do that unless you're swinging. For three or four games I wasn't hitting well at all. But I think I'm back in the groove now."

In fact, McCovey went on another binge that featured 11 home runs in 15 games. Early in that torrent came a May 24 homer off Pittsburgh's Bob Veale, a hard-throwing, bespectacled left-hander who intimidated most hitters. McCovey clouted a 2-run, 5th-inning drive that hastened the Giants' 5–2 triumph. It was significant, given Veale's ability to handcuff McCovey. Before connecting for that round-tripper, McCovey was batting .182 (8-for-44) lifetime against Veale with 20 strikeouts in 47 plate appearances. McCovey's victory in this confrontation added legitimacy to his budding success.

McCovey enjoyed similar results when he faced the league's best pitchers. He homered on May 27 against Chicago's Ferguson Jenkins and on May 30 off the Mets' Tom Seaver. And McCovey hadn't even hit his stride. That occurred in June, his best statistical month of the season. McCovey amassed 11 homers and 29 RBIs in 27 games while posting a .368/.522/.828 slash line. McCovey may have approached his zenith for the season with a June 6 outburst. Philadelphia's Dick Allen articulated what everyone else was thinking after McCovey slugged a pair of homers to back Gaylord Perry in a 4–0 victory over the Phillies. "Willie is simply the best hitter in baseball today," Allen said. Jenkins, who was working on his third of six consecutive 20-win seasons, wasn't about to argue with Allen's assessment. "The number one thing I remember about him was that he was a great low-ball hitter," Jenkins said. "You can't pitch him down. I learned that after a couple of appearances. You had to pitch him up and you had to pitch him in. He didn't miss fastballs. If you hung a pitch, like a curveball or a slider, you got punished." Jenkins performed respectably against McCovey lifetime, yielding 4 home runs to him but limiting him to a .254 batting average (17-for-67). "Studying and rectifying mistakes," was how Jenkins explained it.

Had interested parties known how the season would unfold, the McCovey-Seaver matchups would have been the most widely anticipated confrontations (as well as highly affordable, with box seats costing around $4 at the time). McCovey's reputation had soared—"He dominated the league," Cincinnati superstar Pete Rose said—while Seaver was challenging St. Louis' Bob Gibson and Detroit's Denny McLain for the status of baseball's top pitcher. Said Cubs outfielder Billy Williams of Seaver, "A lot of kids who come to the big leagues are just throwers. He was a pitcher when he first came into the big leagues." Overall, McCovey got the best of Seaver when they clashed in 1969, going 3-for-9 with a homer and a triple in 3 games. But Seaver got the edge from the team perspective, going 2-0 with a 2.63 ERA and a no-decision in 3 outings against the Giants.

As the season unfolded, McCovey began to experience persistent discomfort in his right knee—the one he initially injured during his Double-A season at Dallas in 1957—as well as calcium deposits and bone chips in his hip. "You could always tell that he was in pain," said outfielder Ken Henderson, who appeared in 113 games for the Giants in 1969.

Besides coping with his various ailments, McCovey had to deal with the machinations of opposing teams who knew that their pitching staffs were no match for him. Cincinnati manager Dave Bristol was among those most determined to stop McCovey. Borrowing strategy from baseball's past—and, as it turned out, providing a glimpse into baseball's future—Bristol stationed his defenders where the pull-hitting, powerful McCovey was likely to hit most pitches: extremely deep and heavily to the field's right side. Bristol initially tried this ploy on June 16 in the opener of a 4-game series at Candlestick Park. Reds shortstop Darrel Cheney moved to straightaway center field, left fielder Alex Johnson played the left-center field gap, center fielder Pete Rose defended the right-field power alley, right fielder Bobby Tolan played on the right-field line, first baseman Lee May and second baseman Tommy Helms positioned themselves in dead-pull areas, and third baseman Tony Perez played shortstop. When the count on McCovey reached 2 strikes, Perez sidled to the right side of second base.

Later, defensive metrics spawned shifts (erased by rules changes following the 2022 season) tailored to the idiosyncrasies of each batter, even if he was hitting .220. In bygone eras, only the greatest hitters received such treatment, most notably Stan Musial, Ted Williams, and Eddie Mathews. Bristol explained that he was trying to suppress McCovey's extra-base hit potential. "I had seen him hit so many balls through that hole," Bristol said.

"Well, Dave realized that Willie pulled anybody and anything. It [the shift] was truly ahead of its time," Reds catcher Johnny Bench said. "I thought it was brilliant, until McCovey popped up behind third base just inside the line. I beat Perez to it. I was 20 feet beyond third—almost to the grass—when I made the catch. A typical Mac popup: A mile high—to the moon!"

Said Bristol, "The only thing I did wrong was run out of players. I couldn't put a 10th guy in San Francisco Bay."

Advantage, Reds. They took 3 out of 4 games in the series, though McCovey hit respectably (5-for-14, 1 home run) and even thumbed his nose at the strategy when he bunted for a hit toward the vacant third base area.

Most Giants opponents declined to copy Bristol, who managed San Francisco at the end of McCovey's active playing career, though evidence continued to mount that there was no stopping the big man during his big summer. Giants catcher Dick Dietz disregarded screaming coaches and came up with a novel idea during batting practice at Candlestick Park. As Dietz recalled, "One day we were out there shagging balls and I told them, 'This is the way you've got to play McCovey.' And I climbed up on the fence and sat up on top of the fence in right field when McCovey was taking batting practice. They got mad at that. 'Get on down from there!' I said, 'That's the way you play McCovey. You've got to get up on top of the fence or up in the seats!'"

The 1969 All-Star Game in Washington DC exemplified McCovey's dominance. Not only was he elected to start at first base for the National League in the balloting among players, coaches, and managers, but he also was the NL's top vote-getter, edging out Atlanta's Hank Aaron, 296–295. Though the pair of rosters featured nineteen future Hall of Famers, McCovey alone towered over every participant like the Washington Monument by homering twice in the NL's 9–3 victory.

This Midsummer Classic was different from the rest. Major League Baseball observed the one hundredth anniversary of professional baseball in 1969. What this meant for the All-Stars was special festivities that included a trip to the White House. President Richard Nixon happened to be an avid baseball fan. In fact, then vice president Nixon attended the inaugural game at Candlestick Park on April 12, 1960. "As unpopular as he was, everybody was still thrilled to get to go to the White House," McCovey said. "He signed baseballs for all of us. That was kind of a big deal, to go to the White House."

Steady rain forced postponement of the game, scheduled for July 22, until the next afternoon. McCovey batted fourth, between Aaron and Chicago's

Ron Santo. Though this was McCovey's fourth All-Star selection, he did not take his assignment for granted. "For me to hit cleanup in that lineup was amazing," he said.

McCovey grounded out against Yankees right-hander Mel Stottlemyre in the 1st inning, setting up a rematch against Oakland's John "Blue Moon" Odom with nobody out in the 3rd inning and Hank Aaron on first base via a single. In the '68 All-Star Game at Houston, Odom struck out McCovey, who said "I'm gonna get you" as he returned to the dugout—just loud enough for Odom to hear. Odom welcomed the challenge. "What was on my mind was striking him out again," Odom said. But McCovey got the best of it, clearing the center-field barrier for a 2-run homer that ignited a 5-run NL outburst. "He was a man of his word," Odom said. One inning later, McCovey pulled a drive to right field off Detroit ace Denny McLain, whose 31 victories in 1968 gave him an air of invincibility. McCovey thus joined Arky Vaughan, Al Rosen, and Ted Williams as the only players to homer twice in an All-Star Game. Gary Carter joined the list in 1981.

This was part of a span in which the NL won 19 of 20 All-Star Games from 1963 to 1982. "The National League was much deeper at that point in time with talent," said right-hander Bill Singer, an NL All-Star with the Dodgers in 1969 and a member of the 1973 AL All-Star squad as an Angel. "Billy Williams couldn't make the All-Star team and he made the Hall of Fame." McCovey remained a fiercely proud National Leaguer for the rest of his life. "We wanted to prove to the American League that we were the better league," he said. "So that's the way we approached it every year."

It seemed almost as if McCovey hit that second home run for emphasis. That wouldn't have surprised Singer. "He was that good," Singer said.

Good enough to revive a stratagem that had been around for decades yet rarely employed: the intentional walk. McCovey set a Major League record with 45 intentional walks in 1969, en route to finishing with 260 lifetime.

Issuing the four-finger salute simply wasn't done in bygone eras. Formidable hitters remained supreme beings to reluctantly confront—though some of the following totals might be artificially low, since the intentional walk didn't become an official statistic until 1955. Babe Ruth drew a mere 34 intentional walks during his career. Lou Gehrig had 102. Joe DiMaggio prompted 111.

Mickey Mantle, 148. Willie Mays, 214. Ted Williams, 258—including 33 in 1957, the all-time single-season standard McCovey broke. Not until Barry Bonds established himself as an offensive force in the 1990s did managers again realize that they might have something to gain through bypassing a truly dangerous hitter. Bonds drew 68 intentional walks in 2002, 61 in 2003, and 120 in 2004.

Examples abounded of the sheer fear McCovey aroused in '69. Chicago Cubs manager Leo Durocher, never one to back down from an opponent, intentionally walked him with 1 out to load the bases in a July 30 game. McCovey also walked in his other 3 plate appearances; it's safe to assume that he received little or nothing good to hit in those "unintentional" walks. Durocher outdid himself on August 16 by intentionally walking McCovey with 2 outs and nobody on base in the 8th inning of a scoreless tie. Mets ace Tom Seaver intentionally walked McCovey in an August 21 game; it happened to be McCovey's 33rd of the season, tying Williams's record. The next batter, Bobby Bonds, belted a 3-run homer, his second round-tripper of the game. And on September 21, Los Angeles Dodgers skipper Walter Alston put McCovey aboard with 2 outs and nobody on base with the score tied in the 10th inning, fearing an instant, game-winning home run. The ploy backfired when the Giants proceeded to load the bases and win as shortstop Maury Wills mishandled Jim Davenport's simple grounder.

McCovey's appreciation for this form of respect was limited. "I wanted to swing the bat," he said. "All the teams feared me. I just couldn't get a good pitch to hit. Whenever there was a base open, they put me on."

In fact, the mediocrity of the Giants' 1969 lineup makes McCovey's season look even more monumental. He received relatively little support from teammates. Mays endured one of his worst seasons as a Giant, missing 65 starts due mainly to poor health. He batted a capable .283 but recorded a .362 on-base percentage and a .437 slugging percentage, well below his season-opening career figures of .384 and .578 in those categories, respectively. The diminished Mays denied McCovey the benefits of having a formidable presence in the batting order's third spot who could tax a pitcher's energy, disrupt his concentration, and most importantly, get on base. Moreover, nobody on the Giants' roster was capable of elevating his game even just partially to compensate for Mays's inadequacies. San Francisco's no. 3 hitters posted a slash line of .256/.337/.388 for the season. That paled alongside the league averages of .284/.362/.459. Worse yet was the absence of an assertive no. 5 hitter who could "protect" McCovey by posing enough of a threat to discourage opponents from pitching around him or intentionally walking him. Third baseman Jim Ray Hart filled this role in previous years, averaging 28 home runs and 89 RBIs per season from 1964 to 1968 while producing a .285/.347/.491 slash line through that period. But as was the case with Mays, poor health troubled Hart, whose shoulder ailments limited him to playing 95 games in 1969. His slugging percentage plummeted to a shockingly low .331. Henderson and catcher Dick Dietz were a year away from blossoming as decent fifth hitters. For now, San Francisco would have to cope with no. 5 men who put together an anemic .214/.314/.336 slash line in '69. Only the brilliantly talented Bobby Bonds, who amassed 32 homers and stole 45 bases in his first full Major League season, prevented McCovey from being a one-man band.

McCovey truly stood alone, however, regarding his wardrobe. He seemingly wore a new outfit each day. Would it be a six-button double-breasted suit? Might his ensemble include a pocket handkerchief? What manner of footwear would he be sporting? Said utilityman Bob Burda, "On the road, one of the cool things was, every time we got on the bus to get to the ballpark, we were waiting for McCovey to board because he would be wearing something special. He dressed immaculately. Everybody would 'Oooh' and 'Ahhh.'"

McCovey built his case for the MVP Award with consistency, as his month-by-month totals demonstrated. His prodigious efforts in April (.315 batting average, 8 home runs, and 22 RBIs) and June (.368, 11, 29) surrounded a solid May (.328, 7, 16). Though he batted a season-low .259 in July, his home run and RBI figures (6, 17) were adequate. He then delivered a rousing August (.359, 9, 28). He batted .295 with 4 homers and 14 RBIs in September, his lowest run-production numbers for any month that year. McCovey attributed his drop-off to sore wrists. He said that he jammed one against the wall at Candlestick Park while pursuing a pop fly and hurt the other wrist sliding into home plate in a September home game against the Dodgers. He collected his final homer of the season off Los Angeles' Pete Mikkelsen during an 8–1 victory on September 28. That decision left the Giants 2½ games behind first-place Atlanta in the NL West. But there just wasn't enough season left for San Francisco, which doomed itself with back-to-back, 1-run defeats at last-place San Diego on September 23–24. Atlanta clinched the division title on September 30, sealing the Giants' fifth consecutive second-place finish.

McCovey was no loser, however. He topped the National League with 45 homers and 126 RBIs while finishing with a Major League–best .656 slugging percentage. He thus became only the third player to lead his league in all three categories for at least two years in a row, joining Babe Ruth (1919–21) and Jimmie Foxx (1932–33).

That slugging average was the Majors' best since Mickey Mantle of the Yankees checked in at .687 in 1961. It was the NL's highest since Mays's .659 in 1955. Also, silencing skeptics who considered him just another power hitter, McCovey batted a career-best .320. Not bad for a guy who endured injuries to his knee, hip, shoulder, shin, wrists, and feet. "I've been seeing a lot of doctors since the end of the season. It seems like all I've been doing is seeing them," McCovey told reporters at an off-season news conference.

As the November 20 announcement of the MVP voting approached, some observers wondered whether another pitcher would poach the honor from McCovey, as Cardinals pitcher Bob Gibson did in 1968. Tom Seaver was clearly the glue of the World Series champion New York Mets, fashioning a 25–7 record with a 2.21 ERA. He also went 10–0 in his final 11 starts. Giants manager Clyde King told reporters that he had heard of a fairly large number of voters ready to throw their support behind Seaver. "So I was preparing myself for a letdown the last week or so," McCovey told the Bay Area press. "That made the news that much better."

Hence, McCovey was dressed to celebrate. He was nattily attired in a crisp-looking suit and blue suede shoes at his Candlestick Park news conference. "I've got to dress for the occasion," he said.

McCovey finished ahead of Seaver, 265–243, with each receiving eleven first-place votes (players received fourteen points for a first-place vote, nine for second place, eight for third, and so on). McCovey, the only player named on all twenty-four ballots, received nine second-place votes to four for Seaver.

Additionally, Seaver was not named on two ballots, reviving the argument of whether pitchers should be considered for the award along with position players. After all, infielders, outfielders, and catchers are ineligible for the Cy Young Award, which is reserved for pitchers. At least one New York–based writer believed that Seaver deserved the award. "We wuzzed robbed!" Joe Trimble wrote in the *New York Daily News*. Trimble added that McCovey's victory appeared to be a "miscarriage of justice," since starting pitchers Gibson and Detroit's Denny McLain captured the MVP Awards in their respective leagues in 1968.

Atlanta's Hank Aaron, McCovey's fellow Mobilian, placed third in the voting. Cincinnati's Pete Rose and Chicago's Ron Santo rounded out the top five. "If anything, other than winning the MVP, would make me happier, it would have been winning the pennant. That comes first," McCovey said on the day of his triumph. Nevertheless, McCovey had silenced the skeptics who questioned his abilities at the beginning of his career. "I've never lost confidence in myself, even when I've had poor years," he said. "I've always felt I was capable of real good seasons." For good measure, McCovey captured *The Sporting News'* NL Player of the Year honors in voting held among the league's players.

Four years had passed since a Giant was named MVP—Mays, who bashed a career-high 52 homers in 1965. It would be twenty more years before the Giants produced another MVP—left fielder Kevin Mitchell in 1989. Interestingly, some of McCovey's and Mitchell's statistics from their respective MVP seasons were eerily similar, including plate appearances (McCovey 623, Mitchell 640), runs (McCovey 101, Mitchell 100), homers (McCovey 45, Mitchell 47), RBIs (McCovey 126, Mitchell 125), and slugging percentage (McCovey .656, Mitchell .635). In no way, however, did Mitchell consider himself McCovey's equal. "To be honest, I'm a fan. I'm a big fan," said Mitchell, who, as a youth growing up in San Diego, studied McCovey while he played for the Padres in 1974–76. "You could call me a groupie when it comes to Stretch. I wouldn't care if he cussed me out. Just as long as he acknowledged I was there." Following McCovey's triumph, other Giants who excelled enough to merit MVP consideration were Bobby Bonds in 1973, Will Clark in 1987–89 and '91, and

Barry Bonds, who virtually took sole possession of the award by winning it as a Giant in 1993 and 2001–4.

And what about Willie McCovey in 1970? Asked during his MVP news conference at Candlestick Park about the upcoming season, McCovey said, "I'm capable of having a year just as good. I've established myself now. It's a question of staying in shape and playing enough games."

10

Edging toward an Exit

I'm so happy that someone really wants me.

—Willie McCovey

Rather than train in sunny, warm Arizona to prepare for the 1970 season, the Giants toured Japan. They felt welcome there due to owner Horace Stoneham's various ties to the country's growing baseball establishment. But the sojourn proved to be near disastrous when ace right-hander Juan Marichal not only developed an ear infection but also suffered a severe allergic reaction to the penicillin he was given. His San Francisco–era franchise record of 6 consecutive Opening Day starts (1964–69) ended because he remained too sick to pitch when the regular season opened on April 7 against Houston at Candlestick Park. Marichal was to the Giants what Tom Seaver was to the Mets and Bob Gibson was to the Cardinals. When those men pitched, the team's confidence was almost palpable. Marichal's absence thus left the Giants feeling somewhat rudderless. As Willie McCovey said, "When Juan pitched, it was *win* day." With Marichal convalescing at San Francisco's St. Luke's Hospital instead of staring down the Astros at Candlestick Park, Gaylord Perry, who was good enough to occupy the ace's role on most teams, started the season opener for the Giants. McCovey went 0-for-3 but walked twice and displayed an MVP's grit when he slid home determinedly to score from first base on Ken Henderson's 5th-inning double. This miniachievement was captured by a *San Francisco Chronicle* photographer. "It's McCovey by a Leg," blared a headline accompanying the photo. But pinch hitter Norm Miller swatted a 3-run homer off Perry during a 4-run 7th inning that carried Houston to an 8–5 triumph.

Overall, it was business as usual for McCovey. He went homerless in 33 plate appearances spanning the season's first 8 games, due likely to blurry vision in his right eye that developed when he took oral drugs to relieve pain in his arthritic right knee. He then went deep in 4 consecutive games. His statistical line for 1970 reflected only a slight drop in production from the year before. His performance remained at an MVP level; others elevated their game to match his.

Year	AVG	G	AB	R	H	2B	3B	HR	RBI	BB	SO	OBP	SLG
1969	.320	149	491	101	157	26	2	45	126	121	66	.453	.656
1970	.289	152	495	98	143	39	2	39	126	137	75	.444	.612

"Some people say I'm having a bad season. It seems to me I've been getting a few hits," McCovey said. His two-year streak of leading the NL in home runs and RBIs ended honorably as he finished fourth in both categories. Cincinnati's Johnny Bench, one of McCovey's most ardent admirers, topped everybody by amassing 45 homers and 148 RBIs. Like Bench, two other stalwarts needed to have their most prolific years to surpass McCovey. Cincinnati's Tony Perez ranked second with 129 RBIs and third with 40 home runs. Chicago's Billy Williams, McCovey's Mobile buddy, was second with 42 homers and tied for Perez for third with 129 RBIs.

Though McCovey received ostensibly improved protection in the batting order than he did in 1969, he led the Majors with a career-high 137 walks, including 40 intentionally. Options for opposing managers besides walking McCovey included taking their chances with Dick Dietz (.273/.400/.420 slash line with 3 homers and 31 RBIs in 50 games from the fifth spot) or Ken Henderson (.291/.396./436 with 8 homers and 48 RBIs in 87 games batting fifth). As productive as Dietz and Henderson were, bypassing McCovey was a definite no-brainer.

Sparky Anderson, who succeeded Dave Bristol as Cincinnati's manager after the 1969 season, had the image of McCovey's fabulous Major League debut still lodged in his memory. He wasn't about to let the slugger dismantle his ballclub single-handedly. McCovey recalled seeing Anderson stroll past him by the batting cage or near the dugout, raise his hand, and wiggle four fingers to signify an intentional walk. Hours before the first pitch, Anderson already was informing McCovey that he was taking the bat out of his hands.

In an oft-repeated quotation, Anderson memorably and respectfully said, "If you pitch to him, he'll ruin baseball. He'd hit 80 home runs. There's no comparison between McCovey and anybody else in the league."

One day, after Anderson ordered yet another intentional pass, McCovey's fabled patience finally reached an end. Frustrated after losing more swings, McCovey bellowed at Anderson as he headed for first base, "Who do you think I am? Babe Ruth?" Anderson replied, "No. You're better." Reminded of that exchange about forty years later, McCovey chuckled. "That's a true story," he said.

Henderson tried some insouciant behavior. "One of my ways to motivate myself was, I would get out of the on-deck circle and I'd actually walk really close to home plate—one-quarter or halfway—while they walked Willie to show them that I was anxious to get in there and prove that they made a mistake," he said.

McCovey placed ninth in the MVP balloting that year, marking his final top-ten finish. Meanwhile, the Giants ended their streak of second-place finishes at five (the *Chronicle's* tongue-in-cheek headline read, "Giants Lose; Finish Third for a Change"), but they approached 1971 with optimism after posting a 67–53 record under manager Charlie Fox, who replaced Clyde King after a preposterous 17–16 loss to San Diego on May 23.

The Giants seemed capable of winning almost every day as the 1971 season began. They sprinted from the gate with a 37-14 record, sustaining winning streaks of 9, 4, and 5 games. Willie Mays played like a man half his age, homering in each of the season's first 4 games and batting .389 in his first 25 games. Juan Marichal and Gaylord Perry started 8-2 and 6-2, respectively. Rookie shortstop Chris Speier provided a fresh infusion of energy to a rapidly aging ballclub.

As for McCovey, he batted .172 in his first 9 games, then recovered to hit safely in 14 of his next 17 games. He hit .391 (25-for-64) in that span to lift his average to .333 overall. But it was a troublesome year for McCovey, who played the entire season with torn cartilage in his left knee. He told Mike Mandel in SF *Giants: An Oral History* that he regularly had fluid drained from his knee and took medication to be able to play. McCovey even had season-ending knee surgery scheduled for the middle of the year. But with the Giants striving to win the division, he ultimately resorted to cortisone shots and more frequent rest to make himself available as often as possible.

McCoveyesque moments still occurred throughout '71. They just happened less often. He homered twice on May 2 at Cincinnati, saving the second longball for the 13th inning to lift San Francisco to a 4–3 victory. On June 20, his 3-run, pinch-hit homer sealed a 6–2 victory over the Padres in the first game of a doubleheader. On July 21, he clobbered his 13th career grand slam during a 6-run 9th inning to victimize Dave Giusti and the Pirates in San Francisco's 8–4 win. And, as usual, nobody wanted to throw him a strike. He led the Majors with 21 intentional walks.

Then came the last great night of the Giants empire, one final opportunity for Mays, McCovey, and Marichal to outclass their foes together. It was the regular-season finale, and the Giants, who led the Dodgers by 1 game in the NL West standings, would clinch the division title with a victory at San Diego. It was no contest. Marichal pitched a 5-hit complete game. Mays smacked a 4th-inning RBI double before scoring on rookie Dave Kingman's home run. Tutored by Mays, one of the finest baserunners ever, Henderson sent himself home by forcing Padres pitcher Al Severinsen to commit a 9th-inning balk. The Giants triumphed, 5–1, propelling themselves into the National League Championship Series (back then, they were referred to simply as "the playoffs") against Pittsburgh.

The Giants carried legitimate optimism with them into the playoffs, primarily because they won 9 of their 12 regular-season games against Pittsburgh. But that disparity was somewhat misleading. Each team had its resident all-time great (Mays for the Giants, Roberto Clemente for the Pirates), an indomitable slugger (McCovey for the Giants, Willie Stargell for the Pirates), and a true ace (Marichal and Pittsburgh's Steve Blass finished 18-11 and 15-8, respectively; Blass's 5 shutouts led the NL). Both teams, however, lacked starting pitching depth. The Giants' shortcomings in this area were exacerbated by the need to use Marichal in the regular-season finale to seal the division championship. Had they been able to eliminate Los Angeles earlier, they could have saved Marichal for the playoff opener, followed by

Perry. San Francisco's chances of taking a 2–0 series lead to Pittsburgh would have been much more promising. Instead, this series would be won by the team that more frequently controlled the matchup of the moment—who was swinging the hottest bat, which bullpen proved most effective.

Round 1 went to the Giants, 5–4, with McCovey providing the knockout blow: a 2-run homer that capped a 4-run, 5th-inning uprising. Until the Giants rallied, they looked as meek offensively as they did in their previous postseason appearance—their 1–0, Game 7 loss to the Yankees in the 1962 World Series. Blass was overpowering the Giants, striking out 9 in 4 innings while nursing a 2–1 lead. He didn't yet realize that he was Icarus flying too close to the sun.

"What I learned from that was, because it was my first experience in postseason play, I thought that I had to be better than I was in the regular season," said Blass, who averaged 5.1 strikeouts per 9 innings in 33 starts that year. "And that's a trap. Because you get away from what got you there. I tried to be a power pitcher against the Giants. And it worked for about the first 4½ or five innings. But they got to me and just ripped my face off. You're not going to overpower the Giants. The harder you throw, the farther they'll hit the ball. The Giants really had an aura. And that aura shone brightly over all of them."

McCovey was capable of overwhelming Blass under any circumstance. He all but terrorized the right-hander while accumulating 6 home runs and 16 RBIS off him in 48 career regular-season plate appearances. "When he made contact, it was a different sound," Blass said. While heaping praise upon McCovey, Blass employed a line that numerous pitchers have used when referring to a particular nemesis. But he managed to make it sound original: "When we flew to San Francisco, there was always a limousine waiting for me at the airport, sent by Willie McCovey—so I could get to the hotel safely and not miss my turn [to pitch]."

The Giants needed a full-fledged transportation strike, with Bob Robertson as the lone passenger affected. Compensating for Stargell, who went 0-for-14 against the Giants after leading the Majors with 48 regular-season home runs, Robertson batted .438 (7-for-16) for the series with 4 homers, including 3 in the Pirates' 9–4 victory in Game 2 at Candlestick. The rest of the Pirates mustered 4 homers in 128 at bats for the series. Two of those homers, however, were struck by Richie Hebner and Robertson off Marichal in the series' third game at Pittsburgh, enough to give the Pirates a 2–1 win and a 2-1 edge in the series. McCovey homered off Blass again in the fourth game, this time delivering a 3-run clout in the 2nd inning. But rookie reliever Bruce Kison silenced San Francisco on 2 hits for 4⅔ innings, paving the way for the Pirates' 9–5 decision that clinched the best-of-five playoff and sent them to the World Series.

Anybody paying attention had to be impressed by McCovey. He hit safely in each game, finishing at .429 (6-for-14) with 2 homers and 6 RBIs. He also drew 4 walks, 3 of them intentional. He was by far the Giants' leading offensive force. "To get into the playoffs and have such success . . . was just really good," McCovey told Mandel. "I just felt that I was fortunate to be able to get through the season that year and everything I did was a plus."

Then came 1972, the year when the Giants' world spun off its axis.

The sad dismantling of greatness actually began on November 29, 1971, when the Giants traded right-hander Gaylord Perry and infielder Frank Duffy to Cleveland for left-hander Sam McDowell. The Giants believed that Perry was poised for a decline and that McDowell still possessed the devastating fastball that made him one of the AL's top starters. Wrong on both counts. Perry still had three 20-win seasons and a Cy Young Award left in him as he pitched until 1983. McDowell, who was an alcoholic, didn't last past 1975.

Every team was affected by the work stoppage, which ultimately forced management to increase its contribution to the players' pension fund. The delay caused by the labor dispute forced the regular season to begin on April 15. Not that Giants fans seemed to care. Coming off the NL West Division title, the ballclub drew 16,898 to its home opener on April 21, a 7–3 loss to Houston. That launched a four-year streak in which the Giants' paid attendance in home openers fell short of 20,000.

By then, the start of McCovey's season already had been ruined. Four games into the schedule, he broke his right forearm in a collision at first base with San Diego's John Jeter, who was running out a ground ball, on April 18. McCovey was reaching for a throw from second baseman Tito Fuentes in an effort to complete a double play. Fuentes's relay traveled to the home plate side of first base, leaving McCovey vulnerable to Jeter, who dove into the bag in hopes of coaxing a "safe" call. That's when they collided. The official diagnosis for McCovey: a spinal fracture of the ulna, just above the wrist. "We're not dead. We've got a lot of guys who can play," an undaunted Willie Mays said. Manager Charlie Fox's comment proved more telling: "I can't think of any player we could miss more than McCovey."

Said right-hander Steve Stone, "I remember graphically when we lost him in '72. That was the start of that whole '72 team disintegrating. It took that lineup and made it something it shouldn't have been. To do something to protect Willie Mays, they had to put Bonds behind him. Well, Bonds didn't hit curveballs very well. That lineup literally disintegrated with one injury and that was the injury to McCovey. We thought we were going to repeat as division champions and, of course, we all know it didn't work out that way, largely because of that injury. That's how important he was to that lineup."

McCovey wasn't completely healed on June 3, when he insisted on playing after a 44-game absence. Saddled with a 17-31 record, the Giants were ailing too. Their opponent was Pittsburgh, the pitcher was Steve Blass, and—you guessed it—McCovey belted a 2-run, 6th-inning homer to put San Francisco ahead, 2–1. Blurted Giants broadcaster Lon Simmons, "A man with a broken arm has just hit a home run! . . . Nice to have you back, Stretch!"

McCovey's return was welcome, given the seismic shift in the team's dynamic—on the field and off—that rocked the Giants about a month earlier. On May 11, owner Horace Stoneham, struggling to keep the Giants financially solvent, traded Mays, the very symbol of the franchise, to the New York Mets for right-hander Charlie Williams. McCovey succeeded Mays as team leader, a status he welcomed.

"I could tell there was a noticeable difference when he got traded to New York," McCovey said. "All of a sudden the guys gravitated around me, when before, it was always him."

On the field, however, the Giants lacked a presence—whether it was the legendary Mays or a healthy McCovey. Toward the end of his Giants career, before Mays would start a day game at Candlestick Park, he would play catch with a batboy approximately ten minutes before the 1:00 p.m. first pitch to loosen up. The crowd buzzed with anticipation. Now, Bobby Bonds played catch with the batboy. Crickets could be heard chirping. It wasn't the same.

McCovey reached a milestone on July 2 when he hit his 14th career grand slam, a 2-out, opposite-field drive to left off Los Angeles' Don Sutton. It tied McCovey with Hank Aaron and Gil Hodges for the all-time NL lead in grand slams.

McCovey had gained the respect and accumulated the accomplishments that come with age. So when the franchise structured its 1973 marketing campaign around the "Young Giants"—Bobby Bonds, Chris Speier, Garry Maddox, Gary Matthews, Dave Kingman, Dave Rader, Jim Barr, Randy Moffitt, Tito Fuentes, Ed Goodson, Gary Thomasson—it seemed a tad amusing when the first baseman, who was the initial player summoned to the field in pregame introductions, happened to be McCovey, the team's oldest position player at thirty-five.

For much of the year, McCovey performed as if he were one of San Francisco's youngsters. A hot start helped him erase memories of his injury-filled 1972 season, when he hit a then career-low .213. Consider this 3-game span: On April 11, his 2-run, 9th-inning homer beat the Astros, 5–4. He homered twice in the 4th inning the next day in another win over Houston. And in the April 13 opener of a 3-game series against defending NL champion Cincinnati, his 8th-inning, pinch-hit RBI single contributed to a 3-run rally that generated a 5–4 win.

Only eleven pitchers allowed more home runs to McCovey than Tom Seaver, who yielded 6 roundtrippers to his rival for the 1969 MVP Award. Lon Simmons provided a lively play-by-play call of the final one, which McCovey mashed at Candlestick in the 6th inning to account for San Francisco's only runs in a 5–2 loss to the Mets on May 29, 1973: "Seaver's just been challenging McCovey, just throwing the ball by him. He struck him out in the first and the fourth. And he threw that fastball by him. [The report of bat meeting ball is audible.] He didn't throw that one by him! You can tell it goodbye!" Simmons remained silent for thirty-seven seconds, the better to allow listeners to share the crowd's glee as it thanked McCovey with a delirious ovation.

McCovey grumbled when Fox opted to increase Thomasson's playing time at first base at around midseason. McCovey used July 15, the day he hit his 400th and 401st career home runs, to sound off to reporters. "He said that I was through, that I couldn't play any more up here," said McCovey, who became the fifteenth player to reach 400. Fox stated, "I never have said McCovey was through. I think he needs rest from time to time."

McCovey received 495 plate appearances in 1973, probably a few dozen less than he would have preferred. He nevertheless hit 29 homers, his highest total since he collected 39 in 1970, and his 25 intentional walks topped the Majors.

Bonds pointed out what longtime McCovey aficionados already knew: the man makes an impact under any circumstance. "There's something different about our club when Mac's in the lineup," said Bonds, who had the best season of his career in '73 with 39 homers and 43 stolen bases. "With him at cleanup, the rest of our guys get different pitches to hit. Even when he's not hitting a lot, Mac is a big help to us."

An example of what Bonds meant occurred on June 3. The Giants trailed Philadelphia, 4–1, entering the bottom of the 9th inning, when Giants catcher Dave Rader homered off Ken Brett. The next batter was McCovey, who was pinch-hitting for pitcher Charlie Williams. As Simmons pointed out on the Giants radio broadcast, McCovey might as well have hit a 2-run double. "That one was made possible by Brett getting behind [on the count]," Simmons said. "With McCovey in the on-deck circle, Brett didn't want to walk Rader. At 3–2, he kept throwing fastballs, and Rader finally clobbered one." The Giants proceeded to win, 5–4.

Stoneham appreciated McCovey's value but reluctantly decided that the fifteen-year Giant's $125,000 salary didn't fit in the team's budget. "When Willie Mays was traded," McCovey told the *San Francisco Chronicle*, "I knew I was expendable. Nobody was untouchable. I thought I might get traded then; in fact, I kind of expected it last year. Mr. Stoneham and I talked at the end of the 1972 season and we discussed it. We kicked around what ballparks I might hit well in. That's as far as it went, though. He told me that if he decided to make a move, he would let me know first before pursuing it. Mr. Stoneham is a man of his word."

As a ten-and-five man—ten or more years of Major League service time to go with at least the last five seasons playing for the same ballclub—McCovey had veto power over any deal. When Stoneham approached him with the proposal to send him and outfielder Bernie Williams to San Diego for left-hander Mike Caldwell, McCovey didn't hesitate to okay it. He could remain on the West Coast, play in warmer weather, and escape Candlestick Park's artificial turf, which was unforgiving and thus no good for his knees. The swap was announced on October 25, 1973. Another San Francisco sporting icon, 49ers quarterback John Brodie, announced his retirement on that same day, accentuating the sad reality that the end of a great Bay Area sporting era had arrived. Said an unsentimental Fox, "McCovey has given the Giants a great many years of great service, but there comes a time when you have to give way to the young people."

"They need a leader and they want me to come down and help some of the young players," McCovey told reporters, referring to the Padres. "I'm so happy that someone really wants me."

San Diego Hiatus

Let me follow in his footsteps.
—Hall of Fame outfielder Dave Winfield

Dave Winfield became a big leaguer when the San Diego Padres selected him in the first round of the 1973 draft. Fourth pick overall. Didn't spend a nanosecond in the Minor Leagues. Won Most Outstanding Player honors in that year's College World Series (as a pitcher) with the University of Minnesota. One week after he and his Golden Gophers teammates were eliminated from the tournament, Winfield slapped a single off fourth-year veteran Jerry Reuss for his first Major League hit.

Dave Winfield was a big leaguer, all right. But he wasn't *big league*. That is, he lacked the sophistication that would enable him to curse at umpires and not get ejected from a game, to match white-hot competitors like Bob Gibson and Al Hrabosky stare for stare, to hang with the likes of Pete Rose and Reggie Jackson, to move in and out of gaggles of adoring yet annoying fans.

Fortunately for Winfield, Willie McCovey arrived in San Diego from San Francisco in 1974. It was Winfield's first full season in the Majors, McCovey's fifteenth. For the better part of the next three years, McCovey showed Winfield—largely by example—how to be *big league*.

Coincidentally, Winfield just happened to have torn photographs of McCovey from a sports magazine or two and posted them in his college residence. "Because he was a tall, strong, intimidating, accomplished hitter," the 6-foot-6 Winfield said. "If and when I went to the big leagues, that's who I wanted to emulate."

Winfield described himself as feeling "ecstatic" as McCovey seamlessly slipped into the elder statesman's role for the Padres: "In San Diego at the time, players were too old or too young for us to have a really good team. I thought Willie would add a lot of ability, class, professionalism. I kind of migrated toward him and he kind of migrated toward me." Flights, bus rides, postgame meals—it didn't matter. McCovey found Winfield, or vice versa. "He went out of the way to let me be around him," Winfield said. "'C'mon, Rook. C'mon, kid. We're going to dinner.'" For them, dinner often concluded with their ongoing search for an expertly baked black bottom pie, a delicacy rich in chocolate.

Winfield understood that McCovey no longer could ascend to the heights he occupied when he was regarded as baseball's most feared hitter. "He wasn't 100 percent. But he never complained," said Winfield, who played primarily right field. "Even if he didn't perform admirably or have a good game, he wasn't one of those guys who would break his bat or scream and holler and curse at anybody. He would just set his helmet down, set his bat down, wait for somebody to bring that glove to him, go out to first base and resume his activities."

Watching this paragon of cool, Winfield often repeated something like a prayer.

"I said, 'Let me follow in his footsteps.' Many things he did—'Let me follow in his footsteps,'" Winfield said. "Just being around him helped me mature. I know it did. And I'm forever grateful."

Winfield's credentials, including 465 homers, 1,833 RBIs, 12 All-Star selections, 7 Gold Glove Awards, and 6 Silver Slugger trophies legitimize his status as a first-ballot Hall of Famer. The fact that he was drafted by the Atlanta Hawks of the NBA, the Utah Stars of the American Basketball Association, and the Minnesota Vikings of the NFL speaks to his remarkable athleticism. Winfield also had to summon that McCoveyesque patience while shouldering the hopes of two franchises, the Padres and Yankees.

"I can't tell you there was one bit of sage advice. We'd just talk," Winfield said. "A lot of players did that. Dave Parker can tell you that Willie Stargell did that for him. I'm sure there are guys who would tell you that Billy Williams did it for people with his quiet presence. There were guys in the game who would do that. They'd look out for one another. The next generation."

Winfield remains amused by McCovey's adaptation of baseball's rules at first base. "They called him 'Stretch,' and he would stretch at first base, too," Winfield said. "He'd stretch, and I swear, he'd be a couple of inches off that base when he caught the throw at first base. The [batter-runner] probably thinks he's going to beat it out. And that ball would pop in [McCovey's] glove and he wouldn't even look back. He would fire the ball around the infield as if he were saying, 'I know he's out! I'm not even gonna look.' The umpire would say, 'What do I call here? He's throwing the ball around the infield. I can't dispute Willie McCovey.' So I would laugh internally. Because he would really stretch it out over there. He might be three or four inches off the base, moving forward when he caught the ball and he'd fire it around the infield, like, 'Naaah, the double play's complete.' He'd smooth out the dirt around his position. Wouldn't even look at the umpire. He was something."

McCovey also harmlessly cut corners when he crossed paths with some-body he knew but whose name he couldn't recall. Winfield noticed that McCovey took control of the exchange by initiating contact. "You can't remember everybody that you meet," Winfield said. So McCovey would exclaim, "There he is!" before "he" could say a word.

Gaining an edge in the batter's box proved challenging for Winfield, who didn't hit regularly until his final collegiate season. "So I had a lot to learn, going directly to the Major Leagues," Winfield said. "All these people I'm facing, I only read about. Tom Seaver. Bob Gibson. Don Sutton. Mike Mar-shall throwing a screwball; I had never seen anything like that. Steve Carlton with that disappearing slider that would almost hit you in the back foot. Phil Niekro with his knuckleball."

Ultimately, Winfield met the challenges necessary to achieve entry into Cooperstown. And after making Jackie Robinson the subject of his first thank-you during his 2002 induction speech for paving the way for Black players to perform in the Majors, the next man Winfield acknowledged was McCovey. "I was blessed to be able to have a guy like this on my team," Winfield said, calling McCovey one of the "people who set the bar high" for him. As Winfield observed nearly twenty years later, "When I went into the

Hall of Fame, I had many people to thank. But he was one of the first and most important for my baseball career."

McCovey could prompt similar remarks from the Padres overall, if management were so inclined. In their sixth year of existence as an expansion franchise, the Padres were known largely for the mustard-colored home jerseys they began wearing in 1972. With McCovey on board, San Diego resumed wearing classic white uniforms with script lettering in 1974.

He wasn't the Padres' best player in their early years. That distinction belonged to Nate Colbert, San Diego's previous first baseman, who amassed 163 homers in six seasons. But as the Padres' most distinguished acquisition up to that point, McCovey gave the Padres a distinct "big league" look with his mere presence.

Moreover, San Diego avoided finishing in last place in the National League West for the first time in 1975, ending up in fourth instead of their usual sixth. McCovey, said left-hander Randy Jones, was a primary source of that success. "He taught us to be professionals, to a degree, and a lot of us responded to that," said Jones, who won twenty or more games in 1975–76, led the league in ERA in 1975, and captured the NL Cy Young Award in 1976.

For Jones, San Diego's first true ace pitcher, the mound was his domain when he pitched. He welcomed few visitors bearing well-intentioned advice; after all, he created whatever situation he faced, so he knew best how to handle it. Jones didn't need help escaping a jam or entertaining a pause in his concentration. Unless, from the corner of his eye, he saw McCovey advancing toward him. "I didn't let a lot of people on my mound during a game. I was pretty picky about that," Jones said. "When Mac walked up, I never said shit. I loved the guy. He had that veteran's sixth sense. He knew when he should walk out to the mound and when he shouldn't."

Like many hitters, McCovey believed that a particular pecking order dictated status around the batting cage. McCovey reminded Jones of this before a 1975 game in Cincinnati. That is, pitchers were meant to be held in contempt unless they could handle a bat phenomenally. Hence Jones's memory of a 1975 game in Cincinnati: "I put my five bunts down, maybe take a couple of swings. Here comes Mac around the corner of the batting cage. He walks up to me and said, 'Jonesey, you pitch and get everybody out. We'll do the hitting. Get the hell out of here.'"

The turnstiles also told the story of McCovey's impact. Through its first five seasons (1969–73), San Diego annually averaged 594,052 in paid attendance. The franchise seriously considered moving to Washington DC after the 1973 season. But McCovey, still as classy as ever, and Winfield, improving steadily during his first full Major League season, combined to give the Padres a quality they lacked: charisma. As a result, they helped propel the Padres past the 1 million mark in season attendance for the first time—1,075,399 in 1974. That figure grew to 1,281,747 in 1975.

McCovey's production for San Diego was consistent, albeit a tad diminished from his All-Star-level standard:

Year	AVG	G	AB	R	H	2B	3B	HR	RBI	BB	SO	OBP	SLG
1974	.253	128	344	53	87	19	1	22	63	96	76	.416	.506
1975	.252	122	413	43	104	17	0	23	68	57	80	.345	.460

It's intriguing to note that from 1973, when the Giants began to consider McCovey expendable, through 1975, as both teams strived for consistency, whichever team had him on its roster received better production at first base.

In 1973, Giants first basemen led the NL with 33 home runs. McCovey had 29 of them, followed by Dave Kingman and Gary Thomasson, with 2 apiece. San Diego ranked third with 27. In the category of WAR, which measures the number of victories a player would produce beyond which a replacement-level performer would be responsible for, McCovey and his Giants underlings ranked second with a 3.7 figure. San Diego was fourth at 2.8.

A year later, McCovey's 22 homers accounted for most of the league-high 31 belted by Padres first basemen. Colbert, who started 49 games at first base—compared to 144 in '73—added 8. The Giants sank to ninth with 20. Kingman had 14, Ed Goodson totaled 5, and Steve Ontiveros mustered 1. Worse, San Francisco first sackers recorded a collective WAR of 0.2, which placed them twelfth and last in the NL. The Padres were seventh at 0.8.

The numbers looked similar in 1975, when Padres first basemen outhomered their Giants counterparts, 24–11. San Diego's total was the league's sixth best;

the Giants' was the worst. Of McCovey's 23 home runs, 21 came as a first baseman. Mike Ivie—remember that name—had 2 homers, while Bobby Tolan contributed 1. The Giants received 8 homers in 577 plate appearances from Willie Montañez, who was acquired for center fielder Garry Maddox from Philadelphia in a forgettable May 4 trade. Thomasson and Goodson, who were supposed to make Giants fans forget all about McCovey, homered twice and once that season, respectively. Neither team was impressive in first base WAR. San Diego finished ninth at 1.2, while the Giants were tenth at 0.4.

When McCovey failed to hit a home run in April 1974—his first official month as a Padre—it marked the initial time in his fifteen full Major League seasons that he had not homered in April. Skeptics emerged from their darkened lairs to issue criticism. The first identifying characteristic a power hitter loses, they said, was his power. And McCovey had lost his, they insisted. Release him immediately, they cried. But soon after McCovey ended his home run skid in San Diego's 36th game of the season on May 13 against Atlanta's Roric Harrison, he belted 7 homers in July and 8 in August. This was the McCovey everyone recognized. "I know people have been thinking I'm washed up, but I'm not," McCovey said after a 2-homer outburst on July 21 against the Mets. "I'm 36 years old and I got off to the worst start in my career, so I guess it was natural for people to think I was through." Still, it was significant when Cincinnati manager Sparky Anderson, one of McCovey's most prominent admirers, spoke almost mournfully late in the '75 season of what he perceived to be the big man's decline. "You watch Willie McCovey pop up a pitch that five years ago he would have put into orbit and it hurts," Anderson said. "I see him do it against our kid pitchers and I hear them talk about how they got Willie McCovey out. That was a ghost of Willie McCovey."

McCovey might as well have been a ghost when the 1976 season began. Management clearly wanted Mike Ivie to play first base. Club officials believed that the time was right for Ivie to begin his destiny, and that was to become a star. After all, the Padres selected him first overall in the 1970 draft out of Atlanta's Walker High School. Surely he could build on the talent he showed in 1975, when he batted .241 with 8 home runs and 46 RBIs in 111 games as a Padres rookie while dividing his time between first base (37 starts) and third (58 starts). Though Ivie's statistics fell short of McCovey's, the veteran sensed what was happening before the 1975 campaign ended. He said that management already had indicated that it was "catering" to Ivie toward the end of '75. In fact, Ivie substituted frequently for McCovey at first base that year, coming off the bench to man the position in 41 games. Ivie clearly was serving an apprenticeship.

McCovey approached the situation the only way he knew how: by trying to gain favor through his performance. But the Padres already had reached a verdict. "I had the best spring of my career in 1976," McCovey said. "I figured I would be in the starting lineup [on] opening day, but I wasn't. That really hurt me." Come April, Ivie drew 13 starts at first base during the month. McCovey had 5. He quickly had become basically a nonperson with the Padres, who sold him to the Oakland A's on August 30. He said that neither general manager Buzzie Bavasi nor manager John McNamara telephoned to notify him of the move. "The minor league director called me. I didn't like that," McCovey said. "Bavasi was the one who got me to go to San Diego. He should have told me about the sale."

McCovey had one more alternative to explore that might prolong his career. "I decided that I would play out my option and try to get back with the Giants," he said.

The interest was mutual. The Giants had a new owner, Bob Lurie, who was learning the difficulties of reviving a moribund franchise. Grateful to Lurie for preventing the franchise from moving to Toronto, the Giants' fan base was equal parts loyal and skeptical. Despite a city employees' strike that shut down most concession stands at Candlestick Park, the 1976 season opener on April 9 drew 37,261, San Francisco's largest home crowd since 1973 and biggest for a home opener since 1966. But the Giants drew only two more crowds exceeding 30,000 in '76, demonstrating the importance to Lurie of improving the team's marketability. The Giants nearly traded for McCovey toward the end of the '76 season, but they were unwilling to part with right-hander John D'Acquisto, a San Diego native, in return.

So McCovey endured a wholly unsatisfying end to the 1976 season. He appeared in only 11 games for the A's, batting .208 (5-for-24)—mostly as a designated hitter, a role he disliked. It also happened to be a role he shared with two other longtime National Leaguers—his Mobile buddy, Billy Williams, and ex-Dodger Ron Fairly. However, McCovey's off-season went according to plan. The Giants invited him to spring training. There, newcomer Joe Altobelli, who was receiving his first opportunity to manage in the Majors, would judge whether McCovey had enough bat speed left to compete against National League pitching. A gargantuan home run that McCovey hit in late March during a Cactus League exhibition game against Milwaukee appeared to seal Altobelli's decision. McCovey, thirty-nine, would be San Francisco's Opening Day first baseman, exactly as he was for the first time seventeen years earlier when Candlestick opened. "The main concern we—Bob Lurie, [general manager] Spec Richardson and myself—had was that we didn't want Willie to embarrass himself," Altobelli said. "He has done just the opposite. He's had a super spring and he's a super person."

Said McCovey, "I owe all of what has happened to me to Joe. It was Joe's decision to make—to sign me or to turn me back to Bob to work in the front office. I'm fortunate Joe didn't judge me on my last two years in San Diego, or my age. I went down to Arizona confident I could make the club. And it would have been so easy for Joe to look at my age and assume it was all over."

McCovey expressed the belief that the power of youth is not only restorative but also transferable. "When you are surrounded by young people, you have a tendency to stay young," he said. "I'm still a little boy in a sense. When you lose that, then it's really over."

Triumphant Return

I think when he came back, that might have been the point
when he became the most beloved.
—Giants broadcaster Jon Miller

The cheering cascaded around Willie McCovey as if he were standing in a
waterfall. Opening Day is for new beginnings, and so the 1977 home-opening
crowd of 37,813 at Candlestick Park noisily welcomed McCovey back to the
Giants in a different guise—that of resident legend, capable of generating joy
or pleasure simply by stepping onto the field or in the batter's box. Of course,
fans wanted to see him succeed. But he already had succeeded in capturing
people's hearts. He was Willie McCovey, and that alone sufficed. Nobody
bothered to record the precise length of the ovation that McCovey received
as he stood on the first base line during pregame introductions, but *Sports
Illustrated's* Ron Fimrite clocked it at "a solid five minutes." Said Jon Miller
eloquently of McCovey, "He was who the Giants were—were in the past
and were at that time. He was the face of the franchise. He was beloved as a
great player prior to that. But now there was a different element to it. There
he was, still looking in this uniform, like he did in '62. Or '69. He still looked
great. He wasn't thick in the midriff or anything like that. He still looked the
same. To me, that's when he became larger than life."

McCovey set Giants fans free. They felt free to cheer the memory of Willie
Mays, Juan Marichal, and Orlando Cepeda, which seemed embarrassingly
long ago. "He took you back to that earlier era," Miller said. They could once
again revel in the Giants, who had reached the postseason exactly twice since
arriving from New York in 1958. They could celebrate their favorite ballclub,

despite its below −.500 finishes in four of the previous five years. "It gave us some credibility," longtime Giants executive Pat Gallagher said of McCovey's return. "It restored some of the pride in the uniform. He added a certain amount of respect that the organization couldn't really get any other way." And of course, the fans cherished McCovey himself, particularly because he left *and came back.* Those two years and five months that he spent in San Diego were just a bad dream. Before, during and shortly after that period, life in San Francisco was either short of ideal or downright weird. There was the Patricia Hearst kidnaping in 1974. The People's Temple suicides and murders took place on November 18, 1978, in Guyana but had roots in San Francisco. The Zebra serial killings terrorized the city from October 1973 to April 1974. The Giants nearly moved to Toronto in 1976. And mayor George Moscone, who worked hard behind the scenes to help Bob Lurie keep the Giants in San Francisco, was assassinated along with supervisor Harvey Milk by supervisor Dan White on November 27, 1978. McCovey's welcome presence amid all this provided at least some stability. Others considered the Bay Area a place to flee. Not him.

"I think when he came back, that might have been the point when he was the most beloved," Miller said. No readjustment period was necessary for McCovey, who started at first base, batted fifth, and walked twice in 4 plate appearances in San Francisco's 7–1 loss to the Dodgers. "In a way I felt I never really left," McCovey said of San Francisco. "It's always been home. Since 1959, my rookie year, this has been my home. Even though I was traded away, I was still wrapped up in San Francisco. This is where I belong. I always felt that way. It feels sort of natural to come back here and end my career. I started here and really wanted to be one of the few players who played his whole career in one place. Usually when a guy gets traded away from his original team, he gets traded again and again and again, because the original club is really the only club that cares about him.

"It's like a family in a way. It's like a mother's love. A lot of people may fall in love with you, but it's nothing like mother's love. That's why, once you leave the original club, you're kind of being used after that. . . . That's why I'm coming back to San Francisco. They're the only club that wants me."

Thus, McCovey profoundly appreciated the fans' prolonged roaring for him before the '77 home opener. "I don't think I've ever had a moment in my life like I had Opening Day," he said late in the season. "After suffering through '76 I felt like I was getting down to my lowest point. I felt like a forgotten man. Sure, I expected an ovation just for coming back to San Francisco but I never expected what happened. It might have set the tone for the year I've had."

In fact, 1977 was an admirable year for McCovey. At age thirty-nine, he appeared in 141 games and batted .280 with 28 home runs and 86 RBIs. That output approached the level he reached during his 1965–70 peak. And it featured a performance that remains especially McCoveyesque. It occurred on June 27 at Cincinnati's Riverfront Stadium, where McCovey became the first player to hit 2 home runs in an inning twice. He also accomplished this feat in the 4th inning against Houston on April 12, 1973, at Candlestick Park. This time, McCovey went deep in the 6th inning off Cincinnati starter Jack Billingham before he concluded the Giants' 10-run outburst with a grand slam off left-hander Joe Hoerner. It was the 17th career grand slam for McCovey, who broke a tie with Hank Aaron for the all-time National League record. "To tell you the truth, I could have played five or six more years, not broken the tie with Hank and wouldn't have minded it. I admire him that much," McCovey said. "Anyway, I've always been one of Hank's biggest boosters. We're from the same hometown and played on the same sandlot team, the Mobile Black Bears, although at different times. When I came to the big leagues, I insisted on wearing Hank's number, 44. Breaking one of his records is an honor."

McCovey, who hit his 18th and final grand slam on August 1, 1977, at Montreal off Wayne Twitchell, can be proud of his collection. It truly separates him from the top power hitters of his era. Consider the following list. It compares McCovey's career total of plate appearances with the bases loaded to the number that other players accumulated during the same time frame, with grand slam totals in parentheses. McCovey's average number of bases-loaded appearances per grand slam, also shown, further demonstrates his legitimacy as a slugger:

Brooks Robinson 310 (6)

Tony Perez 240 (6)

Johnny Bench 224 (11)

Ron Santo 211 (6)

Lee May 210 (11)

Carl Yastrzemski 210 (7)

Joe Torre 203 (3)

Orlando Cepeda 201 (9)

Willie McCovey 196 (18)

Paul Blair 191 (3)

Willie Horton 191 (9)

Bases-loaded plate appearances per grand slam: McCovey 10.9, May 19.1, Bench 20.4, Horton 21.2, Cepeda 22.3, Yastrzemski 30.0, Santo 35.2, Perez 40.0, Robinson 51.7, Blair 63.7, Torre 67.7.

There were other highlights for McCovey in a season full of them. Not one who's associated with collecting hits in bulk, he nevertheless recorded his 2,000th career hit on September 7 while homering, doubling, and driving in 4 runs in San Francisco's 6–3 victory over Cincinnati. He said he knew that the milestone was imminent "because there has been some publicity about it, but I didn't go into the season thinking about it. I've never thought about hit totals. I just try to get the maximum out of the minimum of hits. It's not like a guy like Pete Rose. Total hits and batting championships are important to him. The home runs and runs batted in are important to me. I've never in my career thought in terms of 200 hits for a season. I'm not that type [of] hitter. The home runs and ribbies, yes." McCovey reminded everybody on the afternoon of August 28 at Candlestick that baseball's time-honored "book" of strategy can be unreliable. The victim was none other than Herman Franks, the Chicago Cubs manager who piloted the Giants to the first four of their five consecutive second-place finishes (1965–68). With 2 outs in the 3rd inning, Derrel Thomas on second base, left-hander Dave Roberts on the mound, and the score tied, 1–1, Franks ordered Bill Madlock to be walked intentionally. This created a lefty-on-lefty matchup that conceivably should have favored the Cubs. Except that McCovey ripped a 2-run double. The Giants proceeded to win, 4–1.

But the biggest afternoon of all was September 18, which was Willie McCovey Day at Candlestick Park against Cincinnati. Like all celebrations of this sort, which have disappeared amid the proliferation of eight-figure salaries for ballplayers, McCovey was feted by friends, including Golden State Warriors owner Franklin Mieuli, and given a wealth of gifts, such as a television, a golf bag, furniture, wristwatches, and a basset hound puppy. The best gift of all was the presence of McCovey's mother, Ester, who was content to travel by bus from her home in Mobile. "The bus is the only way," she said. "You see more. Who wants to go up there and look at air and clouds?" A second hilarious question was the one Ester received from her son during the ceremony: "Ma, do you still want me to be a lawyer?"

Trying so hard to give the crowd of 27,043 something to cheer about, McCovey went 0-for-3 with a walk in his first 4 plate appearances. He struck out in the 1st inning, stranding runners on second and third. He walked in the 3rd inning, popped up in the 6th, and fouled out in the 8th while his teammates scored twice to forge a 2–2 tie. The deadlock remained intact as Derrel Thomas singled to open the Giants' 9th against Reds reliever Pedro Borbon. Bill Madlock beat out a slow grounder to third base for another single. Then it was McCovey's turn to walk toward the batter's box as the fans hollered in encouragement yet again. The noise grew even louder as his drive to left-center field fell for a clean single. A thrilled Thomas made a bounding leap on his way toward scoring the winning run. "I tried to be calm, not to press when the game started," McCovey said. "But sometimes you just can't make the mind and body do what you want. I was pressing. I wanted so much to thank the fans with a good performance. After my third time up, [manager] Joe Altobelli came to me and suggested if I just meet the ball, not overswing, a home run still could come. And that's what I did in the ninth. I was determined just to make solid contact and the moment I did I knew it was in the gap and that we had won."

Recognition and appreciation continued to pour in for McCovey. On September 26, he became the third opposing player to be honored by the Dodgers for his sustained excellence against them. Hank Aaron and Willie Mays were the first two. The occasion was dubbed "Big Mac" Night. At the time, McCovey ranked third among visiting players in home runs at Dodger Stadium as well as third overall in home runs against the Dodgers. McCovey also defeated Dodgers outfielder Dusty Baker by a ninety-three-vote margin among players to win National League Comeback Player of the Year balloting. Though they compiled remarkably similar offensive totals, the thirty-nine-year-old McCovey (.280/.367/.500, 28 homers, 86 RBIs, 132 OPS+) might have outdistanced Baker (.291/.364/.512, 30 homers, 86 RBIs, 134 OPS+) in the sympathy category. Additionally, McCovey received the Hutch Award, which is given annually to an active Major Leaguer who "best exemplifies the fighting spirit and competitive desire" of Fred Hutchinson by persevering through adversity. The award was created in 1965 in honor of Hutchinson, a former pitcher and manager, who died of lung cancer the previous year. One can assume that "Hutch," who frequently wore a menacing glare, would have ordered his pitchers to challenge McCovey instead of intentionally walking him.

The seeds of McCovey's reputation for Hutch-like toughness were sown years earlier. One particular day in 1971, Giants manager Charlie Fox noticed tears in the big man's eyes. The discomfort in his left knee was almost too much to bear. "He's in pain whenever he goes out there," Fox said. "Some days the pain is greater than other days, but it's always there. The day I saw the tears had to be the worst."

For McCovey, rejoining the Giants meant resuming his role as team leader. "He was a quiet leader," left-hander Gary Lavelle said. "He was one of the type[s] of players you respected because of the way he carried himself. He always carried himself as a great man."

The Giants' March 15 acquisition of left-hander Vida Blue from Oakland for seven expendable players truly buoyed the club's attitude entering the 1978 season, since it gave the pitching staff a legitimate ace. It also spurred several Giants, aware that McCovey was in his final years as an active player, to help him bookend his career with winning clubs. "We're going to show him that we could play the way he did," Barr said, articulating this motivation.

1. McCovey practices his sliding technique during his
first Major League spring training in 1959. Before injuries
robbed him of much of his speed, McCovey hit 40 triples
in the Minor Leagues.

2. McCovey shows off the dimensions that prompted others to nickname him "Stretch." At 6 foot 4, he was among the tallest active players when he broke into the big leagues.

3. (*opposite top*) You can almost feel the power oozing from McCovey's pores as he takes this batting practice cut in spring training. Look closely and notice the absence of a protective screen for the BP pitcher.

4. (*opposite bottom*) McCovey rounds third base and heads for the plate after clobbering the Giants' first home run of the 1962 World Series. McCovey went deep off Ralph Terry in the 7th inning of Game 2.

5. (*opposite top*) McCovey accepts an award from a local sportswriters and sportscasters organization as Giants broadcaster Lon Simmons, who looks like he's awaiting a chance to deliver a punch line, listens.

6. (*opposite bottom*) McCovey crosses home plate for his 6th career grand slam, which he hit off Pittsburgh's Juan Pizarro on September 23, 1967. McCovey ultimately hit an NL-record 18 grand slams.

7. (*above*) A familiar activity for McCovey: off-season exercise, either to help in recovering from an injury or to strengthen to prevent further injuries.

8. McCovey takes a full swing at a pitch during the 1969 season. The 1969 season developed into McCovey's best, largely because he was able to avoid debilitating injuries.

9. McCovey speaking at a Candlestick Park news conference after winning the National League's Most Valuable Player Award for 1969. McCovey batted .320, hit 45 homers, and drove in 126 runs.

10. McCovey finds himself in an unusual position: looking up at someone taller. Here McCovey chats with 6-foot-5 actor Chuck Connors, formerly a first baseman in the Dodgers and Cubs organizations.

11. A lot of people affirmed that this shows how McCovey played first base: with elegance and style. He was not only a sharp dresser away from the baseball field; he also insisted on looking immaculate in his uniform.

12. Everything about McCovey's swing suggested power. Besides generating remarkable bat speed, he managed to maintain his balance much more often than not.

13. McCovey commanded tremendous respect from his teammates. Here catcher Mike Sadek goes to extremes in expressing his high regard for the big man.

14. McCovey and Pittsburgh's Roberto Clemente were revered by teammates and opponents alike. Clemente was a far superior defender and possessed much more speed than McCovey, but McCovey had a tremendous edge in power.

15. The statistical similarities between McCovey and Pittsburgh's Willie Stargell were astounding. Each recorded a lifetime .889 OPS and a 147 OPS+. McCovey totaled 1,555 career RBIS; Stargell had 1,540.

16. A fractured forearm forced McCovey to remain a spectator for most of the first forty-five days of the 1972 season. McCovey is joined on the bench by manager Charlie Fox, coach Ozzie Virgil, and right-hander Juan Marichal.

17. McCovey's "Gentle Giant" persona made him an ideal fit for photos such as this one. Here he and a pair of young fans each cradles an armful of batting helmets to promote Helmet Day at Candlestick Park.

18. Ted Williams, who is as authoritative an expert on hitting as anybody who has ever lived, emphasized to McCovey that bat selection is of paramount importance when trying to hit successfully.

19. McCovey introduces Dave Dravecky, the 1989 Willie Mac Award winner. Dravecky guaranteed himself a permanent spot in Giants lore by recovering from cancer to resume pitching.

20. McCovey delivers his speech during his Hall of Fame induction ceremony at Cooperstown on August 3, 1980. McCovey was only the sixteenth player to gain enshrinement on the first ballot.

21. McCovey is all smiles as he displays a photograph of his Hall of Fame plaque while baseball commissioner Peter Ueberroth stands behind him.

22. (*opposite*) McCovey is a study in concentration as he waits in the on-deck area at Candlestick Park, getting mentally ready to hit.

23. (*above*) Standing beside his mother, Ester, McCovey acknowledges the Candlestick Park crowd on Willie McCovey Day, September 18, 1977.

24. McCovey enjoyed handing out the trophy that bore his name.
Here he bestows the 1984 Willie Mac Award on catcher Bob Brenly.

25. During his final weekend as an active player, McCovey enthusiastically greets legendary Dodgers catcher Roy Campanella in the visitors' clubhouse at Dodger Stadium.

26. McCovey wasn't strictly a slugger, as his career total of 2,211 hits reflects. Here he displays classic hitting form: front leg straight, back leg in an *L* shape.

27. Giants owner Bob Lurie stands with McCovey before the media as McCovey announces his retirement from baseball on June 22, 1980.

Willie McCovey
Final At Bat at Candlestick Park • June 29, 1980

28. McCovey prepares for what is undoubtedly an emotional moment for many people in the stands: his final at bat as a Giant at Candlestick Park. McCovey hit an RBI single earlier that afternoon.

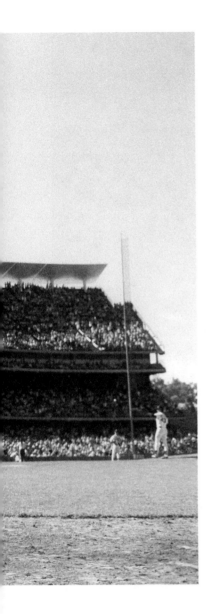

29. McCovey gets ready for the final at bat of his career, a pinch-hitting appearance before a packed house at Dodger Stadium. McCovey launched a sacrifice fly to help the Giants outlast Los Angeles, 7–4, on July 6, 1980.

30. (*opposite top*) McCovey chats with Giants broadcaster Ron Fairly in the home dugout at Candlestick Park. The pair broke into the Major Leagues at the same time as rookies in the 1959 season.

31. (*opposite bottom*) McCovey receives his honorary 2012 World Series ring from Giants CEO Larry Baer. The Giants included all of their living Hall of Famers among their World Series recipients.

32. (*above*) Products of the Giants' rich farm system of the 1950s, McCovey and Felipe Alou appear in a ceremony to celebrate the Giants' sixty years in San Francisco.

33. Mike Felder clutches the Willie Mac Award, which he won in 1992, as a symbolic way of keeping Willie McCovey close to his heart. It was a fitting gesture on the day of the celebration of life held by the Giants in McCovey's honor. The award is given annually to the team's most inspirational player—the one who best mirrors McCovey. Courtesy of Julie Pilossoph.

13

A Hero Departs

It is for the good of the team that I step aside now and allow
the Giants to develop the fine young ballplayers, such as
Rich Murray, who will surely be the backbone of this club in
the years to come.
—Willie McCovey, in the prepared statement announcing his
   retirement

Willie McCovey didn't concentrate on relaxing during the 1977–78 off-season.
He focused on winning. Upgrading themselves to compete against the tradi-
tional powerhouses of the National League West, the Los Angeles Dodgers
and Cincinnati Reds, wasn't feasible for the Giants, who were competitive yet
lacked depth in the form of tradable commodities at the Major and Minor
League levels. Less than a month before opening day, general manager Spec
Richardson strengthened the club's already formidable starting rotation by
sending seven players to the A's for their ace left-hander, Vida Blue. That
still left the Giants' everyday lineup short of those fielded by the Reds and
Dodgers. But McCovey sensed how the Giants could maximize their assets:
move third baseman Bill Madlock to second base and make Darrell Evans
the starter at third. Evans was an effective though somewhat streaky hitter
who had clobbered as many as 41 home runs in 1973. He had a sharp eye for
the strike zone, having led the Majors with 124 walks in 1973 and 126 in 1974.
He also had established himself as a solid defender at the infield and outfield
corners. No wonder sabermetrics expert Bill James later hailed Evans as
"probably the most underrated player in baseball history." Would Madlock,
who had never played second base regularly, struggle to master the position

defensively? Perhaps. But if the two-time NL batting champion could maintain his form offensively, the Giants could tolerate his defensive shortcomings. Rob Andrews, San Francisco's incumbent second baseman, was a decent utility player but wouldn't be missed. And the 77 games that Evans started in left field in 1977 would be better allocated to Terry Whitfield, who was coming off batting .285 in '77.

McCovey approached Madlock with the proposal to switch to second base. Madlock readily agreed. "All because of him," Madlock said. "If anybody else asked me to do it, I wouldn't do it. Like most people around baseball, I had the ultimate respect for him. He was soft-spoken but he obviously carried a big stick. He was the number one San Francisco Giant."

Several Giants took turns being number one in the season's early weeks. Blue won 6 of his first 7 decisions. Right fielder Jack Clark maintained a club-record 26-game hitting streak, eclipsing McCovey's 1963 mark of 24, and was named NL Player of the Month for May. Pitching in his first full Major League season, left-hander Bob Knepper complemented Clark by earning the league's Pitcher of the Month honors for May. This early push helped the Giants spend 95 days in first place in the NL West, almost more than the Dodgers (74) and Reds (28) combined. "What I remember about 1978 was that we were having fun all of a sudden again," McCovey said. "The Giants went through some years when they weren't having any fun. . . . We really re-created the excitement that had been missing around here."

At the outset, the biggest news McCovey made was off the field. Club management initially balked at paying extra to allow him a hotel suite on the road. The previous two owners McCovey played for, San Francisco's Horace Stoneham and San Diego's Ray Kroc, assumed the suite's costs unhesitatingly. Given his relative inexperience as the club's managing general partner, Lurie simply may not have known about McCovey's arrangement. Either way, the issue created controversy that clashed with the club's success on the field. "McCovey May Quit," read the lead headline in the *San Francisco Chronicle's* May 12, 1978, sports section. If team officials were hoping that public reaction would force McCovey to back down, they were wrong. The ovations for him at Candlestick Park grew louder. "Maybe McCovey Should Run for Governor," suggested a *San Francisco Examiner* headline on May 14.

Away from prying eyes, McCovey and the club reached a settlement. He got his suite, and the controversy died quietly.

There was nothing quiet about the evening of May 26—at least not for the Giants, their fans, and their heroes. Knepper recorded his fourth complete-game victory in as many home starts. Evans drew 3 walks, scored twice, and assisted on 6 put-outs. And McCovey proved that he would not stand idly by in this division race, driving in 5 runs off Dodgers left-hander Doug Rau with a 2-run bloop single in the 1st inning and a 3-run homer in the 5th. The latter prompted an ovation from the crowd of 43,646—the largest for a night game in Candlestick Park history—that would have drowned out a spacecraft liftoff. Even broadcaster Lon Simmons joined the fans in their euphoric demand for a curtain call. "Come on out, Will," Simmons said on the air. "C'mon, Will."

A meaningful home run? Certainly. But it actually paled in dramatic comparison to the one hit two days later, when Mike Ivie—the same Mike Ivie who was McCovey's heir apparent at first base in San Diego—belted a 6th-inning, pinch-hit grand slam off Don Sutton that contributed mightily to a 6–5 Giants decision. For Giants fans who experienced it, the Ivie homer stands out because it fueled a come-from-behind rally, it hastened victory in the type of game the Giants were accustomed to losing (that is, any game that the Dodgers led), and it demonstrated inimitable power (possessed by the Giants in general and Ivie in particular).

McCovey's role as a regular was safe for one simple reason: he began contributing. Though he was batting in the low .200s, he accumulated 49 RBIs with the help of his first 51 hits, an admirable ratio. Moreover, he was pursuing his 500th career home run, a milestone that only eleven hitters had reached. And something else: in this era, 500 homers virtually guaranteed election to baseball's Hall of Fame. Each slugger to have reached 500 homers was already enshrined in Cooperstown.

That included Hank Aaron (755 home runs), McCovey's biggest hero and fellow Mobilian.

That included Babe Ruth (714), among the few besides McCovey to lead his league in homers, RBIs, and slugging percentage for at least two years in a row.

That included Willie Mays (660), McCovey's august Giants teammate for 14 seasons.

That included Frank Robinson (586), who, with McCovey, established the pace for slugging in 1969. Robinson set an American League record by hitting 9 April homers; McCovey authored a new NL mark with 8.

That included Harmon Killebrew (573), who out-McCoveyed McCovey by exceeding 40 homers and 100 RBIs in 8 seasons apiece.

That included Mickey Mantle (536), quite possibly the only all-time great player to have performed in as much pain as McCovey, if not more.

That included Jimmie Foxx (534), who struck out a lot without striking out much. Foxx led the AL in 1930 with 66 strikeouts, an acceptable total for a free-swinging slugger. Likewise, McCovey averaged 97 per 162 games and totaled just 66 in his 1969 MVP campaign.

That included Ted Williams (521), McCovey's hitting "mentor."

That included Ernie Banks (512), who was adored in Chicago the way McCovey has been in San Francisco.

That included Eddie Mathews (512), who hit more than 30 homers in 9 consecutive seasons (1953–61).

That included Mel Ott (511), a Giants legend who at the time had more home runs than any left-handed batter in NL history (Mathews hit 9 in the AL).

It was this distinguished company that McCovey joined on June 30, 1978, on a sweltering evening in Atlanta. Starting the opener of a two-night doubleheader, McCovey led off the 2nd inning against left-hander Jamie Easterly and poked an opposite-field drive to left on an o-and-2 pitch. "When I hit the ball, I had no idea it was going to be a homer," McCovey said. "It was a slider, away, and I hit it pretty good, but it was heading for the corner and I figured it was a cinch double." The ball cleared Atlanta-Fulton County Stadium's outfield wall, enabling Giants reliever John Curtis to scoop it up and bring it to McCovey, who already was surrounded by the jubilant Giants at home plate. Said McCovey, "I really wasn't that excited. It was more of a relief than a thrill." That's largely because the media was beginning to shatter the calm he coveted. "I was starting to have a lot of distractions," he said. "People mean well, but they call you at all hours trying to come up with a story. That's why there was this sense of relief when I finally hit it. I really wasn't excited, but all my teammates came out of the dugout and acted as if we had just won the pennant or the World Series." Predictably, Easterly's reaction was quite the opposite. "The 500th didn't bother me," he said. "It was a slider, high and away, but it didn't matter whether it was his first, 341st or 500th." McCovey intended to give the ball he hit for no. 500 to Giants owner Bob Lurie. "He was the man who gave me the chance to return to the Giants two years ago," McCovey said. Singular as his home run accomplishment was, McCovey had some unfinished business awaiting him: "My only concern now is to help this team win a pennant."

Unfortunately for the Giants, they faded in September and finished third in the NL West, 6 games behind division-winning Los Angeles and 3½ games back of second-place Cincinnati. The Giants played an exciting brand of ball, winning a record 42 games by 1 run.

One of the most intriguing late-season aspects of McCovey's '78 season occurred off the field, not on it. In a September conversation with Roger Angell, the outstanding writer from the *New Yorker* magazine, McCovey showed just how keenly he identified with fans. Here's an astounded Angell—What? A star player saying he feels the fans' pain?—telling me about their chat:

"I talked to him once about late-season collapses and the fans dying with them. He said in this voice that was not boastful or humiliating but full of tenderness, 'Yes. We're all they've got.' No other player ever said that to me. How about that?"

And here's what Angell wrote about his conversation with McCovey: "I said that it seemed to have been a painful season all around, for the fans as well as the players. Most ballplayers seem to have almost no awareness of the people in the stands, but McCovey responded at once: 'The fans sitting up there are helpless,'" he said. "They can't pick up a bat and come down and do something. Their only involvement is in how well you do. If you strike out or mess up out there, they feel they've done something wrong. You're all they've got. The professional athlete knows there's always another game or another year coming up. If he loses, he swallows the bitter pill and comes back. It's much harder for the fans."

McCovey's sensitivity didn't matter to a lot of people. A sure way for the Giants to improve on their 89–73 record, many observers reasoned, would be to replace McCovey (.228/.298/.396, 12 homers, 64 RBIs) with Ivie (.308/.363/.475, 11 homers, 55 RBIs) at first base. Ivie also belted 4 pinch-hit home runs, enhancing his image as instant offense personified. In a copyrighted poll conducted by *San Francisco Examiner* beat reporter Glenn Schwarz and released on the eve of spring training 1979, Ivie clearly emerged as the consensus choice to play first. Several Giants refused to speak for attribution, fearing repercussions for saying anything even remotely negative about the revered McCovey. One Giant said privately, "Nobody likes to take down a monument and replace it with a K-Mart, but sometimes it has to be done." However, some expressed themselves freely. "McCovey doesn't have the lateral range to stop balls in the hole or down the line," right-hander Ed Halicki said. "If we're going to build around our pitching staff, we must have good defense. Willie has had great years and he can still drive in runs, but I prefer to have Ivie out there for his RBIs and his defense. You could say Ivie is a better hitter off the bench, but at 26 he's getting better. It's hard for McCovey to get better." Said right-hander John Montefusco, "I think it would be a great year for Willie to become a player-coach. Willie is having trouble walking. If you're having trouble walking, how are you gonna play the game every day? Willie's legs bothered him every day last year, but he's still one of the most feared hitters in the National League. I'd love to see him coming off the bench all the time. I don't want to see him get hurt and go out limping—I want to see him go out with some glory."

He did. With 2 outs and the score tied, 2–2, in the 9th inning of the 1979 home opener, the biggest regular-season baseball crowd at Candlestick—56,196—roared as McCovey laced a pinch-hit single off former Giant John D'Acquisto. Up came another pinch hitter, John Tamargo, whose homer gave the Giants a 4–2 walk-off win. But it was McCovey's hit that sparked the decisive uprising. McCovey seemed to be settling into an off-the-bench hero's role on April 20 when he delivered another 9th-inning pinch single that scored Jack Clark from second base and beat the Dodgers, 3–2. The weird aspect about that one was San Francisco manager Joe Altobelli's setup tactic: he had McCovey squared to bunt on the first two pitches from Dodgers reliever Jerry Reuss. "It wasn't because Willie can't bunt that we took the sign off," Altobelli said. "He can, but with the count 2-and-0 we gave him free rein." McCovey had 5 career sacrifice bunts—and none since 1967, when he recorded 2. That didn't include his occasional bunt hits against defensive shifts.

As for the McCovey-versus-Ivie playing-time issue, no fuss was raised because none developed. They shared activity at first base almost equally. McCovey started 86 games at first and logged 721⅓ innings at that spot. Ivie started 76 games at first while accumulating 704⅔ innings there. He made 98 appearances at first, reflecting his use as a late-inning replacement for McCovey. He also started 24 games in left field and 1 at third base. As predicted, Ivie increased his offensive output, amassing team highs with 27 homers, 89 RBIS, a 152 OPS+, and a .906 OPS. McCovey improved upon 1978, posting a slash line of .249/.318/.402 while totaling 15 homers and 57 RBIS. Yet he still felt disparaged, mostly by the print media. "The criticism has really been getting to me," he said. "After all I've done, I would think I would be treated with some respect. People didn't get on Ted Williams or Stan Musial when they were getting older, so I can't help but wonder if it's a racial thing. I can't understand the press criticism, because I've always treated reporters fairly and I expect the same in return. Maybe I shouldn't have been such a nice guy. If I was getting this sort of criticism when I was 23, I probably would have quit." The livelier bat McCovey swung indicated that he had a point. "All I'm saying is that age doesn't have anything to do with it," he said. "People try to push you out of the way because they refuse to believe you can play well after a certain age. Look at Warren Spahn and Gaylord Perry. Williams won two batting titles when he was 39 and 40. I'm just tired of it. I shouldn't have to convince people that I'm in shape. I feel as good now as I have in several years. I've always taken good care of my body and it's paying off."

The 1980 season began in familiar fashion, with McCovey starting at first base. Ivie, expected to be the regular first baseman, sustained an ankle injury in the April 10 season opener at San Diego. McCovey therefore played every inning of the next 10 games. Now forty-two, he performed as if he were twenty-two in the April 17 home opener, going 3-for-5 and driving in 3 runs in a 7–3 victory over San Diego. He sandwiched RBI singles in the 1st and 5th innings around a 3rd-inning RBI double. This couldn't last, of course, and it didn't. His batting average dipped to .196 on May 2, reached .200 again when he hit career homer number 521 off Montreal's Scott Sanderson May 3, then plunged below .200 on May 4 and stayed there through June 2. The Giants realized that they needed to upgrade themselves at first base. But that help wouldn't come from Mike Ivie. Not only did Ivie accidentally slice off part of his right pinky during an off-season hunting trip, but he also struggled to cope with the mental demands of playing Major League Baseball. Not even an encouraging phone call from McCovey helped lift Ivie's spirits. So Ivie went home with what was described as "mental anguish," which prompted a question for McCovey: Are you surprised that the Giants didn't ask you to reconsider your retirement? "No," he said. It's a young man's game, after all.

This gave Rich Murray a chance to establish himself at first base for the Giants. As the brother of perennial Baltimore All-Star first baseman and future Hall of Famer Eddie Murray, the twenty-two-year-old arrived with a handsome pedigree. Initially, he quite literally appeared intent on making a name for himself. Murray went hitless in his first two games June 7–8, then batted .345 (19-for-55) while hitting safely in 13 of 14 games. That binge included 1 homer, 5 doubles, and 10 RBIs.

Early during Murray's ascent, the Giants' brass decided that the ballclub no longer had room for McCovey. The announcement was made official on June 22. He would remain on the active roster until July 6, then go on the voluntary retired list on July 10 following the All-Star break. "Nobody can go on forever," McCovey said before adding, "I said all along that I would keep playing until some young 'pheenom [sic]' forced me to retire, and it looks like that pheenom has arrived." The news release that reporters received referred to McCovey as "San Francisco's most popular sports figure ever."

McCovey swung a dangerous bat until the very end. A week after he announced his retirement, Giants manager Dave Bristol summoned him to pinch-hit in the first game of a doubleheader against the Dodgers at Candlestick with 2 outs in the 9th inning, Rennie Stennett on first base, Bobby Castillo pitching for Los Angeles, and the score tied, 3–3. McCovey drilled Castillo's pitch up the right-center field alley. The Dodgers quickly relayed the ball home, but Stennett scored the winning run with a sprawling slide. The throng of 50,229 stomped its feet, clapped its hands, and yelled "We want Willie!" for more than five minutes, pleading for a curtain call. This bordered on the stuff of mythology. The spectators yearned to gaze upon their town's great champion, who they had roused from his hero's rest to slay the hated dragon once again. "The early part of my career, every time I faced the Giants, I was convinced their manager manipulated the lineup so McCovey could always come to bat in the ninth inning," Dodgers right-hander Don Sutton said. "Every time the game was on the line, I had to look at McCovey. They had [Willie] Mays, [Orlando] Cepeda and [Jim Ray] Hart. But it always came down to McCovey. He was awesome." Watching from the Dodgers' bench was outfielder Rudy Law, who grew up about a half-hour drive south of Candlestick in East Palo Alto, California, where he attended Ravenswood High School. He admitted to having mixed feelings as San Francisco rallied, having adored McCovey and the Giants as a youth. "I tried to be like him," Law said. "As a kid, he was a big influence in my life." In this 9th-inning situation, Law admitted feeling the tug of ancient allegiances while one of his best friends, Castillo, was pitching. Said Law, "I was like, 'Way to go, Willie' . . . 'Dang, Babo.'" More than four decades later, the memory of the moment remained fresh for Law: "It was a trip. I'll never forget it. It was like yesterday. It amazes me how things come full circle."

Many of the 26,133—39,445, including free admissions—in attendance at Candlestick on July 3 doubtlessly felt the same way. The disproportionately large crowd for McCovey's last home game as a Giant included thousands of people who had never known a San Francisco roster that didn't have McCovey on it. Now they felt compelled to attend this Thursday matinee against the Cincinnati Reds—the final start of McCovey's career, with him batting fourth and playing first base as usual—to watch him unfurl his imposing swing a few times and maybe even stretch for a throw or two. Accompanied by standing ovations for virtually everything he visibly did, McCovey gave the crowd its biggest thrill when he singled to right field off Joe Price to drive in Jack Clark with a 3rd-inning run. McCovey, who hadn't started since June 6 at Houston, also grounded out twice and was called out on strikes, though he kept everybody entertained by hitting a pair of long, loud fouls. "I felt surprisingly good at the plate, considering I hadn't started in so long," McCovey said. "Most guys, when they retire, their bat slows down. If anything, my bat was too quick today."

After grounding out against Reds reliever Doug Bair in the 7th inning, McCovey ran onto the field to start the 8th. But witnesses seemed to realize that this was ceremony, not duty. McCovey was preparing for an early exit by shaking hands with his fellow infielders—Stennett at second base, shortstop Johnnie LeMaster, third baseman Joe Strain, and finally, Rich Murray, who embraced McCovey before taking over at first base. Emotions were almost palpable when Bristol beckoned McCovey back to the dugout—giving fans a final chance to cheer and cry for their beloved Stretch.

"I think what I'll remember most is that so many people came out here today," McCovey said, "to know it means something for them to say, 'I was there. I saw this last game.'" Referring to his run-scoring single, he added, "And I'm glad I got to provide 'em with one last thrill."

McCovey had one more good-bye to endure, and it probably was the cleanest. Not only was it quick, but it also gave the Giants a lead. It was Sunday, July 6, McCovey's last official day as a player. The score was tied, 3–3, with runners at the corners and 1 out in the Giants' half of the 8th inning. Stennett, a right-handed batter, was due to face Dodgers right-hander Rick Sutcliffe. Bristol wanted a better matchup. With mobile Jack Clark as the runner on third, Bristol sought a hitter who could generate even a medium-deep fly ball, since that would mean a sacrifice fly and a run. Bristol just happened to have a guy on the bench who had put enough air under the ball to drive in 1,554 runs. Make that 1,555, as McCovey scored Clark with a sacrifice fly to left-center field. McCovey's soon-to-be-ex-teammates engulfed him in front of the visitors' dugout. Time for one more lingering ovation—this one from the Dodger Stadium crowd, which prompted a stately bow from McCovey. The Dodgers pulled even, which denied McCovey a game-winning RBI, but the Giants rallied in the 10th to win it, 7–4. So McCovey went out as he went in: helping the Giants win with his bat.

Third baseman Darrell Evans compared Aaron to McCovey, who of course was an Aaron acolyte since his youth. "The great ones are better for a reason, more than their physical skills," Evans said. "They've got something that's beyond the rest of us. He's the type of guy you can't forget. I'm very fortunate to have played with Hank Aaron in Atlanta and with Willie here. I'm sad and happy at the same time. I'm glad he went out the way he did, but I wish he could go on playing forever."

Figuratively, the band played on for McCovey. During the game he took a phone call in the dugout from an assistant who worked with Frank Sinatra. Ol' Blue Eyes, a lifelong baseball fan, wanted McCovey to attend his concert that night in Universal City. Marveling at Sinatra's influence, McCovey immediately accepted the invitation. Said McCovey, "He had his guy call the dugout. Who else would be able to ring the dugout during a game but Frank Sinatra?" The opening two songs in Sinatra's set list sounded as if they were selected with McCovey in mind: "I've Got the World on a String" and "The Best Is Yet to Come."

14

A Cherished Honor

After I won that award in '97, everywhere I went, people congratulated me. On the street. In the supermarket. At a restaurant. "Hey, way to go on the Willie Mac Award." Fans knew what it meant. And then it really sank in.

—J. T. Snow, former Giants first baseman

The Giants immediately realized that they missed Willie McCovey. They missed the icon, the legend, and the man—a limitless source of quiet dignity and spellbinding presence. Though McCovey received numerous standing ovations from the day he announced his retirement to his final at bat in Dodger Stadium, he never had a chance to deliver a proper good-bye to the fans—and vice versa. His farewell was spur of the moment—such as his game-winning double against the Dodgers—and scattershot, occurring as it did in three parts: the aforementioned double, his Candlestick home finale, and his actual final pinch-hit appearance at Dodger Stadium. These generated some emotional, feel-good moments, but an organized, scheduled event honoring McCovey would have given everybody a good look at him, something more enduring than a curtain call. Yes, the Giants would conduct a ceremony in his honor, but not until September. "It wasn't necessarily graceful," longtime Giants executive Pat Gallagher said of McCovey's exit.

But the Giants found their stride after staggering from the starting gate. Each year since 1980, they have bestowed the Willie Mac Award upon the team's most inspirational player, selected in a vote among players, the manager and coaching staff, and the athletic training staff. Fan balloting accounts for a small percentage of the vote. McCovey himself received a ballot through 2018, the year he died.

Obviously, the man whose name is linked to the award is celebrated along with its recipients. Said team president Larry Baer, "The Willie Mac Award, what's it about? It's about team. It's about who's the most respected teammate. Everybody respects Willie Mac. In every possible way."

And everybody respects the Willie Mac Award, along with those who prove deserving of it. Through the course of a 162-game season, a ballclub and its players will inevitably reach thrilling heights and endure demoralizing doldrums. A team needs a figure like McCovey who can negotiate a path toward consistency and provide an example while doing so. In McCovey's case, his ability not just to play through pain but to excel despite discomfort won admirers. That's why the award goes annually, by the club's definition, to the player who, "on and off the field, best exemplifies the competitive spirit, ability and leadership" shown by McCovey. "He was sort of a living legend," Gallagher said. "One of the reasons why everybody loved him was, he was a great player, but he was also a regular guy." Wonderfully, players whose careers began with the opening of the ballpark at Third and King Streets or shortly thereafter got to know McCovey, who delighted in spending pregame hours in clubhouse manager Mike Murphy's office and chatting with various Giants as they reported for work. "I loved the guy," first baseman J. T. Snow said. "I cherish my time with him in spring training and in Murph's office. I would just pop in and talk to Willie. 'Hey, I'm struggling with the changeup.' His words of advice were amazing."

It all gets back to what head athletic trainer Joe Liscio repeated about McCovey: "He's a giant among Giants."

As the Giants' director of marketing and business affairs in 1980, Gallagher developed the idea for the Willie Mac Award. The NFL's San Francisco 49ers set a precedent with their Len Eshmont Award, which also is given to an especially inspiring performer. The McCovey/Eshmont comparisons end there. Relatively few fans know that Eshmont was a running back and defensive back who played on the original 1946 49ers squad and scored the first touchdown in team history. "Obviously Eshmont was somebody who commanded a lot of respect," Gallagher said. "But McCovey was different. He was unassailable, the way he carried himself and everything. If you named the award for anybody else, it wouldn't have the impact that it has."

The Giants wasted no time in establishing the Willie Mac Award. The inaugural recipient was somebody who, like McCovey, believed firmly in his own ability, never made excuses, and always, but always, was worth watching every time he stepped in the batter's box, regardless of the result. Jack Clark shared McCovey's sense of what being a Giant meant.

"When it came down to it, I sure would have liked to play my whole career with the Giants. Even at Candlestick Park," Clark said. "The fans treated me very well in San Francisco. I just wish we could have done better."

It's been said that every winner of the award is deserving—that the voters (mostly the players) get it right each year. "It's the guys who are steady," said Giants broadcaster Mike Krukow, a two-time Willie Mac Award winner. "Those are the guys you appreciate playing with."

Here is the roll call of recipients:

1980: Jack Clark, right fielder

If there's anything the Willie Mac Award is not about, it's statistics. But citing a few numbers is necessary to provide a reminder that, at age twenty-four, Clark was a budding star. He compiled an OPS+ of 153, second in the National League only to Philadelphia's Mike Schmidt (171). With Mike Ivie sidelined, the Giants looked to Clark for both consistency and slugging to lead the offense.

He said it: "I didn't know [the award] was going to go on to what it has been. It had a wide base, an orange plaque and a cup. And the cup would always fall off [while changing residences]. You needed a special tool to get at the bottom. I didn't have that tool. I keep putting it back together. It stands by itself." In more ways than one, you might say.

1981: Larry Herndon, outfielder

The always energetic Herndon responded to the leadership of new manager Frank Robinson with probably the best season of his career thus far. He ranked second in the ballclub during the strike-shortened season with 41 RBIs. Herndon also stole a career-high 15 bases in 21 attempts.

He said it: "Willie was just a kind gentleman. He loved the game. He loved playing the game right. But he respected you. He just drew respect because of the way he carried himself. He was a super-kind human being."

1982: Joe Morgan, second baseman

Morgan gave the Giants the veteran leadership they lacked since McCovey's retirement. Fortified with the resilience and confidence that Morgan instilled in them, the Giants remained in the division race until the season's final weekend.

He said it: "I was more impressed with the way those guys handled the pressure down the stretch than any other ballclub I've been with. Obviously, when I was with the Reds, we had the best teams, so we should win. When I was with the Giants down the stretch, we did not have the best team, talent-wise. But I think maybe they had the biggest heart."

1983: Darrell Evans, first baseman

After playing mostly third base since 1978, Evans moved across the diamond to become San Francisco's primary first baseman. He could have griped about how this might affect his status as an impending free agent; instead, he remained as uncomplaining as ever.

He said it: "When Willie and I hit back-to-back in the batting order, which was often, he would encourage us when we were in the on-deck circle by saying, 'You and me, Doody [Evans's nickname].' A couple of years ago I saw him for the first time in a while and he said, 'You and me, Doody.' Willie is Mr. San Francisco Giant. There's no question."

1984: Bob Brenly, catcher

Brenly was known for his genuine never-say-die attitude, which he needed in this season as the Giants finished 66–96 and in the following year when they lost 100 games. He played a team-high 145 games in '84, made the All-Star team, and hit 20 home runs, becoming San Francisco's first catcher to reach that level since Dick Dietz socked 22 in 1970.

1985–86: Mike Krukow, right-hander

One of three two-time award winners, Krukow singled himself out by maintaining a competitive attitude on the mound and as much esprit de corps in the clubhouse as can be mustered by the franchise's lone 100-loss team in 1985.

He said it: "When I got to the big leagues with the Cubs, I never missed watching the Giants take infield practice because I wanted to see McCovey. Nobody moved around the bag like him. He had a style all his own. It was what the name of the award was that made it so special to me, because of who McCovey was to me."

1987: Chris Speier, infielder

The lone link to the Giants' previous postseason qualifier—the NL West champions of 1971, which was his rookie year—Speier emerged as a valuable utility infielder at age thirty-seven.

He said it: "There was a presence about [McCovey] that exuded this confidence and respect. I was in awe of that. He had style and grace, even outside of baseball. A wonderful, wonderful man."

1988: José Uribe, shortstop

Uribe played most of the second's second half in mourning. His wife, Sara, had a fatal heart attack in early June, less than two days after the premature birth of the couple's third child, hospital officials said. She was twenty-seven.

1989: Dave Dravecky, left-hander

Dravecky overcame cancer in his throwing arm to resume pitching in the big leagues, albeit briefly. Told in 1988 that a desmoid tumor was found in his left arm, he underwent surgery in October of that year to remove half of the deltoid muscle in his arm. His rehabilitation proceeded without a hitch, enabling him to face the Reds on August 10. He allowed 3 runs on 4 hits in 8 innings to earn the decision in the Giants' 4–3 victory.

He said it: "Even though I didn't get to know Willie [for] very long, he left me with two very important things: He was a man of integrity, which I desire to be, and he was a man of humility, which I desire to be. I'm just amazed with how gentle a man he was. He was always deferring any attention to himself onto others. He never really talked a lot about himself. That's so important to always be mindful of as we continue to honor this man's legacy."

1990: Steve Bedrosian, right-hander

Bedrosian won the 1987 Cy Young Award while amassing 40 saves for Philadelphia, and he became the Giants' primary closer in their pennant-winning year of 1989 after they acquired him from the Phillies in a trade. But Bedrosian must have handled some of his toughest assignments during this season, as he pitched while his two-year-old son, Cody, battled leukemia.

1991: Robby Thompson, second baseman

The phrase "He plays the game the right way" is synonymous with Thompson, who was fundamentally sound in equal measures at the plate and in the field. He was particularly gritty during this campaign, as he played the season's final month with a cracked bone in his hand.

He said it: "This award is not one you receive and then you go home and stick it under your bed. You put it up on the wall and display it with a lot of pride."

1992: Mike "Tiny" Felder, outfielder

As his nickname indicates, the 5-foot-8 Felder was undersized by Major League standards. But he overcame his diminutive stature with ceaseless determination. He was especially combative on offense, striking out just 29 times in 351 plate appearances.

He said it: "Usually awards like that go to someone who's playing regularly. When they told me I won the award, I was in shock. My heart just melts that I'll always be connected to Willie McCovey."

1993: Kirt Manwaring, catcher

Manwaring hit his best when it counted the most, recording four 4-hit games July 9 and afterward as the Giants competed deeper into the stretch drive. As one of only three regulars to avoid the disabled list, he handled the game's most grueling position admirably.

1994: No award given due to labor dispute

1995: Mark Leiter, right-hander, and Mark Carreon, first baseman

The Giants posted a disappointing 67–77 finish, but this pair didn't allow the club's subpar performance overall to drag them down. Leiter did everything that was asked of him, making a team-high 29 starts while leading an injury- and slump-riddled starting rotation in most major statistical categories. With Matt Williams and Robby Thompson missing significant chunks of playing time due to injuries, Carreon filled the void by hitting .301 with a career-high 17 homers.

1996: Shawon Dunston, shortstop

In his first of three stints with the Giants after thriving as a two-time All-Star with the Cubs, Dunston began the transition from regular to reserve by batting an even .300 in 82 games. Dunston's season ended on August 4 when he was involved in a collision with Houston's Ricky Gutierrez.

He said it: "That's like an MVP award, because when your teammates pick you, that makes you really feel good. The award is not the best player award, because the best players were Barry and Matt Williams. We all know that. I wasn't the best player on any of my teams. Except for high school. But it shows what your teammates think of you and I really appreciate that. It sits at my house so proudly. It's like it makes you part of Giant history when you win the Willie Mac Award."

1997, 2004: J. T. Snow, first baseman

Snow is the only multiple Willie Mac winner to experience an interval of years between honors. In '97, he solidified the infield defense and provided numerous clutch hits. By '04 he remained an asset on the field and by then had developed into a widely respected team leader.

He said it: "He was so supportive of what you did. After I won that award in '97, everywhere I went, people congratulated me—on the street, in the supermarket, at a restaurant. 'Hey, way to go on the Willie Mac Award.' Fans knew what it meant. And then it really sank in. I can't hold a candle to this guy. But he never made you feel like that. [The award] is not about your stats and your home runs and your batting average. It's about the kind of guy you are in the clubhouse and with your teammates. When your career is over and done, not many people will remember your batting average or how many home runs you hit. But when you come back to the city of San Francisco, they'll remember that you're a Willie Mac Award winner."

1998: Jeff Kent, second baseman

Kent established career highs in home runs (31) and RBIs (128) despite missing 24 games with a sprained knee. He had 29 homers and 121 RBIs in '07.

He said it: "I'm proud to have a plaque with my name and his name in the same paragraph. I mount deer heads more than baseball plaques, but I'm proud of this. I really am."

1999: Marvin Benard, center fielder

Another compact Giant, the 5-foot-10 Nicaraguan was a dynamo at the leadoff spot, reaching personal bests in home runs (16), runs (100), RBIs (64), at bats (562), doubles (36), triples (5), stolen bases (27), and games played (149).

He said it: "My whole life, people doubted me. I was told I wasn't supposed to be in the big leagues. If my teammates said, 'You can't play center field,' hey, I'd go somewhere else and do something else. If they think I'm doing a decent job, I guess I can live with that."

2000: Ellis Burks, outfielder

Burks required off-season surgery on both knees before this year. He nevertheless delivered one of his finest seasons to help the Giants post the National League's best record (97–65). He amassed 24 homers and 96 RBIs in just 393 at bats while matching a career best by hitting .344. His slash line (.419/.606/1.025) rivaled his best ever.

He said it: "As much as the guys rag on me, I was surprised to win it. It means a lot coming from my teammates, my manager, the coaching staff and the trainers."

2001: Mark Gardner, right-hander, and Benito Santiago, catcher

Both recipients were relied upon for the quality of leadership they provided as veterans. Gardner, later to become the Giants' bullpen coach, left baseball briefly after this season to spend more time with his family as his wife, Lori, battled liver cancer. She died in November 2003. As for Santiago, the pitchers' 3.84 ERA with him behind the plate was noticeably better than the team's 4.18 figure overall. He appeared in 133 games, his most since he played 136 with Philadelphia in 1996. With the Giants striving for the postseason, Santiago started 100 of the team's final 119 games.

He (Gardner) said it: "Mac could never pass by without saying hello. He always had something positive to say."

2002: David Bell, third baseman

Playing in the NL for the first time since a 39-game cameo with St. Louis in 1995, Bell was one of four Giants to hit 20 or more home runs. His 3.1 WAR was the club's fifth best. His father, Buddy, and grandfather, Gus, both played against McCovey.

He said it: "I didn't win too many awards. But I will say that even if I would've, it is the only personal accomplishment that I ever had that means anything to me for my career. It was *so* meaningful to me. It actually meant more and more over the years, mainly because I had the honor of getting to know Willie. The other part, too, is what he represents, and the way it was voted on. It came from the players, your teammates. My dad had great respect for him. My grandfather did, too. He was an incredible man who represents everything you want every player to be in this game."

2003: Marquis Grissom, center fielder

At age thirty-six, Grissom enjoyed one of the most productive seasons of his fifteen-year career. He batted .300 for just the second time while hitting 33 doubles, clobbering 20 homers, and tallying 82 runs. He also batted .333 with runners in scoring position.

He said it: "I respect the game. I was brought up by great players and coaches, and I was brought up to never disrespect the game. To see them day in, day out, I appreciate it, I really do. It makes me keep trying hard, to do my best."

2005: Mike Matheny, catcher

Playing his last full season before a concussion caused by a foul tip ended his career, Matheny obliterated many of his previous offensive standards, including 13 home runs, 59 RBIS, and 34 doubles. He also won his third consecutive Gold Glove Award for defensive excellence.

He said it: "It's humbling. It's not always your intention [to be inspirational]. You go about your business and have responsibilities. It's how you line them up and prioritize. Whether it's inspiring, I don't know. But it's a huge compliment."

2006: Omar Vizquel, shortstop

At thirty-nine, Vizquel became the oldest shortstop to win a Gold Glove. Errorless streaks of 63 and 53 games helped. His .993 fielding percentage set a franchise record for shortstops. And his .295 batting average was the third best of his seventeen-year career.

2007–8: Bengie Molina, catcher

Nobody ever questioned Molina's status as the pitching staff's ultimate authority due to the respect he commanded. His offensive impact doubled his value to the Giants, who watched him usher Tim Lincecum, Matt Cain, Brian Wilson, and others toward maturity while averaging 18 homers and 88 RBIS in 2007–8.

He said it: "It's just the fact that the guys and the coaches voted for me. That's what gets in my heart. It really touched me. It really did."

2009: Matt Cain, right-hander

Cain's teammates witnessed his metamorphosis from hard-luck loser to All-Star-caliber winner, which was prompted by a transformed attitude toward conditioning. Suddenly, Cain could last deeper into games and reach back for whatever he needed to make the big pitch that would subdue a hitter.

He said it: "It's one of those situations you definitely take to heart, that your teammates are definitely looking at you in big situations. It's pretty cool the way they look at me as a leader and a motivator. All of us starting pitchers want to have that role."

2010: Andrés Torres, outfielder

Few observers believed that Torres would be ready for the postseason—if the Giants progressed that far—after he had his appendix removed on September 12. However, he resumed playing twelve days afterward.

He said it: "I thought I wasn't going to come back. But I've been working my whole life to be where I am now. I wanted to be back with my teammates."

2011: Ryan Vogelsong, right-hander

Vogelsong endured multiple Minor League assignments and a stint in Japan before a foot injury to Barry Zito cleared a path for him to the Giants' starting rotation. His refusal to quit on himself guaranteed him a place in Giants lore, particularly after he made this year's All-Star team.

He said it: "Everyone in that clubhouse has gone through some kind of struggle in their career at some point. Even if it's a couple-week thing or couple years or couple months. They can look to my story as a little pick-me-up to get them through. When you think things are bad, they can always be worse. When you think things can be worse, they can always be better. If It's inspiring people on a daily basis, that's awesome."

2012: Buster Posey, catcher

Posey came back from a broken left leg and sprained ankle ligaments, which he sustained on May 25, 2011. He won the NL batting title and made his first of seven All-Star teams.

He said it: "Hopefully, I'm somebody the guys can look at and say, 'He goes about things the right way.' I'm ready to play, and hopefully I'm a guy people can come up to and bounce stuff off of—really, be the best teammate I can be."

2013: Hunter Pence, right fielder

Pence became the first Giant in the club's San Francisco history (since 1958) to start every game and the franchise's first outfielder to do so since Bobby Thomson in 1949. Pence made the most of his appearances, hitting a career- and team-high 27 home runs while establishing himself as one of the favorite players of the fan base in his first full year with the team.

He said it: "Willie McCovey—the spirit of baseball lives in you. Rest in peace" (tweet on November 1, 2018)

2014: Madison Bumgarner, left-hander

Bear in mind that Bumgarner received this honor before he launched his run of dominance through the postseason, an effort that concluded with his epic relief effort in World Series Game 7. With Tim Lincecum and Matt Cain fading and Tim Hudson slipping more as the season elapsed, it was Bumgarner's turn to assume the ace's role on the pitching staff.

2015: Matt Duffy, third baseman

The first rookie to win the award, Duffy wrested the regular third baseman's job from Casey McGehee in late May. He joined future Hall of Famer Orlando Cepeda, Jim Ray Hart, and Chili Davis as the only Giants rookies to drive in 70 or more runs in a season. Demonstrating his consistency, Duffy batted higher than .300 in May, June, July, and August. He finished the season having started 118 consecutive games, the Majors' third-longest active streak.

He said it: "At the time, I didn't know the award existed. I had zero perspective. There aren't many sports organizations who have what the Giants have. It's hard to beat what the Giants have, in all of sports. To be a small part of that is cool. I feel like in the short time that I was there, I was able to leave a little bit of a mark on the organization."

2016: Brandon Crawford, shortstop, and Javier López, left-hander

Crawford's association with the Giants began when he rooted for the ballclub as a youth while growing up in the Bay Area. His biggest 2016 highlight was going 7-for-8 on August 8 with 5 singles, a double, and a triple at Marlins Park. He was the first player in forty-one years to reach the 7-hit milestone. López, who retired after the 2016 season, ranked among the best left-handed relief specialists in recent big league history.

López formed the "Core Four" along with Jeremy Affeldt, Santiago Casilla, and Sergio Romo and averaged 72 appearances per year in his six full seasons with San Francisco.

He (López) said it: "To share the award with Crawford is special. It's an award you would normally see starters or position players get. Being a reliever and somebody who's respected in the clubhouse speaks volumes."

2017: Nick Hundley, catcher

Hundley helped mold a pitching staff full of disparate parts into a semblance of a cohesive unit. In a year when Matt Cain and Madison Bumgarner finished a combined 7–20, the Giants had to find pitching help from somewhere, and Hundley aided Buster Posey in making the most of what the Giants had. Hundley batted .260 in 66 games as a starter, compared with .135 in 35 appearances as a reserve.

He said it: "This is pretty overwhelming, to be standing here with Giants legends and to be mentioned in the same company with Willie McCovey and these guys up here who I have tremendous respect for—it's incredible."

2018: Will Smith, left-hander

Smith missed the 2017 season after undergoing Tommy John elbow surgery but recovered nicely, excelling for the Giants as a closer and in setup situations. He recorded 14 saves in 18 chances in the former role.

He said it: "I don't know if it's sunk in yet, but it's incredible."

2019: Kevin Pillar, center fielder

Pillar provided experience to an outfield sorely lacking in that quality. The six-year veteran also provided offense, leading the club in runs (82), hits (157), doubles (37), stolen bases (14), and home runs (21, tied with Mike Yastrzemski).

He said it: "First off, I'd like to thank [director of baseball operations] Farhan [Zaidi] for believing in me and trading for me and making me a Giant."

2020: Mike Yastrzemski, outfielder

After spending more than six years in Baltimore's Minor League system, Yastrzemski joined the Giants and quickly became one of their most indispensable performers. He's capable of making significant contributions both offensively and defensively—just like his grandfather, Hall of Famer Carl Yastrzemski.

He said it: "That's the most important thing about this, is that it comes from teammates, from staff—from the guys who mean the most."

2021: LaMonte Wade Jr., first baseman–outfielder

On six occasions, Wade stroked 9th-inning hits that either tied the score or put San Francisco ahead. He thus earned himself the nickname "Late Night LaMonte." He also collected 18 home runs in only 381 plate appearances.

He said it: "I'm truly blessed and honored to receive this award. . . . Of course I'd like to thank Willie, who I know is watching from above."

2022: Wilmer Flores, infielder

Flores's versatility has proven essential to the Giants, who have used him extensively at the infield corners and third base since he joined the team in 2020. He also possesses much-needed pop at the plate, setting personal bests in doubles (28), homers (19), and RBIs (71) this season.

He said it: "It is a true honor to win the Willie Mac Award. I have the greatest teammates I could ever have. I appreciate the fans because you're always cheering. It doesn't matter if we're winning or losing. I always feel you behind us, and that means a lot. It makes me want to come back stronger next year."

2023: Thairo Estrada, infielder

Estrada earned his award in characteristic McCoveyesque fashion: by overcoming injury. He broke his left hand when he was hit by a pitch on July 2. Expected to miss four to six weeks of game action, Estrada managed to make 50 more appearances after he recovered.

15

Bound for Cooperstown

It's an honor for me and for all of San Francisco.

—Willie McCovey, upon being elected to the Hall of Fame

The *San Francisco Chronicle* delivered a welcome holiday gift to its readers on the morning of December 25, 1985. A photograph of Willie McCovey, looking ready for the first tee as he wore a beret, a V-neck sweater, and a jubilant smile, dominated the newspaper's sports section. The occasion for the 8½-inch-by-12-inch photo and the story accompanying it was baseball's annual Hall of Fame balloting, which would conclude the following week. As the most accomplished of the fourteen newcomers to the ballot, McCovey seemed poised to gain entry into Cooperstown. Being the twelfth player to exceed 500 career home runs seemed to improve McCovey's Cooperstown chances, since the previous eleven hitters to gain access to this "club" were all first-ballot selections for induction. "My friends say it's automatic, and they already are making preparations to go to the ceremony," McCovey said. "But I don't know. Some other people thought they were in, and they had trouble making it." The *Chronicle* had few, if any, doubts about McCovey's cachet for glory. The main headline blared, "McCovey's Claim to Fame," accompanied by a secondary headline that read, "Cooperstown Should Be Next for an All-Time Giants Great."

McCovey insisted that he resisted allowing dreams of Cooperstown to cloud his perspective. "The Hall of Fame was never a dream of mine, I have to admit. I never realized the importance of it, I guess," he said. "But after you retire, that's when you start thinking of it, because that's the only honor or award that is left for you."

He did feel confident enough in his Hall of Fame prospects to take stock of his baseball life. "As I look back on my career it is hard to say which of my records is the most important to me. I guess it is for playing 20 years plus," he said.

"That is probably the most important thing because of my love for the game and it is the only thing I have ever wanted to do. I had always dreamed and hoped that I would have a long and successful career. . . . I have had lots of individual awards and good stats. But I think those things become more important to you after you have been in retirement for a few years . . . and you are no longer out there accomplishing anything else, adding to those statistics. These statistics are important, especially if you have any hopes and aspirations of getting into the Hall of Fame. . . . But the stats in the end are not going to be the most important thing of my life. I think what will be the most important thing will be the people I have met along the way and my 20-some plus years of baseball and all things of that sort that I have gotten out of baseball. I owe everything to baseball."

Moreover, people in baseball owed McCovey some credit. True Hall of Famers are originals. That is, they performed so well that they defied comparisons to other players, or they were so good that they were out in front, creating their own category. For instance, McCovey was the leading left-handed-batting home run hitter in National League history when he retired during the 1980 season, with all 521 his long balls being struck against NL competition. He also was the first hitter to smack 2 home runs in the same inning twice as well as the first National Leaguer to hit as many as 18 grand slams. And he drew a Major League record 45 intentional walks in 1969 while establishing himself as the first player to amass 20 or more intentional walks in 5 different seasons. Instilling fear was McCovey's trademark. "I'm proud of the fact that I've done some things more than anybody," he said.

McCovey's pattern of accomplishing singular feats continued when the 1986 Hall of Fame election results were announced on January 8. He was only the sixteenth player to reach the Hall as a first-ballot selection, receiving 346 of 425 votes (81.4 percent) from the ten-year members of the Baseball Writers' Association of America who comprised the electorate. A 75 percent vote total was required. "Only the greatest of the superstars make it the first time they are eligible," said Jack Lang, the BBWAA's secretary-treasurer. Among those who missed out in McCovey's election was his Mobile, Alabama, buddy, Billy Williams. The longtime Chicago Cub outfielder came dishearteningly close, receiving 315 votes, or 74.1 percent. "I was disappointed that Billy Williams and I couldn't make it in together. It would have been good for Mobile." Williams achieved enshrinement in 1987 with a strong 85.7 approval figure.

However, McCovey felt glad to give his hometown fans a thrill. "It's an honor for me and for all of San Francisco," he said. That night, McCovey boarded a red-eye flight to New York to be officially introduced as a Hall of Famer the next day. The number of the flight McCovey boarded? Why, 44, of course.

The Giants staged a dress rehearsal for McCovey in advance of his August 3 induction ceremony at Cooperstown. Willie Mays, Monte Irvin, Chub Feeney, Johnny Mize, and Bill Rigney showed up along with a Candlestick crowd of 40,473 to pay tribute to McCovey before a July 6 game against St. Louis. Feeney, the National League president and former Giants general manager, was asked to explain McCovey's singular popularity among fans. "He's just a lovable guy," Feeney replied. "But I think one of the biggest reasons for his great appeal is [that] he broke in here. He didn't come from New York like some of the others. He would play hurt, he would play anywhere. He never complained, he never whined. He was a perfect gentleman." Said Mays, "He could hit a ball farther than anyone I ever played with. I could hit them more consistently, but I just dropped them over the fence." Bob Gibson, the incomparable right-hander who was present in his role on the Cardinals' broadcasting crew, reserved high praise for McCovey. "He wasn't going to be intimidated by anybody," Gibson said. "McCovey swung harder than anyone I ever saw. Most guys who swung that hard would miss the ball, but he didn't."

The true greats would be outstanding in any era. So it was with McCovey. His career looks just as good when measured by modern metrics as it does when citing home runs and RBIs. A familiar comparison bears this out: McCovey versus Willie Stargell. To a considerable extent, you'd think that they were clones of each other.

Category	McCovey	Stargell
AB	8,197	7,927
Runs	1,229	1,194
Hits	2,211	2,232
HR	521	475
RBIS	1,555	1,550
BA	.270	.282
OBP	.374	.360
SLG	.515	.529

Though their respective on-base percentages don't reflect it, their paths diverged when it came to walks and strikeouts. With 1,345 walks and 1,550 strikeouts, McCovey possessed a keener eye or more restraint or selectivity than Stargell, who went down on strikes 1,936 times and drew 937 walks.

A particular new-wave stat also favors McCovey over Stargell, who was a first-ballot Hall of Famer in 1988. That would be win probability added, or WPA, which gauges a player's impact on eventual victory. McCovey's was 73.3; Stargell's was 54.4. In fact, through 2022, McCovey ranked an impressive eleventh all-time in WPA.

This is not meant to diminish Stargell in any sense. Even players who get equaled or surpassed statistically maintain sterling reputations. It's the rising-tide-lifts-all-boats phenomenon. In 2022, when St. Louis' Albert Pujols became the fifth big leaguer to hit a home run for the same franchise at age twenty-one or younger and forty-two or older, McCovey moved aside to make room for Pujols on this short list along with fellow Cardinal Stan Musial and Boston's Ted Williams and Carl Yastrzemski.

On McCovey's induction day, a crowd estimated at five thousand gathered on the lawn outside the Hall of Fame and museum for the ceremonies that also enshrined hard-hitting catcher Ernie Lombardi and multitalented Red Sox second baseman Bobby Doerr in Cooperstown. The public got its first look at McCovey's plaque, which read, "Top left-handed home run hitter in N.L. history with 521. Second only to Lou Gehrig with 18 grand slams. Led N.L. in homers three times and RBI's twice. N.L. rookie of year in 1959, MVP in 1969 and comeback player of the year in '77. Teamed with Willie Mays for awesome 1–2 punch in Giants' lineup." McCovey's mother, Ester, was present, along with his sister Frances, his brother Clauzell, and his daughter, Allison. Close friends such as the Dudum family, Golden State Warriors owner Franklin Mieuli, and attorney Hal Silen were also present. In fact, McCovey chose family and friends as the theme of his induction speech, which began under stormy skies that turned to sunshine about halfway through his address. Near that juncture, McCovey, known for the impassive mask he wore on the field, had to pause to choke back tears. He did so again at the conclusion of his speech. "I'm a pretty calm person, and I thought I could get through the afternoon without getting too emotional," McCovey said. "But it hit me when I got up on the stage and started thinking about all the special people that passed through my life and what they meant to me."

McCovey's complete remarks were as follows:

I've been thinking about what a perfect kind of day this is for me to be here on this stage, celebrating the pinnacle of my career and my life.

One reason it seems so right is that it's a Sunday afternoon in the summertime, and, to me, it doesn't matter if you're in Mobile, or San Francisco, or Cooperstown, Sunday afternoons in the summertime have always meant two things—it's a time for baseball, and a time for families.

Both of those things have been very important to me throughout my life. Each one has enriched the other over the years. Baseball and family together have shaped my character and my values and my career, and together they have brought me here before you today.

Some of the most important people in both my baseball life and my family life are here today to share these moments with me, and I'm very grateful that they could be here. And some others could not be here today, but I'm sure they're here in spirit.

The people I've come to know through baseball over the years are my family, too, in a way, and I'm going to tell you about some of them a little bit later on.

But when I talk about my family, I'm really talking about two families. There's the one that starts with my dad, Frank McCovey, who passed on 23 years ago. How I wish he could be here with me today. And my mother, Ester McCovey, who is here today and sitting right down here in front of me with my sister, Frances, and my brother, Clauzell, and my lovely daughter, Allison. I was raised with seven brothers, Frank Jr., Wyatt, Arthur, Richmond, Walter, Clauzell and Cleon, and two sisters, Frances and Ethel. All of them, and the others with the McCovey family name in Mobile, Alabama, and throughout the country, are a part of me and share in this occasion today.

I have another "family." It is a family of good, genuine, caring people who opened their hearts and their homes to me over the years. I guess you might say they "adopted" me and made me a part of their families, too.

Come to think of it, I'm not sure how I ever got to be known as a loner type of guy when I was actually surrounded by so many special, loving people. Let me tell you about some of them.

I was "adopted" in this way by:

A warm and unselfish San Francisco family, the Dudums: Rocky and his wife, Nada, are my closest friends in the Dudum family. Paul, who is here today, Audie, Jack, George and Jimmy—all my adopted brothers.

By a bright young lawyer and his wife, Harold and Helen Silen, who not only managed my finances, but invited me into their home as part of their family.

By honest, compassionate men of dignity like Franklin Mieuli, Bill Rigney, Salty Parker, Lon Simmons and Ed Nagourney . . . men who offered only friendship, counsel and understanding and expected nothing in return. These guys were always there for me.

By loving, nurturing women like Ruth Stovall, whom I call my "San Francisco mother," by the late Mary Cross in Phoenix and by Charlotte Kahn in San Diego, who is here today. These ladies took me under their wing and saw to it that I took care of myself, ate right, got my rest and had plenty of motherly advice when I needed it away from home.

By loyal teammates. I had four decades of them, some closer than others, but all of them are part of my Giants family.

By Horace Stoneham and Bob Lurie, the two gentlemen who owned the Giants during my career. It was Horace who brought me up through the system and supported me throughout my career, and I've always been grateful to Bob for bringing me back to San Francisco in 1977 to finish out my career where I started it. And, of course, in between I'm grateful to Buzzie Bavasi for the three years I spent with him and the San Diego Padres and I especially thank Buzzie for crediting me for turning around the franchise in 1974, '75 and '76. Horace, unfortunately, is not well enough to travel, but if he could hear me today, I'd let him know how much he means to me. Bob and his lovely wife, Connie, are here today and I appreciate that very much. I know you all join me in congratulating Bob and the Giants on the very special season they're having in San Francisco. And hopefully, with the support of the people in the Bay Area, we can get that stadium built and keep the Giants where they belong.

I've been adopted, too, by all the thousands of great Giants fans everywhere and by the city of San Francisco, where I've always been welcome and, like the Golden Gate Bridge and the cable cars, I've been made to feel like a landmark, too.

There are some other people I can't help but remember fondly on this day as I think way back to the beginnings of my career in Mobile, Alabama, more than thirty years ago.

I'm thinking of Jackie Robinson, who broke the color line and made our dreams of being major leaguers a reality.

I'm thinking of Jesse Thomas, a playground director in Mobile who arranged for me to have a tryout in front of the Giants' scout down in Melbourne, Florida.

And the late scout, Alex Pompez, and Jack Schwarz of the Giants who, together, signed me to my first contract.

And, of course, my first manager, Pete Pavlick. Pete was the skipper of the Class-D Sandersville club in the Georgia State League, where I broke into the pros in 1955. He and his wife were the first to adopt me. They used to invite me to their house after the games and became very close to me. I also remember one of my teammates there, Ralph Crosby, out of New York. We were the only two black players on that team and we had to stay in separate parts of town back then, so Ralph and I became good friends.

I first met Salty Parker in 1956 when I went to Danville in the Carolina League and he was the manager. He also managed me in 1957 at Dallas in the Texas League. Salty became somewhat of a father figure to me. I'll never forget the day he called me into his office and told me, "Big 'un, you're tall, and because you're tall, you'll always be respected and you'll always stand out in a crowd. . . . You're not a very outgoing person and you have an easygoing manner . . . people may interpret that as though you're not caring.

"But whatever people say, stay the way you are and just be yourself. Don't ever change or let somebody try to make you something you're not."

I've always remembered those words and tried to live by them, and I'll always feel close to Salty because of the way he treated me.

When I went on to Phoenix in 1958, the manager there was Red Davis, who was a low-key, easy-going guy. I don't know a person who played for Red who didn't like him, and I'm no exception.

Of course, I'll never forget how my big league career got started. after a twilight doubleheader in Phoenix on July the 29th, 1959, Rosy Ryan, who was the general manager of the Phoenix club at that time, came to my locker and said, "You're going to the big club. . . . They have a day game tomorrow and they want you to play."

I was up all night packing and I flew up the next morning. Horace Stoneham sent someone to the airport to pick me up and we drove right to Seals Stadium. I got uniform number 44 because I'd always admired Hank Aaron, and I was getting dressed when Bill Rigney came to me and said, "How do you feel?" I said, "Fine," not wanting to tell him I'd been up all night. He said, "Good. You're in there and you're hittin' third. And you know whose spot that is. I'm moving Mays up to second today, so you know what we're expecting of you." Well, that was the first of many days that season I was to make Bill look like a genius.

I was fortunate enough to go 4-for-4 off Robin Roberts that day, with two triples and two singles.

The next night I'm facing a tough left-hander, Harvey Haddix of the Pirates. With the score tied in the bottom of the eighth inning, Mays leads off with a single. Bill comes storming out of the dugout waving his hands. So I step out of the batter's box and say to myself, "Now I know he's not crazy enough to take me out for a pinch hitter, is he?" So he says, "If you be patient and take a couple of pitches, that guy at first will steal second for you and you can win the game."

So I take the first pitch, strike one. I take the second pitch, and Mays steals second. The next pitch I single to right, Mays scores the go-ahead run and we win the game. I went to hit .354 and win Rookie of the Year.

The next year I hit .238 and got Bill fired. But the fact that he's here today tells you that he didn't hold it against me. We've both come a long ways since then.

My first few years in San Francisco I became very close to Rocky Dudum and his family and they're still my closest friends today.

I also got to know Ruth Stovall, Franklin Mieuli and Hal Silen at that time and they remain very special people in my life.

All of the people I've mentioned today have played a part in the successes I've been fortunate enough to have throughout my life and my career in baseball.

I wanted you to know who they are because without them I certainly would not be standing here now.

They are the most valuable players in my life.

They are the champions of my world.

They are the people in *my* Hall of Fame.

I would be remiss if I failed to acknowledge and extend my thanks and appreciation to the members of the Baseball Writers' Association of America, not only for electing me to baseball's highest shrine, but for many years of kind words and generous praise. The same holds true for all of the sports media. It's been my distinct pleasure through the years to have met and become friends with many of the nation's best and brightest sports journalists.

And now, I have become a player on the most distinguished team of all. It's a new family, in a way. A family of men whose accomplishments in baseball—and in life—set them apart from all others. I am truly honored and blessed with this ultimate "adoption," if you will, by the game I played so hard and that I love so deeply.

For many warm summer Sunday afternoons in the years to come, I will cherish the memories of my baseball career and the closeness of my relatives, friends, teammates, fans and my fellow Hall of Famers.

And I know my mother would not want me to leave this stage without thanking God almighty—thank you, Jesus.

Thank you.

16

The Cove

The new park wouldn't be complete without a tribute to
Willie McCovey.

—Larry Baer, longtime Giants executive

As the San Francisco Giants approached their bright and shiny future, Willie McCovey was being left behind. The club's transition from Candlestick Park to Pacific Bell Park was moving forward with fanfare and nostalgia as Pac Bell's inaugural season in the year 2000 drew closer. The 1999 season was full of pomp, circumstance, and tributes at Candlestick Park to former Giants. Little of this sentimental mood involved McCovey, despite his status as the franchise's most popular player ever. He did nothing to cause this. It just happened. He merited a full-page biography in the Giants' 1994 media guide as a special assistant to the president and general manager, along with Willie Mays. That evaporated into nothingness in the guide's 1995 version. McCovey remained absent from the guide in the year after that. And the year after that. And the year after that. And the year after that. By contrast, the Giants honored Mays, their most treasured legend, with a statue at the new ballpark's main entrance on Third and King Streets. Mays's godson, slugger Barry Bonds, was being credited as the man who, figuratively speaking, "built" the yard by recording one standout season after another that helped launch the successful fall 1996 vote to approve the ballpark's construction. Vida Blue and Orlando Cepeda, hugely popular Giants from decades past, maintained their roles as community representatives as the ballclub changed addresses.

McCovey? He had vanished by then, as far as the Giants were concerned. The colossus who authored the Game 7 drama in the 1962 World Series,

Candlestick Park's all-time leader with 237 home runs, one of a small handful of truly dynamic hitters in the 1960s . . . he wasn't as much fired as he was simply overlooked.

How a 6-foot-4 Hall of Fame first baseman ever could be overlooked defies belief. But certain factors perpetuated the celebration of Mays's greatness, which contrasted with the tendency to take McCovey for granted. Peter Magowan, the Giants' managing general partner, grew up idolizing Mays. Magowan appreciated McCovey but not with the same unconditional love that his most ardent fans clung to through all four decades that his playing career spanned. Also, McCovey's worsening knee problems prevented him from visiting Candlestick as much as he would have liked. Thus, he wasn't very visible. Contrast that with the last twenty or so years of McCovey's life, when he learned to cope with his various ailments smoothly enough to make it to Third and King for almost every home game.

Moreover, McCovey may have preferred to keep the curtain drawn on his life during the mid-1990s. On July 20, 1995, he and Brooklyn Dodgers legend Duke Snider pleaded guilty to tax evasion stemming from cash they received for signing autographs at baseball memorabilia shows. The *New York Post* reported that McCovey failed to disclose $69,800 that he received in cash from 1988 to 1990, including $33,000 at a January 1989 event in Atlantic City, New Jersey. McCovey and Snider faced one to seven months in prison and $250,000 in fines. Baseball insiders insisted that McCovey simply received bad advice and had no intention of deliberately cheating the Internal Revenue Service. In fact, he received two years of probation and a $5,000 fine when he was sentenced by a federal judge in Brooklyn on June 7, 1996. "The only thing I'd like to say is, well, I've always tried to do the right things," McCovey told Judge Edward R. Korman. "I have never willingly tried to cheat the government, and it's one of those things that was overlooked at the time and I do accept responsibility for it. I have never in my life deliberately tried to cheat the government or do anything wrong." McCovey received staunch support in absentia from many prominent San Franciscans who sent letters to the court citing his high moral character and numerous good deeds. Those offering such backing included San Francisco Mayor Willie Brown, former mayor Art Agnos, and Congresswoman Nancy Pelosi. Brown's letter read, in part, "Willie McCovey has been, above all else, loyal to the good things that matter in life: loyal to a set of values that put the right priority on giving to others, loyal to fans and the hometown that cheered him on, and loyal to children and the needy who need a champion to be there for them." This chapter in McCovey's life officially ended on January 17, 2017, when he was one of sixty-four people to receive a pardon from President Barack Obama. Three days later, Obama left office. "I want to express my sincere gratitude to President Obama not only for this kind gesture on my behalf, but also for his tireless service to all Americans," McCovey said in a statement issued through the Giants. "He will be deeply missed and I wish him all the best in the future."

By then, McCovey's popularity had emerged intact from the memorabilia fuss, and the Cove was well established as a ballpark landmark. Just a little bit of prodding was necessary to make it a reality. The cartographer who put the Cove on the map, so to speak, was San Jose *Mercury News* sports columnist Mark Purdy, who couldn't understand why McCovey didn't play a more prominent role in Giants ceremonies as they bade farewell to Candlestick in 1999 and approached the opening of Pacific Bell Park in 2000. "What about McCovey?" Purdy said. "I knew what an impact guy he was. I think even then I knew that he had hit more home runs as a San Francisco Giant [469] than Mays [459]."

These thoughts gnawed at Purdy in early May 1999 as he and his fourteen-year-old son, A.J., crossed the recessed portion of the Bay—then known as China Basin Channel—to attend the X Games at San Francisco's Pier 39. The Purdys and other extreme sports connoisseurs crossed the channel by taking a shuttle bus over the Lefty O'Doul Bridge—formerly the Third Street Bridge, but renamed to honor O'Doul, another San Francisco baseball celebrity—from Parking Lot A. If the city could do this for O'Doul, couldn't the Giants do something to recognize McCovey? Yes, the Willie Mac Award had been created to honor McCovey's spirit. But it wasn't something he kept for himself.

The day after his X Games foray, Purdy was at Candlestick Park, where the Giants honored their 1960s All-Decade Team. Most of the usual suspects showed up, including Mays, Orlando Cepeda, and right-hander Juan

Marichal. But McCovey felt too physically infirm to make the short drive from his home in Woodside to Candlestick, and then to negotiate the relatively short walk onto the field to acknowledge the fans' cheering. He sent in some videotaped remarks instead.

That inflamed Purdy's passion even more. Making good use of China Basin Channel was very much on his mind. Pointing out that McCovey would have routinely hit baseballs into the drink or perhaps beyond it, Purdy wrote a column suggesting renaming the channel for McCovey. Asked Purdy, "Why shouldn't left-handed hitters be able to launch homers into 'McCovey Channel' or 'McCovey Stream' or 'McCovey Run'?" Purdy related a conversation he had with veteran baseball scribe Leonard Koppett, who distinguished himself with the *New York Times* and the *Peninsula Times Tribune*. Koppett proposed a smoother-sounding alternative: "McCovey Cove."

Purdy took the renaming concept to Giants executive vice president Larry Baer, who was described as "cautiously supportive." Baer noted that honoring McCovey in this manner would have a desirable side effect: restoring him to his rightful place in the Giants' pantheon. "We're trying to reach out to him," Baer said. "He's the one person, of all our great alumni, who does not have as much direct involvement as we would like."

The immediate impact of this column wasn't exactly what Purdy sought. "Nothing happened," he said. However, an assistant of McCovey's called Purdy and scheduled a lunch appointment at Green Hills Country Club near San Francisco. "If a Hall of Famer wants to have lunch with you, you say, 'Yes,'" Purdy observed. His column stirred some deep feelings within McCovey, who spoke mostly off the record. "He told me some things that he didn't want printed," Purdy said. "These are not his words but I'll paraphrase. He was hurt the way that the Giants rolled out the whole ballpark thing without him. Willie's personality was that he wasn't angry. But I think I could say that he was hurt, that he felt kind of left out at that point from the organization. And he didn't know whether it was because of the tax-evasion stuff. I don't think Peter meant it this way. But McCovey's impression was that Peter was a Willie Mays guy and not a Willie McCovey guy and had not really thought much about McCovey, if at all. I'll just leave it at that. McCovey was hurt by that. He didn't want me to write that. But he really appreciated, whether this went anywhere or not, that I would write this column proposing this. I was very humbled by that."

Some three months later, Baer delivered the good news: the portion of China Basin Channel beyond right field at Pacific Bell Park will officially be referred to as "McCovey Cove." Thus, every watery home run conceivably would serve as a reminder of the dynamic McCovey himself.

"The new park wouldn't be complete without a tribute to Willie McCovey," said Giants chief operating officer Larry Baer. "Arguably, he was the most popular San Francisco Giant ever. In our minds, this is a very appropriate thing to do." Said Purdy, "It made me happy, not because it was my idea, but because it brought Willie back into the organization in a cool and worthy and wonderful way. Otherwise, it might be Taco Bell Cove." Said McCovey, "It's a big honor. Let's face it. To know there's going to be something left behind after you leave with your name on it, it's all you can ask. I thought it was an honor when the little league field in Woodside was named after me, but this is even better. The only people who know about that are the people in Woodside. Everybody will know about this."

Everybody, including the revelers on sail- and engine-propelled craft that hover outside the right-field wall for a few innings or even longer. Everybody, including the athletic types in scuba gear accompanied by their swimming dogs who chase home run balls or prodigious, pulled fouls. Everybody, including the hundreds of fans who come out every season to rent kayaks and soak in the sun or stare languidly at the ballpark's upper deck. Everybody, including the dozens of sluggers who, as Purdy envisioned, try to emulate McCovey's power by clearing the twenty-four-foot-high right-field wall with a drive that sinks into the drink. But reaching the Cove on the fly isn't as easy as Barry Bonds, baseball's all-time home run leader whose total includes 35 "splash hits" into the water, may have made it seem.

"As a left-handed hitter, you think, 'ok, I can pull something down the line and get it out there,' but the way pitchers pitch you in those ballparks, you end up hitting more balls to right-center field, into that 'Triples Alley,'" said outfielder Luis Gonzalez, the first visiting player to hit two homers into the cove on the fly while playing for the Arizona Diamondbacks. "The dimensions are huge in right- and left-center field. But it's pretty awesome if you're one of the guys that end up hitting one out there into the water. It's kind of like your stamp—'Hey, I hit one into McCovey Cove.' It's a cool thing if you can hit one into McCovey Cove. The guy was one of the greatest players to play the game. They named the Cove after him, so you knew he was an impact player. It's just kind of a prestigious thing."

Kevin Mitchell, who won the 1989 NL Most Valuable Player Award as a Giant, relied on colorful imagery to describe conditions in the cove if McCovey were still playing: "You mean the river out there? The ocean? He'd be sinking boats out there. They'd be thinking they're in World War V."

Bay Area Symbol

Like the Golden Gate Bridge and the cable cars, I've been made to feel like a landmark too.

—Willie McCovey, in his Hall of Fame induction speech

San Jose Sharks executives realized that they wouldn't enjoy the luxury of a honeymoon period when their team joined the NHL as an expansion franchise before the 1991–92 season. They also knew that they risked the possibility of an annulment if they didn't woo Bay Area fans in exactly the right manner.

Succeeding in the competitive Northern California market presented a challenge. Sheer novelty wouldn't be enough to enable a team to thrive. Each of the San Francisco Bay Area's five franchises in major professional sports leagues had learned this.

The Giants ranked among the National League's elite during the 1960s, but five consecutive second-place finishes from 1965–69 disillusioned their fan base. Their season attendance dropped nearly in half during that span, and the ballclub nearly moved to Toronto and Tampa–St. Petersburg following the 1975 and 1992 seasons, respectively.

The A's captured three World Series championships from 1972–74 while reaching the postseason for five consecutive years. Yet one of the most accomplished teams of the modern era drew one million in attendance only twice in its first thirteen years in Oakland. That was due largely to widespread public antipathy toward owner Charles O. Finley, who stubbornly refused to promote the A's as richly as they deserved. They were expected to play their final season in Oakland in 2024 before an eventual move to Las Vegas.

The 49ers built a season-ticket waiting list that extended from the Golden Gate Bridge to Los Angeles, but it took four Super Bowl triumphs between 1982 and 1990 to make that happen. The Niners began their breakthrough 1981 season playing to less-than-sellout crowds.

The Warriors moved from Philadelphia before the 1962–63 season with the National Basketball Association's most prolific scorer, Wilt Chamberlain, in tow. But the franchise was anything but stable. For nearly a decade, the Warriors played home games at three different sites: the Cow Palace, Civic Auditorium, and the Oakland-Alameda County Coliseum, where they finally settled in the early 1970s.

The team that may have sustained the Bay Area's most consistently rabid fan support, the NFL's Oakland Raiders, remained susceptible to the whims of owner Al Davis as he pursued a lucrative stadium deal. The Raiders meandered to Los Angeles in 1982 and returned to Oakland in 1995 before finally moving to Las Vegas in 2020.

The Sharks avoided such drama, though they had virtually no pro hockey legacy to draw upon. The Seals, who materialized in 1967 as an NHL expansion team based in Oakland, lasted only until 1976. The ubiquitous Finley purchased the team before the 1970–71 season but couldn't bring the A's lofty fortunes to the ice. Brothers George and Gordon Gund bought the team from Finley and moved it to Cleveland. Eventually, in an example of circular history, the Gunds were awarded the Sharks franchise.

The Sharks' San Jose arena was under construction, forcing them to open their 1991–92 inaugural season at the dowdy Cow Palace on the outskirts of San Francisco in Daly City. Unfazed, the Sharks packed various fan-friendly promotions, including an innovative laser light show, into the home schedule.

They also had a league-wide mandate to fulfill.

As part of its observance of its seventy-fifth anniversary, the NHL requested each team to name an honorary captain for the season. Two categories of individuals tended to be chosen for this role. They were hockey legends who conjured memories of the greatness they demonstrated on behalf of his former team. Or they were local celebrities who symbolized the charms of their respective geographical region.

Being a brand-new organization, the Sharks had nobody to fit the "hockey legend" description. But they nevertheless had an ideal candidate to help welcome the team into the Bay Area sports realm. This man could draw standing ovations in San Francisco, Oakland, or San Jose. This man represented the stability that the new franchise sought. This man's mere presence in Sharks colors inspired fans to embrace the team, just as they embraced him and the ballclub he represented throughout most of his playing career.

Willie McCovey, put on your teal jacket.

Some thirty years later, Matt Levine remains proud of the Sharks' selection.

"We were pretty lucky in that we, pardon the expression, hit it out of the park with our first choice," said Levine, who served as the organization's vice president of business operations at the time. "We were trying to find athletes who not only spent their careers or most of their careers in the Bay Area, but also somebody who remained in the Bay Area."

To Levine and the Sharks, image was everything. The sight of McCovey at the Cow Palace, beaming as he faithfully sported Sharks gear, buoyed the souls of the freshly minted fans.

"We wanted someone with a clean-cut reputation," Levine said. "There were ex-athletes from the Bay Area whose reputation wasn't consistent with the one that we wanted to communicate coming on board, new to the marketplace. We wanted the player we selected to have a reputation with all segments of the population, and families, as well as just hardcore, 35-and-under, male sports gluttons. Willie met all the criteria. He recognized what was going on. He recognized that we were trying to capitalize on his reputation. But he also was sympathetic that we were trying to come on board in a very tough market and he liked the values that we stood for and the spirit and energy that we were bringing to how we positioned the franchise in people's minds."

Said Sharks broadcaster Dan Rusanowsky, "He was really a good guy. That's the thing everybody remembers."

That's indeed the thing virtually everyone remembers about McCovey.

"Once you create loyal fans I don't think they ever really leave you," McCovey said.

Another instance of McCovey's enduring popularity occurred on October 13, 2017, when he served as grand marshal of the parade celebrating the

Half Moon Bay Art & Pumpkin Festival. The event is an annual rite of autumn that draws highway-choking throngs to Half Moon Bay, a friendly town of about eleven thousand located on the Pacific Coast about twenty-five miles south of San Francisco. The festival's highlights include a pumpkin weigh-off, pumpkin pie eating contests, jack-o'-lantern carving competitions, 5K and 10K road races, and a Halloween costume contest.

And, of course, there's the parade. McCovey perched himself in the back of a Ford Mustang convertible as he waved to spectators and beamed at them with his familiar smile. He wasn't the first ballplayer to be honored as grand marshal. Cameron Palmer, who has served as president of the festival committee for more than thirty years, cited Willie Mays, Joe DiMaggio, Bobby Bonds, Barry Bonds, Jim Davenport, Orlando Cepeda, and John "Blue Moon" Odom as previous honorees. But McCovey surely ranked among the most welcomed guests in the festival's annals. Said Palmer, "Boy, did he bring out the crowd! People loved that guy."

Indirectly, McCovey's popularity enabled him to bolster the 49ers' success. On May 31, 1982, he and All-Pro guard Randy Cross of the reigning Super Bowl champion 49ers were among the participants in a celebrity sports challenge competition for charity at Marine World / Africa USA, an animal-themed amusement park then located in Redwood City, California. Bound for his destination on a zip line at an attraction called Whale of a Time World, Cross fell and landed with his left leg bent awkwardly underneath him. McCovey was the first person to reach Cross's side. Cross sustained multiple injuries in the leg—a broken fibula, torn ankle ligaments, and a dislocated foot—but McCovey may have prevented the damage from being more severe. It was a good thing that he was invited to this event.

"I can't remember exactly what he was saying. I was obviously in shock," said Cross, who did recall that he was wearing Puma athletic shoes. Alarmingly, as he stared at the top of his foot, he saw the trademark Puma stripe that appears on the side of the shoe. That showed the sickening extent to which his foot was wrenched out of shape.

So Dr. McCovey went to work. "My lasting memory, as far as him, were these gigantic, first baseman glove-sized hands. And him grabbing my foot. I don't know if it was just him, or if there was somebody else, but I remember those hands were there, and they basically put the foot semi-back in place."

Otherwise, medical attention for Cross was scant and a tad sloppy. Nowadays, paramedics aplenty would have descended upon him immediately. Then, only a wheelchair was available. "They started wheeling me and I remember hearing Willie say, 'Wait, wait, stop! Look at his leg.' Because as the chair was moving, the fibula was moving back and forth because it was snapped in half. That was pretty important."

McCovey's treatment impressed Dr. Fred Behling, the 49ers' team physician. As Cross related, Behling told him, "I don't know who did it, but when they put your foot back in place, they completely isolated the ligament." Explained Cross, "The ligament was laying inside the joint when they went back in. So it hadn't shriveled up. It hadn't reduced. It hadn't anything. It was just sitting there kind of flattened up inside the joint."

Cross made a full recovery, enabling him to earn two more Pro Bowl selections and win two additional Super Bowl rings. He retired from playing following the 1988 season, then embarked upon a successful broadcasting career.

"I'll always have a very positive, loving memory of Willie McCovey," Cross said. Referring to his leg injury, he added with a dash of humor, "As a lifelong Dodger fan born in Brooklyn, it took something like that to happen to do it."

You might call Willie McCovey an aspiring two-way king of swing. He particularly merited the crown, of course, in the batter's box. The other venue where the title applied was a stage, concert hall, or anywhere that progressive, "hip" musicians might have convened. Early in 1968, a couple of Northern Californians released songs on vinyl discs that bore the label of "Stretch Records." Could that have been the same "Stretch" McCovey who patrolled first base for the San Francisco Giants? Why, of course. Nothing was heard from Stretch Records thereafter. But for a while, the slugger seemed enthusiastic about at least dipping his toe into the music-producing business. This was, after all, the same McCovey who worried about how he would return the records he had borrowed from friends after the Giants initially summoned him to the Major Leagues in 1959. And this was the same McCovey who, with Orlando Cepeda, prowled the nightclubs that composed San Francisco's then lively jazz scene.

"I like the business," McCovey said. "I spent most of the winter months looking around for fresh talent all over the Bay Area. I'd go to rock spots, jazz places and just regular clubs looking for young people who sounded good enough to go on records. It was very enjoyable work. I like music, but jazz, rock 'n' roll and then soul music are my favorites. Jazz is my speciality, though."

A handful of big leaguers, including right-hander Jim "Mudcat" Grant, outfielder Lee Maye, and shortstop Maury Wills, tried performing themselves. Nobody should have waited for the soft-spoken McCovey to join them onstage. "I leave all that business to those guys," McCovey said. "I'll just stick to the production and management side of the operation and be satisfied doing that."

McCovey was dedicated to the Giants' causes off the field and on. His involvement in various programs helped raise more than $2.5 million over the years for the Giants Community Fund, which helped sustain the Junior Giants baseball leagues for thousands of underserved youths around the Bay Area and fund the construction of baseball fields. Building ballfields was extremely meaningful to McCovey, who often lacked decent fields to play on as a youth because racist Jim Crow laws denied young Blacks access to regulation fields.

McCovey, who hosted a golf tournament sponsored by the March of Dimes early in his retirement, stayed active in this realm by presenting the Willie McCovey Golf Classic annually. More than twenty celebrities, including Giants alumni and local notables, join donors to participate in this major event benefiting the Giants Community Fund.

Another signature effort is the Junior Giants Stretch Drive, which of course gets its designation from McCovey's famous nickname. The organization, which conducts this event during a midseason home series, regards this as an "all-in" endeavor to educate fans, team employees, sponsors, vendors, and players about the Junior Giants program.

McCovey was deeply woven into San Francisco's fabric. He attended Beach Blanket Babylon, the San Francisco–oriented musical revue that ran for forty-five years. According to his daughter, Allison, he laughed uproariously and almost nonstop throughout the performance. He rubbed elbows with the city's socialites as he attended the September 1980 opening of the Louise M. Davies Symphony Hall. One year, McCovey attended the opening night performance of the opera, which in San Francisco is tantamount to the World Series, Super Bowl, July 4, and New Year's Eve all rolled into one. "I've always had a connection here in the city from the first day I arrived," said McCovey, who lived in San Francisco for nearly twenty years before moving approximately thirty miles south to Woodside in 1977. "I stayed in the city. I made San Francisco my home. I was seen in the offseason at a lot of different functions and people liked that."

18

Double Trouble at First Base

Another season at least, never forever.
—Willie McCovey

McCovey's durability and other circumstances put the Giants in a unique position: they had to replace him in the lineup not once—but twice. He was such a constant presence. Fans grew from childhood to adulthood with McCovey playing first base for the Giants.

Willie McCovey's career arc traced a path that made him truly singular or, at the very least, highly unusual. He essentially forced the San Francisco Giants to replace him twice—both times with little success. The trade to the San Diego Padres following the 1973 season brought the Giants left-hander Mike Caldwell, who finished 14–5 in 1974. He proceeded to win 102 games and place second in the 1978 Cy Young Award voting. However, Caldwell compiled those admirable credentials with the Milwaukee Brewers, two stops after his 1974–76 Giants stint. San Francisco not only missed out on Caldwell's best but also, as previously mentioned, could not develop a replacement for McCovey from a quartet of homegrown candidates: Ed Goodson, Dave Kingman, Steve Ontiveros, and Gary Thomasson. History proved that each was inadequate in some way. "Steve Ontiveros, my roomie," right-hander John D'Acquisto reflected. "He could throw the ball to first base, but he couldn't catch it." Goodson was injury-prone, Thomasson was a better fit as an outfielder, and Kingman . . . well, Kingman was another story entirely.

Following McCovey's 1977–80 return to San Francisco, the Giants searched and waited for another exceptional first baseman until 1986, when Will Clark, the second choice overall in the 1985 draft, took over the position and solidified it for eight years (1986–93). San Francisco also struggled to fill the spot after J. T. Snow's reign (1997–2005) until Aubrey Huff had an excellent season for the 2010 World Series champions and Brandon Belt remained a solid presence from 2011 to 2022.

It could be said that failing to nurture Kingman's apparently abundant talent was the Giants' biggest shortcoming during his 1971–74 tenure with the ballclub. Rewind to the paradoxical 1971 season. The Giants captured the National League West title but also squandered George Foster, a future NL Most Valuable Player and a potential heir to the power-hitting throne of Willie Mays and McCovey. Foster departed for Cincinnati in a senseless trade—senseless because the Giants acquired infielder Frank Duffy, who was a redundancy with rookie Chris Speier emerging as an electrifying presence at shortstop.

As for Kingman, the Giants would not have captured the division title without him. He hit a grand slam off Pittsburgh reliever Dave Giusti in his second major-league game, a wild 15–11 San Francisco victory on July 31. He also clobbered an essential 2-run homer in the season finale, a 5–1 decision at San Diego that clinched the West for San Francisco. Overall, he drove in 24 runs in 41 games while recording a .557 slugging percentage and a 148 OPS+. At 6 foot 6 and 210 pounds, Kingman certainly possessed a first baseman's build, and in fact, he started 15 games at that spot when McCovey needed a break. Kingman also started 13 games at the outfield corners. He seemed capable of playing everywhere. The truth was, Kingman's best position was with a bat in his hands. He accumulated 442 career home runs, hitting 30 or more 5 times in 16 seasons. But the designated hitter came to the NL about fifty years too late for the Giants to take advantage of it with Kingman in that role.

So the Giants tried to find a position that Kingman could play adequately. Either the coaches lost patience with him or he displayed insufficient aptitude while San Francisco tried to help him survive at one of the infield or outfield corners. Due to McCovey's 44-game absence with the fractured forearm in 1972, Kingman started 46 games at first base, along with 59 at third base and 22 in left field. Kingman started 56 games at third and 29 at first in 1973. With McCovey gone to San Diego, Kingman finished his Giants career in 1974 with 70 starts at first base, 19 at third, and 2 in right field. Clearly cash-poor at this juncture, Giants owner Horace Stoneham sold Kingman to the Mets for $150,000 on February 28, 1975.

D'Acquisto suggested that the Giants wasted their time hoping that Kingman could function as a position player. As a guy whose fastball exceeded 102 mph, D'Acquisto sensed where Kingman truly belonged. "Dave probably could have been a better pitcher than a position player," D'Acquisto said. In fact, Kingman posted an 11–5 record as a sophomore at the University of Southern California before switching to the outfield. "As a position player, he was 6-foot-6 and very stiff with his hands. He had a great, great arm to first base, but that great arm could have been better on the mound. Like as a closer. Dave Kingman could throw the ball about as hard as I could. And they didn't want to have anything to do with it."

Clark addressed the futility of assigning one-dimensional athletes to play first base. "That's the one thing that I want to say started probably a little bit before me, when Keith Hernandez [of the Cardinals and Mets] first got going," Clark said, "where first basemen had to be more athletic, they had to be better fielders and not be just ex-outfielders that you put over there."

Snow, who won four of his six Gold Glove Awards for defensive excellence while with the Giants, reinforced the notion that thriving at the position is an art. "I've always said that first base is a hard position to play if you want to be really good at it, or if you want to be great," Snow said. "If you just want to fit in and do the normal, it's not that hard, right? Stand over there and catch throws. Balls in the dirt, you can scoop 50 percent of them. If you don't turn the 3-6-3, it's no big deal because it's a hard double play. But if you want to be good or great at it, it's one of the hardest positions on the field. You're involved in every throw—bunt plays, relays, pickoffs, double plays. I think when you've had someone that's played it and who's really good at it, it's tough to bring somebody in because they get exposed. I know Willie played it great; Will played it great; I came in after Will; Brandon Belt was a very good first baseman. All of the guys who play it well make it look easy."

Though McCovey wasn't renowned for his defense, he earned his nickname "Stretch" for his skill at using his size around first base. "They talk about all his offensive statistics, but this guy was a very, very good first baseman," said Joe Amalfitano, a teammate of McCovey's in the Majors and Minors. "If he got his glove on the ball, you were out." Said right-hander Bob Bolin, "He could catch a lot of your mistakes." Shortstop Hal Lanier said, "I don't think I ever threw a ball over his head." Said another shortstop Chris Speier, "My first year I made 30 errors and I bet I would have made 50 if he weren't over there. 'Jump, Stretch, jump.'"

As pointed out earlier, McCovey largely outperformed the Giants' first basemen during his San Diego tenure. If any replacement from that period was going to stick, it would have been Willie Montañez, obtained from Philadelphia for center fielder Garry Maddox on May 4, 1975. But Montañez accumulated only 10 home runs and 105 RBIs during his 195-game Giants stint, along with a slash line of .306/.357/.412. That helped open the door for McCovey's 1977 comeback. Meanwhile, the Giants sent Moñtanez to Atlanta as part of a four-player package in exchange for a pair of players on June 13, 1976. One of them happened to be Darrell Evans, who proceeded to become one of the most valuable Giants through 1983.

The Giants' succession plan once McCovey's skills began to falter should have gone smoothly. But Mike Ivie, who amassed 27 homers and 89 RBIs in 1979, sustained an ankle injury on opening night, 1980. Ivie ultimately went between May 28 and July 17 without appearing in a game due to "mental exhaustion."

Murray, who turned twenty-three during the 1980 season, was anything but exhausted. In fact, the Giants went 24–27 in games he started—which might not sound like much until one considers that San Francisco finished 75-86 that year.

Murray played in 4 more Major League games after 1980, going 2-for-10 with the Giants in 1983. He believes that Frank Robinson, who replaced Dave Bristol as the Giants' manager after the 1980 season, didn't give him enough of a chance. As Murray related, Robinson told him, "Hit .300 and you'll be back." Murray batted .326 in 1981, .299 in 1983, and .287 in 1984 in Triple-A with the Giants organization and received just that brief call-up in '83. "For some reason, Frank Robinson didn't want me there," said Murray, younger brother of Hall of Fame first baseman Eddie Murray. "I knew I could play. I never got an opportunity. I never thought of [Robinson] as a man of his word. He'd say something just to kind of get you away. He never stood by what he said. I don't know what his reasoning was. Because it wasn't me. I never had a fight with him. He didn't give me a chance to have an argument with him or any kind of confrontation."

Murray thoroughly enjoyed his 1980 experience with the Giants. He cited Evans, Vida Blue, Jack Clark, Larry Herndon, and Mike Sadek as among his more supportive teammates.

And what of McCovey, the legend he was replacing? Did they discuss the situation? Was there any animosity? Did McCovey try to convey advice to Murray?

"Willie was very quiet," Murray said. "He was in his 40s and I was in my 20s. What do you discuss?"

Playing in Pain Part of the Game

He wanted to be a whole person.

—Allison McCovey on her father, Willie McCovey

Willie McCovey, double amputee. This never became a reality. But it was an option that physicians presented to McCovey during the last years of his life. Severing both legs above the knee would spare McCovey the infections in his knees that troubled him more as he aged. But, as is the case with so many people faced with a similar choice, he wanted to cling to one of the last shreds of normalcy that he had available to him. Moreover, approaching eighty, he would not have experienced the improvement in his quality of life that a younger person might have through prosthetic devices. "No, he did not want to be amputated," said Allison McCovey, Willie's daughter. "It was harder for someone of his age, if he was amputated, to have artificial legs placed on. Because he was the man that he was, he wanted his legs. He wanted to be a whole person."

It is difficult to imagine a baseball player who performed on a Hall of Fame level while enduring as much physical hardship as Willie McCovey. The renowned Mickey Mantle also played in constant pain. McCovey's ailments extended literally from head to toe, from blurred vision (reported in 1970) to fallen arches in both feet (which lingered from 1964 through the end of his playing career in 1980).

McCovey's body continued to betray him until his last day on earth. When he died on October 31, 2018, at Stanford University Medical Center at age eighty, the Giants cited his cause of death as "ongoing health issues." He was undergoing dialysis at home and had been hospitalized for an infection the previous week.

Asked in late 2017 how he refrained from complaining about his luck, or lack of it, regarding his ailments, McCovey said, "I don't like to dwell on that. I would like to be able to walk and I still miss playing golf. The things you do after your retirement, I miss that. I guess going to the game gets my mind off of that." McCovey attended nearly every home game after the Giants moved into Pacific Bell Park in 2000.

Early in his career, McCovey was a slugger with speed to hit triples. He lashed 8 triples with Class A Danville in the Carolina League in 1956, 9 with Double-A Dallas in the Texas League in 1957, and 10 for Triple-A Phoenix in 1958. He somehow continued this progression in 1959, tripling 11 times in 349 at bats with Phoenix before the Giants promoted him to the Majors. Of course, he tripled twice in his 4-for-4 big league debut on July 30 as the Giants trounced future Hall of Famer Robin Roberts and the Phillies, 7–2. McCovey proceeded to total 5 triples in 219 plate appearances as a rookie. By then, McCovey had undergone his first knee operation. He hurt himself while running the bases for Dallas but received conservative treatment until the Giants decided that surgery was necessary in the 1958–59 off-season. Even then, McCovey's knees wouldn't threaten to limit his activity for close to another ten years, though they never ceased to be an issue.

Before that, intense foot pain posed a problem for McCovey. Distressingly, it reached a crisis level in 1964, when he hit .220 with 18 homers and 54 RBIs. Just one year earlier, he enjoyed an apparent breakthrough season when he batted .280, scored 103 runs—which would remain a career high—and tied his idol, Milwaukee's Hank Aaron, for the NL lead with 44 homers. Customized shoes meant to ease the pain provided only partial relief. Early in the 1965 season, he decided that playing through the pain was his best alternative. "I've got to live with it," he said.

McCovey could say the same thing about his knees. Both nagged him in 1968, when he led the NL with 36 homers and 105 RBIs. He also missed 13 games in May after Chicago's Ron Santo inadvertently spiked him during a rundown play on May 17. The wound on his right ankle required twenty stitches to close. McCovey increased his home run and RBI totals to 45 and 126, respectively, while winning the league's Most Valuable Player Award in 1969. The gains can be attributed, at least in part, to a relative absence of aches and pains. "It makes a big difference when you can play with nothing else on your mind," he said. Yet even during that charmed year, sore wrists diminished his power late in the season. His 4 September home runs represented his lowest total for any month that year.

McCovey's injury demons struck back with a vengeance in 1970. The aforementioned blurry vision didn't last long. But the knee pain returned, and his feet still ached. Worse, his hip required frequent treatment. He nevertheless approached or matched most of his 1969 numbers.

The 1971 season was a trying one for McCovey. When he wasn't resting his left knee, he was having fluid drained from it. That contrasted with the health and optimism that buoyed him before the season began. "I was in the best shape of my life," he recalled. "I felt great. It was almost too good to be true." That was proven when McCovey aggravated the knee three times late in spring training and early in the regular season.

Plans were made for McCovey to undergo midseason surgery so Dr. Robert Kerlan could repair his torn cartilage. Then McCovey was told that the procedure would be season ending. With the Giants driving toward the NL West Division title, he had no desire to miss a significant amount of activity. So he played on, managing to make his sixth and final NL All-Star team while contributing 18 homers, 70 RBIS, and a .277 batting average to the Giants' division-winning effort. He underwent knee surgery shortly after the Giants' season ended, an operation that left him feeling even more confident than ever about his health.

In fact, McCovey belted a 2-run homer in the Giants' 1972 season opener at Houston. He doubled in their second game and went 2-for-3 in the series finale. Then it was on to San Diego—where McCovey sustained a fractured right forearm when he was involved in a collision with Padres baserunner John Jeter. The mishap sidelined McCovey for six weeks and basically ruined the Giants' season. Jeter's wounds were psychological. "I feel like I killed Santa Claus," he said, aware of McCovey's popularity.

From then on, McCovey's aches and pains resulted mostly from the erosion in his knees, which left him unable to walk or play golf. The physical trauma wore down McCovey's knees but not his spirit. Shortly before the

1999 season ended, almost twenty years after playing his last game, McCovey announced that he had undergone fifteen knee operations—nearly one for each of his eighteen grand slams—but had planned three more procedures in the hopes of walking normally again. Unfortunately for McCovey, nothing succeeded conclusively.

20

Quiet? Yes. Shy? Not Really.

He didn't say much of anything to anyone at all. He wasn't an extrovert. But, sometimes, he wouldn't sugarcoat it.
—Allison McCovey

Given the choice between silence and speaking, Willie McCovey almost always opted for the former. This reticence made him comparable to his father, Frank, who typically found speech unnecessary unless one of the children was behaving out of line. And in the McCovey household, nobody ever did. "Most of the time, he didn't have much to say," Clauzell McCovey, one of Willie's brothers and the family's ten siblings, said of Frank McCovey. "But when he was saying something, you knew it. And Willie was just like my father."

True to form, Willie McCovey indeed spoke up when he had a point to make. Most often, McCovey cleared his throat when he felt compelled to defend somebody he felt had been wronged. He grabbed more than his share of headlines, for instance, when he felt that all-time home run leader Barry Bonds was the object of unfair innuendo regarding his alleged use of performance-enhancing drugs. Through the years, Bonds and McCovey forged a kinship based on their exalted status as sluggers and simply through personal association. When McCovey and outfielder Bobby Bonds, Barry's father, were Giants teammates from 1968 to 1973, the younger Bonds often accompanied his father on visits to the clubhouse. Barry had to temper his youthful behavior around McCovey, who preferred a placid pregame atmosphere.

Allison McCovey, Willie's daughter, pointed out that the Jim Crow laws, which created a racist atmosphere for most of the twentieth century, discouraged free speech among Black men, particularly those living in the South. It explained Willie McCovey's choice to reside in California—where racism exists but takes benign, more subtle forms—and limit his Alabama visits to a bare minimum. "Black men had to swallow their pride and self-respect or else risk being lynched," Allison said. "If you want to stay alive, keep your mouth shut. If you want your family to stay alive, keep your mouth shut. He didn't say much of anything to anyone at all. He wasn't an extrovert. But, sometimes, he wouldn't sugarcoat it. He wasn't going to make any false statements."

Such was the case with McCovey's unqualified endorsement of Barry Bonds as a Hall of Fame candidate. It's impossible to argue with Bonds' credentials—762 homers, 7 Most Valuable Player Awards, 8 Gold Glove Awards for fielding excellence, and 14 All-Star selections. But McCovey took umbrage with a letter written in November 2017 by Joe Morgan urging tenured members of the Baseball Writers' Association of America who possess Hall of Fame ballots not to vote for Cooperstown candidates who were linked to steroid use.

Interestingly enough, McCovey and Morgan, a Hall of Fame second baseman, had a warm relationship that survived this minicontroversy.

"Joe and I are really close, too. He's one of my best friends," McCovey said. "I went back and forth with him on it. I told him how much I disagree with him. I told him I won't let that hurt our friendship. But don't include me on the ones who are not going to show up if they go in."

It's also intriguing that McCovey and not Willie Mays, Bonds's godfather who's more closely associated with Barry, figuratively rushed to Bonds's side more publicly and quickly than anyone else.

"I just think it's a sin he's not in there," McCovey said of Bonds. "If anybody deserved to be in the Hall of Fame, it's Barry."

On November 21, a day after the ballot including thirty-three names was released, Morgan's letter was emailed to voters by the Hall of Fame, pleading with them not to support players who admitted using steroids, flunked drug tests, or were mentioned as users in the 2007 *Mitchell Report*, which published findings of an MLB investigation headed by former Senator George Mitchell.

Morgan, then the hall's vice chairman and a member of its board of directors, wrote that some Hall of Famers wouldn't attend induction ceremonies "if steroid users get in," refusing to share a stage with them.

"That letter Morgan wrote sure is not going to help Barry," McCovey said, "but I'm glad to hear a lot of the writers say the letter is not going to influence their vote because I know a lot of it is aimed at him. I wasn't too happy about it."

Concluded McCovey, "You're naive if you don't think it was aimed at Barry."

Bonds's eligibility for election to the Hall by BBWAA members expired with the 2022 vote. In December of that year, the Contemporary Baseball Era Committee, which consists of former players, baseball executives, and members of the media, did not elect him to Cooperstown. He must wait until 2026 for his next chance to receive the committee's consideration.

McCovey also minced no words when he cited what he considered to be the overall superiority of Black ballplayers, as evidenced by the National League's dominance in All-Star games. He regarded it as an affront when asked to explain the NL's All-Star Game superiority: "We had more black players, man!" Led chronologically by Willie Mays, Hank Aaron, and Roberto Clemente, the NL won 25 of 29 Midsummer Classics with 1 tie from 1960 to 1985. The NL possessed such an abundance of talent that a handful of players would knock one another off the All-Star roster—particularly in the 1960s, when voting was in the hands of the players, not fans. Both McCovey and Billy Williams were six-time All-Stars who could have made a couple of more teams apiece. Reds center fielder Vada Pinson made four All-Star squads but did so in 1959 and 1960, when MLB played two All-Star games annually. Surely he was good enough to find his way onto another team or two. Meanwhile, AL teams were slow to obtain and develop talented Black prospects, leaving the league without a transcendent star once Mickey Mantle began to decline in 1965. Baltimore outfielder Frank Robinson filled that void in 1966, but only because Cincinnati virtually gave him to Baltimore in one of the most lopsided trades ever.

The NL's All-Star hegemony over the AL had a little less than a decade remaining when McCovey addressed the subject in 1978. "I don't know if the National League is as dominant as the recent games indicate, but at one point a few years ago it was, I think," he said. "About six or eight years ago, when Clemente and Aaron and those sort of fellows were in their prime and making the All-Star team every year, I think the National League was superior. *That* superior. If you looked around, the National League just had that many more true superstars—and I don't mean guys they call 'superstar' today—and you couldn't find a real superstar in the American League, not since Mantle retired. . . . The only good team in the American League was the Yankees and at one time you had to be lily-white to play with them. It was a big breakthrough when they brought up Elston Howard. So all your great black superstars went to the National League, with the Giants and with Brooklyn."

McCovey likely would not have spoken so boldly about Black dominance in baseball in 1968, when he made the following remarks in a *Sport Magazine* profile: "I am not actively involved in the race problem. I am not a member of any organized group. I do what I think is right. I have experienced prejudice. I know something's got to be done, but I am not knowledgeable as to what should be done. No matter what, I am a Negro. I'm not going to put them down. But I don't condone violence on any side. I do not support anybody who believes in violence. It is not my bag."

McCovey remained capable of saying a lot with a little. During the 1964 season, racial tension mounted in the Giants' clubhouse and nearly overflowed in late July when manager Alvin Dark delivered some highly flammable comments in a two-part interview with *Newsday*'s Stan Isaacs. Dark was quoted as attributing what he considered to be the club's underachieving performance to faulty efforts and poor attitudes on the part of its Black and Hispanic players. Willie Mays, recently appointed team captain by Dark to quell the controversy he knew was coming, called a meeting of his Black and Hispanic teammates. He urged them to suppress their loathing for Dark and keep playing hard. Firing Dark in midseason, Mays emphasized, would embolden bigots who backed Dark. "Don't let the rednecks make a hero out of him," said Mays, who guaranteed his teammates that Dark would not be back for the 1965 season. McCovey said nothing until Mays set up a hypothetical situation that illustrated Dark's color-blind side: "Suppose him and a lady friend went to a picture show together in Birmingham, where I'm from, and one of them passes out. And somebody shouts, 'Is there a doctor in the house?' And it turns out the only doctor is colored. You think Dark's gonna turn him away?"

McCovey's deadpan humor decompressed the stress. "Be a while for him to get there, that doctor, seeing as he'd have to make his way down from the balcony," he said.

21

Friends and Family

You couldn't ask for a better set of friends.

—Allison McCovey

McCovey cherished his privacy, but that didn't mean he always preferred to be alone. He had a group of faithful friends who made sure his needs were being met, both social and personal. And if he needed help from his daughter, Allison, all he needed to do was ask.

Willie McCovey's all-star team never wore a fielder's glove or swung a bat. This was McCovey's group of friends who reciprocated his warmth and gentle candor, who simplified his life by providing everything from necessities such as food and childcare to rarer needs such as advice and love.

"The people he chose to surround himself with were very genuine," said McCovey's daughter, Allison. "You couldn't ask for a better set of friends."

First and foremost on the list was Rocky Dudum, who McCovey met shortly after his promotion to the Majors. The Dudum family operated Ramallah Wholesale on San Francisco's Mission Street, which provided Giants players with furniture and textiles. McCovey's apartment on Washington Street looked somewhat threadbare; the Dudums were all too happy to help him fill it. Pretty soon, the Dudums invited McCovey into their family. "He and Rocky were like brothers," Allison McCovey said. And McCovey served as godfather to Jeff Dudum, who accompanied him on most of his public appearances during the last twenty years of his life.

In his baseball Hall of Fame induction speech in August 1986, McCovey said of the Dudums, "They're still my closest friends today."

Dudum occasionally offered some brotherly advice to McCovey. For example, Dudum suggested to McCovey while he was playing for the Padres that moving to San Diego or at least establishing some sort of base there might be a good idea. McCovey, who happened to be visiting the Bay Area at the time, would have none of it. Said McCovey, "Are you kidding me? This is my home." It truly was home for McCovey, who joined and was baptized into the Dudums' church, St. John's Syrian Orthodox.

The longtime Giants hero wove himself into the local fabric even more deeply when the Dudums opened McCovey's Restaurant in Walnut Creek. Jeff Dudum, Rocky's son and a successful restaurateur, told his godfather that he wanted to build a restaurant that resembles the Hall of Fame. He succeeded, as McCovey's became known for its remarkable array of memorabilia as well as its cuisine. The establishment opened in September 2003 and closed in February 2015. Dudum had hoped to reopen the restaurant in the Mission Rock complex adjacent to Oracle Park, the Giants' home field. But Dudum said that planning delays forced him to cancel that idea.

McCovey's "team" had other members, as he said in his Hall of Fame speech. Ruth Stovall was his "San Francisco mother," helping him with personal affairs and practical matters. Attorney Hal Silen assisted him with his finances. Golden State Warriors owner Franklin Mieuli, broadcaster Lon Simmons, and Bill Rigney, McCovey's first Major League manager, were among other close associates.

Allison particularly enjoyed attending Giants games with Mieuli. "He had snacks and made me laugh all the time," she said.

Like many city dwellers, when McCovey felt compelled to make a major relocation, he headed for the suburbs. His pad in Woodside, nestled in the foothills about thirty miles south of San Francisco, cost a then pricey $500,000 to build by the time it was complete in 1977. "I wanted a place where I could relax," McCovey said, who was doing exactly that in one of the house's fourteen rooms as he spoke. McCovey wasn't the first Giant to consider moving into the neighborhood. That was Juan Marichal, the marvelous right-hander who opted to spend more time at his ranch in the Dominican Republic instead. Addressing the fleeting possibility of becoming neighbors with McCovey, Marichal amended the remark by saying, "*Good* neighbors."

Thousands of Giants fans were overjoyed to have McCovey as their neighbor again, so to speak, once he rejoined the Giants before the 1977 season. None of them was happier than Allison, who, understandably, missed her father during his 1974–76 stint in San Diego. "He was definitely not around when he was playing for the Padres," said Allison, who was born in 1965. "During that period of time, when I tried to write him letters, there was really no communication." This was not the same McCovey who, according to Allison, was the first father in the annals of San Francisco's Mt. Zion Hospital to be in the delivery room when his child was born. Fathers were not yet frequent spectators at childbirths. Understandably, Allison cast a cold eye toward baseball at that juncture of her life: "When he went to the Padres, I didn't really see him that much anymore until junior high school. I resented baseball because I felt like when my dad went to the Padres, it took my dad away. I didn't realize that's his career; that was his love. But as a young child in the third grade or fourth grade, that [resentment was] how I felt. People would ask me questions and I couldn't answer them. So how could you not answer questions about your dad? He was famous; he was on TV. So was I supposed to watch TV or look at the newspaper when I was in the third grade?"

The McCoveys had been striving to juggle the baseball schedule with personal time together for several years. The conclusion of Giants night games at Candlestick Park inevitably coincided with young Allison's bedtime. That usually doomed Alllison's hopes for postgame quality time with her father. It didn't help that McCovey was usually the last player to leave the clubhouse, since he was so meticulous about his appearance. Said Allison, "I'd tell myself, 'I'm going to keep my eyes open,' and it was disappointing because I would always fall asleep. That's a long day for a four- or five-year-old."

Allison shared the contempt of fans who grew disgusted when McCovey had the bat taken out of his hands. "I do remember what I hated to watch were intentional walks," she said. "I couldn't stand that. I was like, 'This is not fair.'" However, Allison remained mostly subdued in expressing her emotions. "I didn't want people asking me questions," she said. In turn, she pointedly refrained from quizzing her dad about his job. "I wasn't a baseball fanatic," she said. "My dad didn't talk to me a lot about baseball and I just didn't ask questions because I wanted my dad as my dad, not Willie McCovey, the baseball player."

Time helped father and daughter bond. "We became closer because I saw him more when I was older than when I was younger," Allison said. They traveled together on special occasions, such as Allison's high school graduation, when McCovey gave her a trip to Maui and Oahu as a present. Allison also accompanied her father to Washington DC for an old-timer's game. On their flight, the McCoveys sat alongside U.S. Senator Barbara Boxer of California, who gave Allison an insider's tour of the Capitol Building a day or two later. "What an incredible woman," Allison said. And of course, she was on hand for her father's Hall of Fame induction ceremony at Cooperstown. "I loved my dad's speech," she said. "It was the pinnacle of his career." Other Cooperstown highlights for Allison included meeting Negro Leagues legend "Cool Papa" Bell and Linda Ruth Tosetti, Babe Ruth's granddaughter.

She acknowledged that caddying for her father could pose a challenge. "He would hit that little white ball so high it looked like it reached the sky where the clouds were and I could never find it," she said.

The quiet dignity that became one of Willie McCovey's hallmarks also became a characteristic of Allison's. "I didn't want anything to ever come back to my dad that was disrespectful," she said. "I wanted to uphold his name. I never wanted to disappoint him."

Disappointment was not an option as Allison's January 1998 marriage to Philip Patrick approached. McCovey was coming off one of his major surgeries but toiled especially hard in his rehabilitation so he could uphold his obligation to walk Allison down the aisle. "He didn't want to walk me down the aisle in a wheelchair. He said he had to walk," Allison recalled. "And, boy, did he."

22

The Final Year

When I was growing up, that seemed ancient, to be eighty.
But I don't feel any different than when I turned forty, really.

—Willie McCovey, a month shy of turning eighty

Though Willie McCovey showed the effects of age during his final year on this earth, he felt as ageless as ever. Still unable to walk, he remained bound by a gurney or wheelchair. Neither could confine his spirit. Rather than tiptoe toward death, McCovey continued to pursue life with the same gusto that distinguished the powerful swing that made him a San Francisco Giants legend.

The year began with a party. On January 10, 2018, McCovey turned eighty, an occasion that the Giants organization observed by hosting a private reception for him at Oracle Park's Gotham Club. McCovey's luminous smile seemingly never left his face as he basked in the love expressed by friends, relatives, and former teammates. A little more than a month after his birthday party, he visited Giants training camp in Scottsdale, Arizona, a trip he hadn't made for several years due to health reasons. The man who amassed 521 home runs and intimidated legions of pitchers during his twenty-two-year career as a Hall of Fame first baseman watched batting practice intently, eager to see the ballplayers attempt to perpetuate the legacy he left as the National League's most feared hitter of his era.

McCovey's passion for baseball was rivaled only by his ardor for Estela Bejar, his girlfriend of seven years. They got married, with Giants president and CEO Larry Baer officiating. Shortly afterward, McCovey's health worsened. Besides the back and knee problems that numerous surgeries never eased, he remained susceptible to infections, which nearly killed him in 2015. He spent most of the last two months of his life in hospitals.

Ernest Hemingway once remarked, "As you get older, it is harder to have heroes, but it is sort of necessary." That statement fits McCovey as neatly as the Giants cap he wore almost perpetually. McCovey the ballplayer was exemplary for the excellence and class he displayed on the field. McCovey the man was worth emulating for reasons that transcended baseball. He never complained publicly about his health, which fluctuated at best and declined overall. He married Estela just ninety-two days before his death, eager to affirm the love he had found. We all can learn something from the dignified, joyous way Willie Lee McCovey chose to keep living right up to the very end.

McCovey didn't mind sitting still for a pair of Bay Area sportswriters who visited his Woodside, California, home in early December 2017. The writers sought material for feature stories to commemorate McCovey's milestone birthday. "When I was growing up, that seemed ancient, to be eighty," McCovey said genially. "But I don't feel any different than when I turned forty, really."

McCovey did mind what he considered to be the excessive efforts of a photographer, employed by the same news organization as one of the writers, to get decent shots. "That's enough. Come on," McCovey protested at one juncture. Of course, the ever-polite McCovey was incapable of expressing his annoyance more forcefully. He even mustered a couple of jokes. "One [photo] for the Christmas card," he said. After another minute or two passed, he remarked, "I didn't know I was going to become a male model."

Feeling much more relaxed later, McCovey demonstrated a trait that was familiar only to those closest to him: he liked to laugh. It wasn't belly-busting, thigh-slapping laughter but instead soft chuckling that proved he relished his memories. Here are a few examples:

Recalling a long discussion he had during the early 1960s with St. Louis legend Stan Musial about hitting, McCovey said, "I think he went out and got five hits that day. Heh-Heh-heh." On whether he ever felt he was in Willie Mays's shadow: "Well, I was. Ha-ha-ha." On being sent to New York for knee surgery during the 1958–59 off-season and meeting Mays for the first time: "A lot of people don't know, but I stayed in Willie's house in New York when I was just a teenager. Heh-heh-heh." On that particular surgery: "I think it was the first of many. Ha-ha." Plainly, this was no grumpy old man.

At the Giants' private birthday party for McCovey, a handful of Giants alumni, including Terry Whitfield and Jim Barr, showed up to honor their former teammate. "I gave him a big hug and then a kiss on the forehead or the cheek, I don't remember," Whitfield said. "Right after that, Barry Bonds did the same thing. Willie looked at us like he was shocked and said, 'What's going on here?' Those are memories you never forget."

Too soon—because nobody wanted the night to end—the time arrived for spoken tributes from some of the more illustrious guests. Orlando Cepeda, who signed with the Giants in 1955, recalled meeting McCovey, whom the organization signed the same year. "I didn't know anything about nothing. Willie [didn't] either," Cepeda teasingly said, prompting laughter. Bonds declared, "I love you to death," and gave McCovey another peck on the right cheek. Mays maintained his role as the proud team captain. "It's important for me to see all these guys come back and be a part [of] the Giants," Mays said. "That's what I said to Mac—I love you, and I'll be right there with you."

McCovey was equal parts graceful and grateful. "It's been a great career," he said. "Here I am today, from 17-year-old kid to now 80. It's been a long ride. Thanks, everybody, for coming. I hope there are going to be many more like this."

About two months later, he visited Scottsdale, Arizona, to watch the Giants play a couple of Cactus League exhibitions. A few years had passed since his previous spring training appearance, since his health had made long-distance journeys all but impossible. Yet there he was, perched in a wheelchair and watching with unwavering concentration as the Giants took batting practice. "He could not travel on a plane anymore, so we got a van and drove," said McCovey's wife, Estela. "For some reason, he really was so eager to come. Before, when he says he does not want to go, you cannot force him. This time? Maybe there was a reason behind that. Before he died, maybe God wanted him there. He was so happy."

Occasionally during batting practice, a player would approach McCovey and shake his hand. Among those who paid homage to McCovey was catcher Nick Hundley, who articulated the thrill derived from a legend's presence. "Any time that he showed up or came into a room, the dynamic of that room changed," Hundley said. "He didn't have to say anything. Once Willie entered the room, everybody kind of started to pay attention. That's pretty special. You have to have serious clout, when everything stops in a place that's filled with guys who have accomplished a lot of things. He had that aura around him, you know? Everybody, to a man, was inspired by him." Of course, McCovey welcomed each greeting. "Sometimes if you have some stature as a baseball player, you could be viewed as unapproachable, just because they're such a big, iconic figure," Hundley said. "But he was really approachable. It was awesome." Darrell Evans, one of McCovey's San Francisco teammates, was in town to raise funds for the Fergie Jenkins Foundation. Evans happened to stop by Scottsdale Stadium and was treated to a surprise reunion with McCovey, who didn't skip a beat. "Me and you, Doody?" McCovey said. He and Evans—nicknamed "Doody" for his resemblance to the 1950s-era puppet character Howdy Doody—often batted consecutively in the Giants' order. On these occasions, McCovey asked Evans this question as a form of friendly motivation to generate offense. "When he saw me, he just lit up," Evans recalled. "'Hey, me and you, Doody?' He was just like a brother."

The person who truly illuminated McCovey's life was Estela, who he met in 2010. Recovering from back surgery at the time, McCovey needed some extra care around his house. He was directed to a company operated by Estela's sister, Eunice. On the day that the office manager was initially scheduled to meet McCovey in person, she asked Estela to accompany her. Estela had other appointments that day; moreover, as a native of the Philippines, she knew nothing about baseball or Willie McCovey. But she changed her plans and took the drive to Woodside.

Lacking any real obligation to be present, Estela faded into the background after she and the office manager arrived at McCovey's house. Eventually, though, McCovey got around to introducing himself to Estela. As she recalled, McCovey said, "By the way, I'm Willie. W-I-L-L-I-E." They made small talk before he asked her, "Have you ever been to a baseball game? I can bring you." Estela expressed concern about ticket prices.

Said McCovey, who watched nearly every Giants home game from a private booth on the broadcast level of the press box, "Oh, you don't have to worry about that."

Estela attended about one or two games a month as McCovey's guest through most of the 2010 season. Though he formerly watched entire games in virtual silence, he gladly spoke up to teach her baseball's basic rules. She also visited McCovey at his home occasionally. "Little by little, he would tell me stories about himself," Estela said. Estela rode with McCovey in the vehicle that took him to city hall in the victory parade following the Giants' five-game triumph over the Texas Rangers in the World Series. As he explained to Estela, "You're my lucky charm."

A few months later, McCovey and Estela became a couple. As Estela related, he told her, "I just want to be happy for the remaining days of my life." At that time, McCovey still could walk with a cane but had begun experiencing heart problems. His health further declined in 2014, when sepsis infected both of his artificial knees and nearly killed him. He needed three surgeries in a one-week span at Stanford University Medical Center. His heart stopped twice.

It's not too corny to say that in the years immediately following, McCovey's ardor for Estela kept his heart beating. "I still want to live because of her," he told a physician after one of his surgeries. Giants public address announcer Renel Brooks-Moon, whose press box booth neighbored McCovey's, witnessed their mutual affection. "She made him so happy in the last years of his life," Brooks-Moon said.

Kidney failure added dialysis to McCovey's survival regimen in 2018. That was determined when he checked into Stanford Hospital in early May. But McCovey wouldn't allow illness to dominate his life. On June 11, Estela's birthday, he had a present for her: a marriage proposal. "I was so surprised," Estela said. "I cried so hard. I told him, 'Of course, baby, I'll marry you.' He told me, 'You know you are the love of my life.'"

The ballpark was the site of the ceremonies. "That's his home," Estela said. The wedding was held in the Field Club lounge. The reception, with Brooks-Moon serving as emcee, took place in the Giants' clubhouse. The guest list of approximately seventy included U.S. Congresswoman Nancy Pelosi and former San Francisco mayors Willie Brown and Art Agnos.

The relatively small gathering made it easier for everyone to share in the McCoveys' bliss. "They were like high school kids at that wedding, like high school sweethearts. And it was palpable," Brooks-Moon said. "There was not a dry eye during that celebration. The room was just filled with such love. It was amazing." Baer described the honor of officiating the wedding as "beyond incredible." He added, "Willie was always a deeply thoughtful person. His heart was full of gratitude to Estela and all she meant to him in his life."

McCovey couldn't restrain his enthusiasm. Miked for sound, he declared as Estela's brother Eduardo escorted her down the aisle, "How about a hand for my bride?" Later, Estela sang "I Just Fell in Love Again." Exclaimed Brooks-Moon, "None of us saw that coming. She's a beautiful singer!" Former Giants pitcher Dave Dravecky was among the overwhelmed guests. "What I watched was the most beautiful expression of love that, quite frankly, I think I've ever seen," said Dravecky, whose saga involving cancer remains stirring. "What I experienced was two people who actually laid their lives down for each other. They gave the best of themselves to each other."

McCovey's health continued to worsen, though that wasn't evident at the ballpark on September 28. He participated in the pregame ceremony to bestow the Willie Mac Award upon left-hander Will Smith. Evans, the award's 1983 recipient, was present. "Nobody was going to ask him how he was feeling because he was just a happy guy," Evans said. "I walked up to him and it was the same thing—'Hey, you and me, Doody.'" Two days later, McCovey and Estela went to the ballpark for the Giants' season finale against the Dodgers. But he felt exceedingly ill, prompting them to leave for Redwood City's Sequoia Hospital before the game's first pitch so he could be treated for pneumonia and low blood pressure. He stayed there for nearly a month. Back home for a few days, the always stoic McCovey complained to Estela that his knees ached. He was admitted to Stanford Hospital on October 25. Requesting a chair for Estela was one of his last acts before losing consciousness. "All the time, he cared for me," she said. Placed in the intensive care unit, McCovey was revived after his heart stopped. He was given a breathing tube and survived for a few days. But doctors could do nothing about the infection that undermined his powerful body. He died on October 31 at 4:04 p.m., a figure eerily close to the jersey number 44 that became part of his identity.

The Giants held a celebration of life in McCovey's honor on November 8 at Oracle Park. The variety of ballplayers attending the two-hour function reflected the breadth and depth of McCovey's nineteen-year Giants career. Those attending ranged from the obscure (pitchers Rich Robertson and Don Carrithers) to the legendary (Willie Mays and Barry Bonds). Jim Barr, who McCovey called one of his favorite pitchers to play behind, was fittingly present. For each Giant of recent vintage who showed up, such as outfielder Randy Winn or manager Bruce Bochy, there were older ones, including infielder Tito Fuentes and right-hander Bill Laskey, who wanted to pay their respects. Dusty Baker and Tony LaRussa, intense rivals as managers, shared common ground on this particular day.

Then there were the winners of the Willie Mac Award given annually to the player considered to be the season's most inspirational Giant. Representing this cadre were outfielders Jack Clark (the award's inaugural recipient in 1980), Mike Felder (1992), and Marvin Benard (1999); Dravecky (1989); utilityman Shawon Dunston (1996); and catchers Buster Posey (2012) and Hundley (2017). Numerous speakers paid tribute to the slugger, including Brooks-Moon, Baer, Dravecky, Bonds, McCovey's godson Jeff Dudum, San Francisco mayor London Breed, and broadcaster Mike Krukow, a two-time Willie Mac Award winner. Former teammates came from near and far, including Gaylord Perry, Felipe Alou, Orlando Cepeda, and Joe Amalfitano. "No Giants player has ever been more beloved in our community than Willie McCovey," Baer proclaimed. "He was so warm and gracious, so authentic that soon after meeting him, you'd swear he was a regular guy. And he was. . . . Permanence. Permanence. Willie's persona is chiseled in our collective souls." Dravecky concluded his remarks by saying he had prayed for "a baseball field like this in heaven." He continued, "The greatest gift that God could give me is having the opportunity to pitch to Willie McCovey. And the greatest joy of my life in heaven will be watching him hit that hanging slider into the universe." Dudum drew laughter by conveying McCovey's thoughts when he was asked about the possibility of moving to the East Bay: "I'm a Giant. What would my fans think of me if I lived in the A's territory?"

Barr pondered an unsettling reality as he listened to the speeches and watched dozens of videotaped highlights from McCovey's career being replayed on the scoreboard. "It was one of those things like, 'I can't believe he's gone,'" Barr said. "I can't believe I'm not going to see him anymore."

Table 1. McCovey's year-by-year Major League statistics

San Francisco Giants

Year	G	PA	AB	R	H	2B	3B	HR	RBI	BA	OBP	SLG	BB	IBB	SO
1959	52	219	192	32	68	9	5	13	38	354	429	656	22	1	35
1960	101	307	260	37	62	15	3	13	51	238	349	469	45	4	53
1961	106	374	328	59	89	12	3	18	50	271	350	491	37	3	60
1962	91	262	229	41	67	6	1	20	54	293	368	590	29	1	35
1963	152	627	564	103	158	19	5	44	102	280	350	566	50	5	119
1964	130	434	364	55	80	14	1	18	54	220	336	412	61	5	73
1965	160	639	540	93	149	17	4	39	92	276	381	539	88	5	118
1966	150	588	502	85	148	26	6	36	96	295	391	586	76	10	100
1967	135	539	456	73	126	17	4	31	91	276	378	535	71	17	110
1968	148	608	523	81	153	16	4	36	105	293	378	545	72	20	71
1969	149	623	491	101	157	26	2	45	126	320	453	656	121	45	66
1970	152	638	495	98	143	39	2	39	126	289	444	612	137	40	75
1971	105	402	329	45	91	13	0	18	70	277	396	480	64	21	57
1972	81	304	263	30	56	8	0	14	35	213	316	403	38	5	45
1973	130	495	383	52	102	14	3	29	75	266	420	546	105	25	78

San Diego Padres

Year	G	PA	AB	R	H	2B	3B	HR	RBI	BA	OBP	SLG	BB	IBB	SO
1974	128	443	344	53	87	19	1	22	63	253	416	506	96	9	76
1975	122	475	413	43	104	17	0	23	68	252	345	460	57	8	80
1976	71	251	226	20	41	9	0	7	36	203	281	351	21	7	39

Oakland A's

Year	G	PA	AB	R	H	2B	3B	HR	RBI	BA	OBP	SLG	BB	IBB	SO
1976	11	27	24	0	5	0	0	0	0	208	296	208	3	1	4

San Francisco Giants

Year	G	PA	AB	R	H	2B	3B	HR	RBI	BA	OBP	SLG	BB	IBB	SO
1977	141	548	478	54	134	21	0	28	86	280	367	500	67	16	106
1978	108	390	351	32	80	19	2	12	64	228	298	396	36	8	57
1979	117	394	353	34	88	9	0	15	57	249	318	402	36	2	70
1980	48	132	113	8	23	8	0	1	16	204	285	301	13	2	23

Table 2. McCovey's year-by-year Minor League statistics

Sandersville—Class D Georgia State League

Year	G	PA	AB	R	H	2B	3B	HR	RBI	BA	OBP	SLG	BB	IBB	SO
1955	107	478	410	82	125	24	1	19	113	305	387	507	56	N/A	89

Danville—Class B Carolina League

Year	G	PA	AB	R	H	2B	3B	HR	RBI	BA	OBP	SLG	BB	IBB	SO
1956	152	630	519	119	161	38	8	29	89	310	415	582	90	4	113

Dallas—Class AA Texas League

Year	G	PA	AB	R	H	2B	3B	HR	RBI	BA	OBP	SLG	BB	IBB	SO
1957	115	455	395	63	111	21	9	11	65	281	372	463	52	N/A	52

Phoenix—Class AAA Pacific Coast League

Year	G	PA	AB	R	H	2B	3B	HR	RBI	BA	OBP	SLG	BB	IBB	SO
1958	146	594	527	91	168	37	10	14	89	319	387	507	52	N/A	83
1959	52	219	192	84	130	26	11	29	92	372	459	759	51	N/A	48

Tacoma—Class AAA Pacific Coast League

Year	G	PA	AB	R	H	2B	3B	HR	RBI	BA	OBP	SLG	BB	IBB	SO
1960	17	77	63	14	18	1	2	3	16	286	390	508	11	N/A	6

Table 3. McCovey's career grand slams

No.	Date	Inning	Opponent	Site	Pitcher	(Threw)
1	June 12, 1960	7th*	Milwaukee	Candlestick	Willey	(RH)
2	June 22, 1964	6th	Cincinnati	Crosley Field	Tsitouris	(RH)
3	September 10, 1965	6th*	Chicago	Candlestick	Abernathy	(RH)
4	April 27, 1966	5th	Cincinnati	Candlestick	Pappas	(RH)
5	April 22, 1967	8th	Atlanta	Candlestick	Hernandez	(LH)
6	September 23, 1967	8th	Pittsburgh	Candlestick	Pizarro	(LH)
7	September 27, 1967	3rd	New York	Candlestick	McGraw	(LH)
8	May 4, 1968	3rd	St. Louis	Candlestick	Jaster	(LH)
9	June 28, 1969	1st	Cincinnati	Crosley Field	Fisher	(RH)
10	August 26, 1969	3rd	Philadelphia	Candlestick	Johnson	(RH)
11	April 26, 1970	1st	Montreal	Candlestick	Stoneman	(RH)
12	May 10, 1970	4th	New York	Shea Stadium	McGraw	(LH)
13	July 21, 1971	9th	Pittsburgh	Three Rivers	Giusti	(RH)
14	July 2, 1972	7th	Los Angeles	Candlestick	Sutton	(RH)
15	May 19, 1974	5th#	San Francisco	Candlestick	Bradley	(RH)
16	May 30, 1975	8th*#	New York	Shea Stadium	Apodaca	(RH)
17	June 27, 1977	6th	Cincinnati	Riverfront	Hoerner	(LH)
18	August 1, 1977	3rd	Montreal	Olympic	Twitchell	(RH)

* as pinch-hitter; # as member of Padres

Note: McCovey hit 18 career grand slams, more than any player who spent his entire career in the National League. He also hit at least 1 grand slam in each of 9 consecutive seasons, a streak matched only by Alex Rodriguez, and the 4 slams that he recorded consecutively off left-handed pitchers from 1967 to 1968 reflected the mastery he developed against southpaws that enabled him to escape the fate of being platooned.

Table 4. McCovey's top 10 home runs (multiple-homer games as single entry)

1	July 11, 1962, off Don Drysdale	This is entirely fitting, since Drysdale allowed more home runs to McCovey (12) than any other pitcher. Though it was only July, McCovey's Giants and Drysdale's Dodgers already were locked in a ferocious pennant race—which became tighter when McCovey connected for a 3-run, pinch-hit clout in the 6th inning that carried San Francisco to a 5–4 triumph.
2	Game 2, 1962 World Series, off Ralph Terry	The Giants clung to a 1–0 lead when McCovey led off San Francisco's half of the 7th inning. The Giants' edge quickly grew to 2–0 when McCovey drilled Terry's first pitch far over the right-field fence. That would be the final score. Until McCovey went deep, Terry had pitched magnificently, yielding just 2 hits. He and McCovey would confront each other again, most notably at the conclusion of Game 7.
3	Game 1, 1971 National League playoffs, off Steve Blass	It's a shame that McCovey didn't receive more chances than he did to perform in the postseason. The frequency with which he excelled when he appeared in October suggested that he could have added to his already con- siderable legend with more postseason opportunities. In this instance, McCovey followed a 2-run, 5th-inning homer by Tito Fuentes, who wasn't known for his power, with a soaring 2-run homer that proved essential to the Giants' 5–4 win over Pittsburgh.

(*continued*)

Table 4. McCovey's top 10 home runs (multiple-homer games as single entry) (*continued*)

4   October 2, 1966, off Steve Blass   Though this was a must-win game for the Giants, whose hopes of capturing the National League pennant remained alive, McCovey was on the bench when the game began because Pittsburgh's starting pitcher was Bob Veale, a hard-throwing, bespectacled left-hander who gave him fits. To that point in their careers, McCovey was batting .150 (3-for-20) with 13 strikeouts off Veale. However, Veale was long gone when the 11th inning opened, and Blass entered the game in relief with the score tied 3–3. Pinch-hitting, McCovey belted his 36th homer of the season, a 2-run drive that propelled the Giants to a 7–3 decision. That forced the Dodgers to use Sandy Koufax at Philadelphia to preserve their lead in the standings over the Giants. Koufax earned a complete-game victory, pitching Los Angeles to the pennant and obscuring McCovey's heroics.

5   September 10, 1965, off Ted Abernathy   See no. 4. McCovey had proven that he couldn't find his swing against Cubs left-hander Dick Ellsworth, against whom he would bat .050 (1-for-20) in his career. So with another Giants-Dodgers pennant race providing the backdrop, McCovey received a rare day off until Ellsworth left the game in the 6th inning with 1 out and 2 runners aboard. Batting for Jack Hiatt with the bases loaded, McCovey launched an 0-1 pitch over the right-field fence from Cubs right-hander Ted Abernathy, he of the deceptive submarine pitching motion. It was McCovey's third career grand slam and second as a pinch hitter. It also kept San Francisco a ½ game ahead of Los Angeles in the NL standings. "That was one of the most satisfying hits I ever got," McCovey said. Referring to the '62 blow off Drysdale, McCovey added, "I can only think of one that was really bigger."

(*continued*)

Table 4. McCovey's top 10 home runs (multiple-homer games as single entry) (*continued*)

6	May 2, 1965, off Claude Osteen and Bob Miller	McCovey verified multiple strengths with this multiple-homer effort. First, he reinforced what experts already knew: he could indeed hit left-handers. His 2-run, 7th-inning homer off Osteen, a southpaw, erased the Dodgers' 1–0 lead. Later, McCovey demonstrated his penchant for wielding a clutch bat when he homered off Miller to snap a 2–2 tie leading off the 10th inning to enable the Giants to cruise to a 4–2 victory. That's what the great ones do: they beat you twice, if that's what it takes.
7	June 27, 1977, off Jack Billingham and Joe Hoerner	The Cincinnati Reds should have been relaxed on this summer evening. They led 8–3, entering the 6th inning. Then the Giants scored 3 instant runs, 2 coming on a McCovey home run off Billingham. The Giants chased him two batters later; reliever Joe Henderson lasted only 4 hitters. By the time McCovey's turn to hit again arrived, the Giants led 9–8, the bases were loaded, and Hoerner was striving to retire McCovey for the inning's final out. Hoerner had to wait one more batter to accomplish that goal as McCovey planted his pitch deep into the right-field seats for his 17th career grand slam. It concluded San Francisco's 10-run inning and marked the second time during McCovey's career in which he homered twice in an inning.
8	July 23, 1969, off Blue Moon Odom and Denny McLain	Since the season belonged to McCovey, who won that year's National League MVP Award, it figured that he should have dominated the All-Star Game too. He hit roundtrippers off Odom in the 3rd inning and McLain in the 4th to become the fourth player to homer twice in an All-Star Game. The NL triumphed, 9–3. It was the second of four consecutive All-Star appearances for McCovey, who had six overall. McCovey batted fourth, one spot behind Hank Aaron and one ahead of Ron Santo. "For me to hit cleanup in that lineup was amazing," he said.

(*continued*)

Table 4. McCovey's top 10 home runs (multiple-homer games as single entry) (*continued*)

9	June 1, 1962, off Roger Craig	A throng of 43,742 came to the Polo Grounds to (1) see the Giants make their first regular-season appearance in New York since they fled for San Francisco in 1958 and (2) feast their eyes on Willie Mays, who remained a demigod in New York. But the fans went home buzzing about McCovey, who homered to right in the 1st inning, then homered to left in the 3rd. Both clouts were yielded by Roger Craig, the future Giants manager. How would McCovey have fared in the Polo Grounds had the Giants stayed in New York? Well, he hit .286 (16-for-56) there, with 4 home runs and a slugging percentage of .571. You make a guess.
10	May 3, 1980, off Scott Sanderson	This was McCovey's final career homer—number 521, which proved significant. It tied McCovey for eighth on the all-time list with Ted Williams, who was among his mentors early in his career. This was McCovey's lone homer of the 1980 season and sixth all-time at Montreal's Olympic Stadium. He also went deep off Sanderson, an Expos right-hander, on July 10, 1979.

SOURCES

Introduction

"I've known Willie McCovey all my life," said Jeff Dudum, the slugger's godson. "He's like family to me." Janice De Jesus, "Restaurateur Pays Tribute to McCovey," *Contra Costa Times*, September 13, 2003.

Chapter 1

"Nice going, Stretch! The drinks are on you." Such on-the-scene quotations and details, such as McCovey's flight schedule from Phoenix to San Francisco, come from Curley Grieve's postgame story in the *San Francisco Examiner*, July 31, 1959.

"I dropped him into a tough spot," Giants manager Bill Rigney said. The origin of the quotation is uncertain, though there's no denying the veracity of this remark.

Chapter 2

"You could very easily go walking in the wrong house, they all looked so much alike. It was an all-black neighborhood that some people might call a ghetto, but I've seen some areas now since I've grown up that are considered ghettos and I think we were a lot better off than some of those neighborhoods." McCovey quotation from Mike Mandel, SF *Giants: An Oral History* (Santa Cruz CA: Self-published, 1979), 76.

Details of the Giants' signing of McCovey provided by Art Rosenbaum, interview with farm director Jack Schwarz, *San Francisco Chronicle*, July 3, 1980.

A very brief report of the window-breaking incident at McCovey's San Francisco residence was published in *The Sporting News*, July 20, 1963.

Chapter 3

McCovey quotation in the epigraph comes from Charles Einstein, *A Flag for San Francisco* (New York: Simon & Schuster, 1962), 45.

Bill Rigney's comments on McCovey's susceptibility to the "sophomore jinx" ("He's one guy who I'd say would be immune") and projected home run total ("a conservative 30") come from a Jack McDonald column in the *San Francisco News Call Bulletin*. This was an actual newspaper clipping that did not include a publication date, but it obviously ran sometime during the 1959–60 off-season.

Rigney quotation ("In 1960 we were two or three games behind Pittsburgh. And a lot of people thought that if the Russians didn't attack we'd win the pennant by 15") from Mandel, SF *Giants*, 16.

Chapter 4

Orlando Cepeda quotation ("When Willie McCovey came up") from "This Great Game: The Online Book of Baseball."

McCovey quotation on Charles McCabe ("How can I hit him? I don't even know who he is") from Einstein, *Flag for San Francisco*, 130.

Horace Stoneham remarks from Milton Gross's syndicated column appearing in *San Francisco Chronicle*, April 27, 1962.

McCovey outburst ("This is the greatest moment of my life!") from David Plaut, *Chasing October: The Dodgers-Giants Pennant Race of 1962* (South Bend IN: Diamond Communications, 1994), 187.

Chapter 5

McCovey's visit to Fack's cited in Art Rosenbaum and Bob Stevens, *The Giants of San Francisco* (New York: Coward-McCann Inc., 1963), 15.

As opposed to OPS, which is the sum of a player's on-base percentage and slugging percentage, OPS+ takes ballpark factors into consideration.

Jack Sanford's bitter insistence, "That walk to Terry did it," appears in Rosenbaum and Stevens, *Giants of San Francisco*, 190.

Mays's quotation ("I was going for the bomb") comes from Rosenbaum and Stevens, *Giants of San Francisco*, 190.

McCovey quotation ("Not only did I have a whole team on my shoulders in that at-bat, I had a whole city") from Karen Crouse, "Slugger Who Just Won't Stop," *New York Times*, October 18, 2010.

Chapter 6

Don Drysdale quotation in the epigraph comes from *San Francisco Chronicle*, August 12, 1962.

Casey Stengel quotation ("I'll give any of you $250,000 for him") from Joe Williams column, *New York World-Telegram*, October 6, 1962.

McCovey quotation on Drysdale ("Why I hit him consistently is hard to explain") from Jack McDonald column, *San Francisco News Call Bulletin*, June 12, 1963.

McCovey quotation ("I am tired of people saying my output is against one pitcher") from Jim Murray column, *Los Angeles Times*, June 13, 1963.

Alvin Dark's comments on McCovey's outfield defense ("He's done a great job for us") from Louis Duino column, affiliation unidentified.

Charlie Fox ("When Willie learned to handle this pitch") and Mel Harder ("When it comes to sheer strength") quotations from Bob Stevens in *The Sporting News*, June 1, 1968.

Chapter 7

The St. Louis bus anecdote is archetypal. All of it seems completely likely.

Ray Sadecki quotation ("All I had to do was to win five ballgames, and we would have won the pennant") from Mandel, SF *Giants*, 155.

Bob Gibson's remark about McCovey being "the scariest hitter in baseball" comes from Bob Gibson, Reggie Jackson, and Lonnie Wheeler, *Sixty Feet, Six Inches: A Hall of Fame Pitcher & a Hall of Fame Hitter Talk about How the Game Is Played* (New York: Doubleday, 2009), 212.

McCovey's Crosley Field homer is another archetypal tale, this from respected Cincinnati scribe Greg Hoard. This one sounds a tad embellished.

"I followed the ball all the way, but apparently the umpire didn't." McCovey quotation from Jim Kaplan, *The Greatest Game Ever Pitched: Juan Marichal, Warren Spahn, and the Pitching Duel of the Century* (Chicago: Triumph Books, 2011), 91.

Chapter 8

"Yes, I am aware I am the number-one Giant." McCovey quotation from Arnold Hano, "The Arrival of Willie McCovey," *Sport Magazine*, June 1969.

"Mays was the type of guy, I don't know what it was about him . . ." McCovey quotation from Mandel, SF *Giants*, 89.

"He's the best slugger right now. McCovey has been doing the job for us." A Mays quotation on McCovey from Lee Biederman, *Pittsburgh Press*, August 15, 1968.

Chapter 9

McCovey quotations ("It still comes up just as fast as before" and "It makes a big difference when you can play with nothing else on your mind") come from United Press International interview, "McCovey Claims It's Not Easier," *Los Angeles Herald Examiner*, April 27, 1969.

Dick Allen quotation ("Willie is simply the best hitter in baseball today") comes from Phillies-Giants game story, "McCovey Hits 2 More—SF Wins, 4–0," *San Francisco Chronicle*, June 7, 1969.

Sometimes there's no laughing in baseball, as Dick Dietz learned when he climbed an outfield fence to demonstrate how best to defend McCovey. Mandel, SF *Giants*, 161.

A ballplayer's slash line consists of, in this sequence, his batting average, on-base percentage, and slugging percentage.

Giants beat writer James K. McGee of the *San Francisco Examiner* captured details of McCovey's award-winning outfit in "McCovey Is Named MVP," *San Francisco Examiner*, November 20, 1969.

Chapter 10

The divergent reactions from Willie Mays and Charlie Fox regarding McCovey's fractured wrist come from Giants correspondent Pat Frizzell in *The Sporting News*, May 6, 1972.

In his dispatch to *The Sporting News* dated September 1, 1973, Frizzell captured the verbal
jousting between McCovey ("He said I was through") and Fox ("I think he needs rest
from time to time").

Bobby Bonds's remarks about McCovey ("There's something different about our club
when Mac's in the lineup") appeared in Pat Frizzell's contribution to *The Sporting News*,
August 18, 1973.

Chapter 11

Slightly different versions of WAR exist. We used baseballreference.com's.

McCovey's quotation ("I know people have been thinking I'm washed up, but I'm not")
appears in the file of press clippings provided by the Hall of Fame's research depart-
ment. The name of the publication in which this particular comment appeared was
omitted, though the date July 23, 1974, was scrawled on it—two days after McCovey
homered twice against the Mets and was actually quoted.

Sparky Anderson's mournful recollections of McCovey's power hitting appeared in the
Padres' regular installment in *The Sporting News*, September 27, 1975.

Remarks from McCovey and Giants manager Joe Altobelli appeared in Giants correspondent
Art Spander's report, "Giants Revive Memories with Return of McCovey," *The Sporting
News*, late March 1977 (precise date was omitted).

Chapter 12

The five-minute estimate of cheering for McCovey during pregame introductions at Candlestick Park on Opening Day, 1977, was delivered by Ron Fimrite, "The Cable Cars, the
Fog—and Willie," *Sports Illustrated*, April 17, 1978.

McCovey quotations ("In a way I felt I never really left" to "It might have set the tone for
the year I've had") from Stephanie Salter, *San Francisco Examiner*, September 18, 1977.

McCovey's respect for Hank Aaron is captured in Giants correspondent Art Spander's
report, "McCovey's Grand Slam Stirs Ghost of Gehrig," *The Sporting News*, early July
1977 (precise date was omitted).

Quotations from Willie ("Ma, do you still want me to be a lawyer?") and Ester McCovey
("He's a good son") appear in Art Rosenbaum, "Her Son, the Ballplayer," *San Francisco
Chronicle*, September 19, 1977.

McCovey's comments about his big day and his game-winning hit came from Bob Stevens,
"McCovey's Hit Beats Reds in Ninth," *San Francisco Chronicle*, September 19, 1977.

Giants manager Charlie Fox's comments on the pain McCovey endures appeared in Phil
Pepe, "Through the Press Gate," *New York Daily News*, August 21, 1971.

Chapter 13

"What I remember about 1978 was that we were having fun all of a sudden again." McCovey
quotation from David Bush, "Near Great in 1978," *San Francisco Chronicle*, May 31, 2003.

McCovey's thoughts and feelings about smacking his 500th career home run were captured
by Giants correspondent Nick Peters, "Willie's 500th HR More Relief Than Thrill," *The

Sporting News, June 22, 1978. Peters also reported Atlanta pitcher Jamie Easterly's reaction to allowing the historic hit. Reporter Bob Stevens told of McCovey's plans to give the home run ball to Giants owner Bob Lurie. Bob Stevens, "It's Willie's Big Night, but a Giants Nightmare," *San Francisco Chronicle*, July 1, 1978.

Through Giants manager Joe Altobelli, Stevens conveyed McCovey's role in another Giants-Dodgers thriller. Bob Stevens, "McCovey's Hit Beats the Dodgers," *San Francisco Chronicle*, April 21, 1979.

The quotation from Giants third baseman Darrell Evans ("The great ones are better for a reason, more than their physical skills") was generated by Tom Singer of the *Los Angeles Herald Examiner* for a July 6, 1980, farewell feature about McCovey.

Chapter 14

Joe Morgan quotation comes from a 1986 video, "A Giants History: The Tale of Two Cities," available at https://www.youtube.com/watch?v=jDNdb2xHxCI.

Remarks from Jeff Kent, Marvin Benard, Ellis Burks, Mark Gardner, and Marquis Grissom come from *San Francisco Chronicle* archives; others obtained by author.

Chapter 15

McCovey quotations ("As I look back on my career it is hard to say" and "The Hall of Fame was never a dream of mine" through "I owe everything to baseball") come from William Flynn, "McCovey on McCovey," *San Francisco Sunday Examiner and Chronicle*, July 6, 1980.

Jack Lang quotation ("Only the greatest of the superstars make it the first time they are eligible") from "Hall of Fame: Few Enter on the First Knock," *San Francisco Examiner*, January 3, 1986.

Information on McCovey's coast-to-coast red-eye flight designated as Flight 44 from Rick LaPlante, "McCovey Isn't Fazed by His 'Fame,'" *Peninsula Times Tribune*, January 8, 1986.

Comments from Chub Feeney, Willie Mays, Bob Gibson, and McCovey come from "Warming Up for Cooperstown," *San Francisco Chronicle*, July 7, 1986.

Chapter 16

McCovey's address to Judge Edward R. Korman, the list of prominent San Franciscans who wrote supportive letters on McCovey's behalf, and details of Willie Brown's letter appear in Lynda Richardson, "Baseball Hall of Famer Is Sentenced in Tax Case," *New York Times*, June 8, 1996.

McCovey's "acceptance speech" regarding having the cove named for him ("It's a big honor. Let's face it. To know there's going to be something left behind after you leave with your name on it") appeared in Mark Purdy, "McCovey Cove to Be Part of Pac Bell Park," *San Jose Mercury News*, August 26, 1999.

Chapter 17

McCovey wasn't talking about the Sharks when he made this remark in 1999, but the sentiment that he expressed ("Once you create loyal fans I don't think they ever really leave you") certainly applied to the fledgling franchise. The quotation comes from Mandel, sf *Giants*, 92.

Chapter 18

This chapter's epigraph was contributed by the *San Francisco Chronicle*'s Art Rosenbaum, who, in terms of longevity, was the Willie McCovey of Bay Area sportswriters. Rosenbaum's column appeared in the Sunday Punch section of the *Examiner and Chronicle*, where sports-related items rarely appeared. It was the date of McCovey's "Day" at Candlestick Park—September 18, 1977—and so an appreciation piece was appropriate.

Chapter 19

San Diego outfielder John Jeter's dark humor about his first-base collision with McCovey that fractured the big man's wrist ("I feel like I killed Santa Claus") gained national attention when it was published in *Sports Illustrated*'s "Week in Review" baseball column, May 1, 1972.

Chapter 20

I initially encountered the anecdote about McCovey defusing the tension during the meeting Willie Mays called to avoid an Alvin Dark–prompted insurrection in James S. Hirsch, *Willie Mays: The Life, the Legend* (New York: Scribner, 2010).

Chapter 22

The pair of baseball writers who interviewed McCovey in early December 2018 were the author and John Shea of the *San Francisco Chronicle*. We felt comfortable in jointly requesting an audience with McCovey because this wasn't a dog-eat-dog competitive journalistic situation. We also reasoned that we would gather better material while talking to McCovey together rather than risk taxing his energy and his patience by making him sit through two interview sessions. I also used material from McCovey (and other interviewees) that I steadily gathered since 2005, when I covered the Giants for the *San Jose Mercury News* (2005–6) and mlb.com (2007–18). However, I did not begin actively working on the book until 2021, when I received Allison McCovey's blessing to undertake the project.

Page numbers in *italics* refer to tables.